CITY SCHOOLS

HOW DISTRICTS AND COMMUNITIES
CAN CREATE SMART EDUCATION SYSTEMS

CITY SCHOOLS

HOW DISTRICTS AND COMMUNITIES
CAN CREATE SMART EDUCATION SYSTEMS

Edited by
Robert Rothman

HARVARD EDUCATION PRESS
CAMBRIDGE, MASSACHUSETTS

The poem "Paul Robeson" by Gwendolyn Brooks on page 173
is reprinted by consent of Brooks Permissions.

Library of Congress Control Number 2006939815

Paperback ISBN 978-1-891792-41-0
Library Edition ISBN 978-1-891792-42-7

Published by Harvard Education Press,
an imprint of the Harvard Education Publishing Group

Harvard Education Press
8 Story Street
Cambridge, MA 02138

Cover Design: Alyssa Morris

The typefaces used in this book are ITC Slimbach for text
and Adobe Chaparral for display.

CONTENTS

ACKNOWLEDGMENTS

I f the notion of smart education systems is, as Warren Simmons puts it in this volume, a "new old idea," then the most recent incarnation of the concept emerged during a series of discussions and seminars held at the Annenberg Institute for School Reform at Brown University. I am indebted to all those who participated, in person or virtually, for honing the ideas and framing the components of smart education systems and suggesting illustrative examples. Those who helped shape the idea include the authors of this volume, as well as Susan Fisher, Norm Fruchter, Margaret Balch-Gonzalez, Deborah King, David Nerenberg, and Alethea Frazier Raynor. I would also like to thank Dana Borelli, a master's student in Brown University's program in urban education policy, who supported our work with research and writing, and Kenneth Jones and Kris Kurtenbach, who facilitated the discussions.

At Harvard Education Press, Caroline Chauncey championed the project from the outset, even while the editor was thousands of miles away. Doug Clayton, director of the Press, was also a strong supporter.

On behalf of my fellow authors, I dedicate this book to the 13 million children in urban U.S. schools, with a hope that their opportunities, and those of the next generation, will be brighter.

ACKNOWLEDGMENTS

INTRODUCTION

As the nation's unprecedented push to reform and improve education approaches the midpoint of its third decade, reformers can claim some success. Overall student achievement is up, particularly in mathematics. Thousands of new schools that provide a vast array of educational options have opened their doors. And an idea that represented the fondest aspiration of educators—that all children can learn—is now national policy.

Yet despite these advances, few would argue that education in the nation's cities remains a challenge. To be sure, urban schools have made substantial gains, and The Broad Foundation has recognized (with $500,000 worth of scholarships) large cities that have shown improvement in student achievement and in closing achievement gaps.Boston; Norfolk, Virginia, and Long Beach, California, are among the winners of the Broad Prize for Urban Education. Yet even these cities would acknowledge that they and their counterparts around the nation have a long way to go toward ensuring that every child receives an excellent education and develops the knowledge and skills needed for a fulfilling, productive future.

Indeed, some of the most dramatic reform efforts under way are aimed squarely at improving education in cities. In 2006, the mayor of the nation's second largest city, Los Angeles, won legislative approval to exert substantial authority over that city's schools, joining his counterparts in Boston, Chicago, and New York City. New York and other cities have been at the forefront of the effort to break down large high schools into more intimate units and in creating new small schools. In other cities, like Dayton, Ohio, and Washington, D.C., charter schools have proliferated and now educate a substantial proportion of the city's youth.

Even some national policy concerns and initiatives have a particularly urban beat. The national concern over closing the achievement gap, to take a prominent example, addresses the fact that poor children and children of color achieve academically at levels far below those of their white and more affluent peers. Moreover, cities educate a far higher proportion of students at the low end of the achievement gap than do other geographical areas. According to the U.S. Census Bureau, some 30 percent of urban children live in poverty, compared with 22 percent in rural areas and 13 percent in the suburbs.

Attempts to address the needs of urban education and close the achievement gap have sparked considerable debate, however. On the one hand, some researchers contend that the economic and social barriers children in poverty face are so daunting that no amount of school reform can hope to eliminate achievement gaps. They argue that we can only hope to do so by addressing the health and well-being of children and eliminating widening economic inequalities.[1]

On the other hand, another group of researchers has examined schools that have managed to beat the odds and show dramatic results in student achievement, despite the social and economic disadvantages of poverty. These authors maintain that schools that hold high expectations and address the educational needs of all of their students can overcome the barriers these children face outside of school and enable them to learn at high levels.[2]

No one would deny that the barriers faced by children who live in poverty are substantial and have profound effects on their educational opportunities and ability to learn well. For example, poor children are more likely than others to have health problems that affect their ability to learn, such as asthma, poor vision, or impairments associated with lead exposure. Poor children also tend to be mobile, and thus frequently find their schoolwork disrupted in the middle of a school year.[3]

Poor children also lack many of the advantages their more affluent peers have that can enhance achievement, such as books in the home, access to stimulating out-of-school activities, and exposure to well-educated adults who can socialize children into the world of school and hold high expectations for their future.

Yet the debate over whether in-school or out-of-school factors are more salient in children's learning—a debate that has raged at least since the 1966 publication of James Coleman's *Equality of Educational Opportunity*—is in many respects a false one. Both factors are important and both must be addressed if the nation is to make good on its 60-year-old promise to guarantee equal educational opportunity and its more recent pledge to ensure that all students learn at high levels.

A number of reform initiatives over the past two decades have attempted to address both the in-school and out-of-school needs of children and youths, but they have not succeeded in ensuring high levels of learning and development for all children. The reasons they have not succeeded are instructive and point to a solution that might be more effective.

One such initiative was New Futures, an effort launched by The Annie E. Casey Foundation in 1988 to integrate health and social services and education in five cities. The initiative had some success in creating new relationships across sectors and a new willingness to address common concerns. But the cities involved had less success in developing meaningful changes that improved outcomes for their children.[4]

From the outset, the initiative faced the daunting challenge of asking large, entrenched bureaucracies to operate differently, all at the same time—an approach a foundation review of the effort called "the path of most resistance."[5] School districts faced particular challenges because they struggled with low achievement and graduation rates and often reacted defensively.

Other efforts started at the school level and attempted to graft health and social services onto other educational supports in schools. The Beacons in New York City offer a range of recreation, cultural, and family support and health services on school campuses at more than seventy-five locations around the city. An evaluation of the program found that the Beacons yielded positive outcomes for children and families, such as helping them avoid negative behaviors, but were less successful at linking the schools to noneducational services.[6] As those involved in New Futures found, the Beacons had academic challenges that overwhelmed their ability to integrate services with other sectors. In addition, many of the services and supports the students and families needed were not well suited to being provided in school buildings.

What would a system look like that effectively supported children both in and outside of school? In 2000, the Annenberg Institute for School Reform's Task Force on the Future of Urban Districts, known as School Communities that Work, began to address that question and come up with a vision for an effective system. The task force, and particularly its design group for developing family and community supports, recognized that such a system must include both a highly functioning and effective school district—which the task force called a "smart district"—and a comprehensive and accessible web of supports for children, youth, and families.[7] We refer to such a system in this volume as a "smart education system."

The task force also recognized that such a system did not exist in any city in the United States but that there might be two pathways for getting there. First, districts could redesign themselves to become "smarter" and serve schools and students more effectively. The Annenberg Institute has developed a number of tools and frameworks to help districts do this and is working with several districts to implement their designs and make significant improvements.

Second, communities within cities could form a network of supports and services around a set of schools in a neighborhood or a focused area. They could work to influence the district and city agencies, helping them to become "smarter" and more effective, and to help create and nurture such networks throughout the city. Networks of this type, which Steve Jubb of the Bay Area Center for Equitable Schools has termed Local Education Support Networks (LESNs), are being developed in New York City, Sacramento, Oakland, and other cities.

This book lays out a vision for a smart education system and outlines its components. Using examples from a number of cities, the authors outline some of the approaches that might be effective in building such a system, and some of the challenges cities face in doing so.

OVERVIEW OF THE BOOK

The book is organized into four sections. In Part I, we consider the challenge cities face in educating all students to high levels and the opportunities they offer to meet that challenge. In chapter 1, I consider the achievement gap and analyze the kinds of knowledge and skills all students should attain to become "proficient." I suggest that the achievement gap in fact reflects the vastly different opportunities students have to develop proficiency, both in and out of school.

In chapter 2, Dennie Palmer Wolf and Heather A. Harding examine the opportunities for learning and youth development available in cities. Looking through the eyes of parents in Providence, Rhode Island, they find that many opportunities exist for children outside of schools, but that these opportunities are not available equitably. They suggest ways the city—and all cities—could build on their assets to create pathways for learning for all students.

Part II looks at schools and school districts in a smart education system. One of the reasons for the growing attention focused on school districts is the recognition that a school-by-school approach to improvement is not likely to be effective on a large enough scale to ensure that all students achieve at high levels. Nor does such an approach enable schools to connect to communities and city resources that would support them and their students. But a redesigned district—one focused on results, equity, and community—can in fact work for all children.

In chapter 3, Marla Ucelli, Ellen Foley, and Jacob Mishook lay out the case for "smart districts" that operate on the principles of results, equity, and community. They show what these principles mean in practice and provide examples of districts that are getting "smart" by providing appropriate and timely supports and interventions for schools; ensuring an equitable distribution of resources; using data wisely for accountability; and engaging with partners.

Deanna Burney and Kenneth Klau, in chapter 4, examine the way smart districts go about their primary mission: improving teaching and learning. Using data from Baltimore and Portland, Oregon, Burney and Klau consider the match between the "intended" curriculum and the "enacted" curriculum, and they address some issues that emerge as districts tackle the difficult problem of teaching all students to high levels. They also note that an element of what makes districts "smart" is the importance they place on community involvement in the examination of teaching and learning, and in providing appropriate supports to students and schools.

In chapter 5, Kenneth K. Wong and David Wishnick highlight the role of diverse service providers in operating schools. Looking at the experiences of Chicago and Philadelphia, the authors note that smart districts seek out community resources to augment their capacity to manage schools and to provide additional options that parents and families might seek. While such providers can offer a new options and some important innovations, the way the diverse provider model works depends in large part on the political environment and district culture.

Part III focuses on the community side of the equation. The involvement of community organizations and agencies gives students, parents, and community members a voice in how supports are selected and allocated. It connects students and schools with the environment outside the classroom and puts agency in the hands of grassroots organizations while holding the community accountable for their connection to the system. Smart education systems with strong community partnerships show the engagement of all constituents.

In chapter 6, Richard Gray and Lamson Lam show how grassroots organizations can break down the barriers that have traditionally kept schools and community members apart, and how partners such as universities and local organizations can support their efforts.

In chapter 7, Kavitha Mediratta, Amy Cohen, and Seema Shah examine the role of youth organizing in engaging a critical sector of the community. They show how engaged youth provide the necessary demand and support that lead to sustained improvements in education, and how youth organizing enhances young people's sense of efficacy and engagement in school.

If communities are to address the educational needs of all children, particularly those who have been underserved, civic capacity is a necessary component. In chapter 8, Jeffrey R. Henig and Clarence N. Stone illustrate ways that low-income communities in California and Philadelphia have developed civic capacity and produced improvements.

How can cities engage communities and mobilize the resources necessary to support children and schools? Mayors play important roles, as Michael K. Grady and Audrey Hutchinson note in chapter 9. They draw on case studies from four cities to show how mayors, even those without formal authority over schools, have attracted resources and support for education in and out of school.

Part IV provides in-depth case studies of two cities that are building smart education systems. In chapter 10, Jesse B. Register describes the efforts the Chattanooga-Hamilton County, Tennessee, schools have made over the past decade to create a "smart district." Following a merger of the city and county school systems that was viewed with skepticism by both communities, the newly created district crafted a common vision to support high levels of learning for all students and aligned its structure and services to support that vision. The district's success has strengthened community support and enabled the district to attract partners and supporters who can provide additional resources for children and schools.

In chapter 11, Dennie Palmer Wolf and Jennifer Bransom show how arts and cultural institutions in the city of Dallas worked with the school district and city agencies to provide equitable and enhanced learning opportunities for children throughout the city. They also show how the strategic use of data has enabled these partners to strengthen teaching and learning in and out of school and produce better outcomes for all students.

In Part V, Warren Simmons lays out a vision of a "smart education system." Citing the need for sustained support for high-quality educational opportunities, Simmons argues for a new kind of partnership among schools, community agencies, and local organizations that will provide the support for all children that affluent children currently enjoy. He concludes with steps that communities can take to begin to build the infrastructure for such a system.

Such efforts will not be easy, but with these and other steps, cities can begin to address the gaps in opportunities that have produced the achievement gap, and help ensure that all young people do, in fact, learn at high levels.

PART I

URBAN EDUCATION:
THE CHALLENGE AND THE PROMISE

THE REAL ACHIEVEMENT GAP

Robert Rothman

A century ago, the schools of Gary, Indiana, drew national attention. Led by a dynamic superintendent, William A. Wirt, Gary had developed an innovative system that introduced students to all manner of vocational trades, health and hygiene, as well as academic subjects. The schools also moved students around the buildings during the day instead of keeping them at desks. At night, the buildings were kept open for use by the community.

The Gary Plan, known as "Work-Study-Play," attracted the attention of John Dewey, Wirt's former teacher, who included a chapter on the idea in his book *Schools of Tomorrow*. The plan also drew visitors from all over the United States as well as from other countries. Ultimately, some two-hundred cities adopted some version of the Gary Plan. In New York City the proposal met heated—and violent—opposition that the plan robbed children of academic instruction and forced them into vocational training. When a leader of the opponents, John Hylan, won the mayor's race in 1917 after riots broke out in the city, he scrapped the plan, and it faded away in other cities as well over the next few years.

Despite the criticism, the Gary Plan was initially attractive to urban educators in the early part of the twentieth century because it was designed to address an issue that all cities faced at that time: a sharp rise in immigration. When the United States Steel Corporation built the world's largest steel mill in Gary in 1906, émigrés from many nations flocked to the city for jobs, and with them came their school-age children. The plan addressed the needs of the émigrés by trying to tap their varied interests; for example, it allowed youths who might not be facile in English to show their talents by working in a woodshop. Not coincidentally, the plan also attempted to "Americanize" students by introducing the children, many of whom came from impoverished backgrounds, to American social mores and sanitary practices in ways that traditional instructional methods could not.

With its rapidly growing immigrant population, Gary was hardly unique. In New York City, for example, some two-thirds of students in the first decade of the twentieth century had fathers who were born outside the United States.[1] Many of these recent immigrants came from Eastern and Southern Europe and were poorer than the immigrants from Western Europe who had arrived in the previous century.

Moreover, many of these new students struggled in school. In New York City in 1904, nearly half the fourth and fifth graders were overage for their grade, suggesting that they had been held back because they failed to master grade-level material. Dropout rates were high; of every 1,000 students who entered New York City schools in 1908, only 263 reached eighth grade, and only 56 reached the end of high school.[2]

URBAN SCHOOLS TODAY

Today, city schools face many of the same challenges as those of their early twentieth-century counterparts, and many new ones as well. Like the schools of the 1900s, the urban schools of the early twenty-first century include large numbers of students who have recently arrived from other countries and who speak languages other than English at home. Among the 65 large cities that belong to the Council of the Great City Schools, a national organization of large urban districts,17 percent of students are English-language learners, compared with 7 percent nationwide. Now, though, immigrants are more likely to come from Latin America, Africa, or Southeast Asia than from anywhere in Europe. In 2000, the top ten countries of origin for immigrants were Mexico, China, the Philippines, India, Cuba, Vietnam, El Salvador, Korea, the Dominican Republic, and Canada.[3]

City students now also resemble their earlier counterparts in economic status. In the 1900s, many immigrants settled in tenements that lacked even the most basic amenities, let alone what we would consider appropriate conditions to support children's learning. Today, some urban families live in dire circumstances, and many more struggle to survive from day to day. The rise of the suburbs after World War II and the migration of middle-class families from cities to outer-ring communities left poor families in the cities. Today, a disproportionate number of urban children come from low-income households.

In fact, some 30 percent of urban children live in poverty, compared with 22 percent in rural areas and 13 percent in suburbs. More than three in five urban students receive free and reduced-price lunches, and urban students are much more likely than students in other communities to attend schools with large concentrations of poor children. Some 40 percent of urban children attend high-poverty schools (those in which 40 percent or more of the students are eligible for subsidized meals) compared with 10 percent of suburban students, and 25 percent of rural students.[4]

Significantly, urban children are much more likely than others to live in concentrated poverty—that is, in neighborhoods with large numbers of poor families. Although poverty rates declined in the 1990s, the number of children in severely distressed neighborhoods—those with high poverty rates, high percentages of female-headed families, high percentages of high school dropouts, and high percentages of males unattached to the labor force—increased during that period. In 2000, 5.6 million children lived in distressed neighborhoods; this was 18 percent more than in 1990.[5]

URBAN ACADEMIC ACHIEVEMENT

Another factor urban children have in common with their counterparts from the last century is low academic achievement. Like the New York City children of 1908, large numbers of city students in 2005 are retained in grade and drop out of school. In Chicago, for example, where the district in 1996 adopted a policy to promote students in third, sixth, and eighth grades based on scores on standardized tests, some 7,000 to 10,000 students have been retained in their grades each year—one in five third graders, and one in ten sixth and eighth graders. Students who were retained in grade 8 were more likely to drop out of school by age seventeen. A number of other cities, notably Long Beach, California, and New York City, have adopted similar policies.[6]

Dropout rates are difficult to determine, because few districts track students who leave schools, but there is considerable evidence that large numbers of students leave school early in many cities. Perhaps the most reliable study of national graduation rates found that the graduation rate in central cities is 58 percent, compared with 73 percent in suburban school districts. In some cities, though, the rate may be much lower. A separate study of the "promoting power" of high schools—the extent to which students entering ninth grade actually graduate four years later—found that in nearly 1,000 schools, less than half the fresh-man class of 2002 earned a diploma that year. Of particular significance is the fact that most of these schools were in large and medium-sized cities, primarily in the Northeast and Midwest. In some cities, notably Indianapolis and St. Louis, all students attended schools with weak promoting power.[7]

The low level of academic achievement among urban students is also re-flected on tests, which are prevalent now but which barely existed in the early 1900s. Results from the National Assessment of Educational Progress show that students from central cities consistently perform lower in core subjects than those in suburbs and rural areas. For example, in 2003, 18 percent of fourth graders in large central cities performed at the proficient level or above in read-ing, compared with 30 percent nationwide: and 23 percent of fourth graders per-formed at the proficient level or above in mathematics, compared with 31 per-cent nationwide.[8]

On state tests, the story is similar. A study by the Council of the Great City Schools found that only seven of forty-nine member cities had scores in math-ematics that were equal to or higher than state averages in grades 4 and 8; and in reading only five cities equaled or outperformed state averages.[9]

Of course, as many studies have shown, academic performance is related to the demographic characteristics of students. On most measures, limited English proficiency and poverty are associated with low academic achievement. Thus, it is not surprising that cities, which have high concentrations of immigrants and poor children, also perform less well on tests and demonstrate higher drop-out rates.

During the 1990s, closing the gap in test performance between white and relatively affluent students, on the one hand, and poor students and students of color, on the other hand, became an urgent public-policy objective. At the beginning of the decade, the eight national education goals adopted by Presi-dent George H. W. Bush and the nation's governors and later ratified by Con-gress, pledged to raise achievement for all students. The third goal, on academic achievement, stated that "all students will leave grades 4, 8, and 12 having dem-onstrated competency in challenging subject matter," and an objective for the goal stated that "the distribution of minority students in each quartile will more closely reflect the student population as a whole." (A separate goal, on high school graduation, had as an objective that "the gap in high school graduation rates between American students from minority backgrounds and their nonmi-nority counterparts will be eliminated.")

By the end of the decade, however, eliminating the disparities in academic achievement was also a national goal. The No Child Left Behind Act of 2001

(NCLB), passed by large majorities in both houses of Congress, was aimed explicitly at closing the gap:

> The purpose of this title is to ensure that all children have a fair, equal, and significant opportunity to obtain a high-quality education and reach, at a minimum, proficiency on state academic achievement standards and state academic assessments. This purpose can be achieved by . . . closing the achievement gap between high- and low-performing children, especially the achievement gap between minority and nonminority students, and between disadvantaged children and their more-advantaged peers.

Yet in focusing on academic achievement, particularly achievement on standardized tests, the framers of NCLB, and other similar policy efforts under way at the same time, took a narrow view of educational opportunity and achievement. Like the critics of the Gary Plan, these policymakers rejected the idea of multiple pathways for youth success and instead addressed their efforts at improving academic outcomes only.

To be sure, test scores are important indicators of youth development, but they are indicators, not outcomes. By focusing on the indicator, rather than on the abilities the policymakers wish to develop, the policies risk constricting opportunities for young people and hindering their development.

A LONG-STANDING DEBATE

The debate over whether schools should focus solely on academic outcomes or include other pathways has a long history within which debate over the Gary Plan plays a prominent role. In the 1890s, for example, the Committee of Ten, a panel chaired by Charles Eliot, the president of Harvard College, advocated a common academic curriculum for all students. In its 1893 report, the committee noted "a very general custom in American high schools and academies to make up separate courses of study for pupils of supposed different direction," but argued that, instead, "every subject which is taught at all in a secondary school should be taught in the same way and to the same extent to every pupil as long as he pursues it, no matter what the probable destination of the pupil may be, or at what point his education is to cease." In fact, the members of the committee were concerned with the education offered to students who were *not* college bound.[10]

While this recommendation had some influence on high school instruction—enrollments in Latin increased sharply during the 1890s—a countermovement that proposed varied courses of study for students, depending on their interests and perceived abilities, ultimately held greater sway. The idea of a differentiated curriculum reflected the role of education in a rapidly growing industrial economy and answered the call from business for vocational training to prepare youths for the factories that were sprouting throughout America's cities, like Gary. The idea also helped school systems of the early twentieth century deal with rapidly exploding school populations resulting from immigration to large cities.

The idea of differentiated instruction was bolstered by the nascent science of mental testing, which coincidentally emerged at the same time as the rapid growth in the secondary school population. By enabling educators to rank students according to supposed ability, tests could allow them to channel students into a course of study that was considered appropriate. In many cases, unfortunately, school administrators held racially biased ideas about which students were best suited to vocational or academic coursework.

The notion of differentiation received its clearest expression and strongest boost with the publication of the *Cardinal Principals of Secondary Education*, the 1918 report of the National Education Association's Commission on the Reorganization of Secondary Education. That report declared, "The work of the senior high school should be organized into differentiated curriculums. . . . The basis of differentiation should be, in the broad sense of the term, vocational, thus justifying the names commonly given, such as agricultural, business, clerical, industrial, fine arts, and household-arts curriculums. Provisions should be made also for those having distinctively academic needs and interests."[11]

It is worth noting that, in the commission's view, such a program would open opportunities for young people. The goal, the report stated, was to enable each individual "to find his place and use that place to shape both himself and society toward ever nobler ends." Thus, the idea was to create multiple pathways for learning and development, not to choke off opportunities for learning or advancement.

Nevertheless, the advocates of academic instruction saw programs for differentiated instruction, like the Gary Plan, as dead ends, and they succeeded in killing the plan in New York and other cities. In the long run, though, to use the words of historian Jeffrey Mirel, "the *Cardinal Principles* team won." Mirel notes that, beginning in the 1930s, when economic opportunities dried up and school enrollments surged, the number of students taking academic courses in high schools declined, while enrollments in nonacademic courses, such as health and physical education, rose dramatically. According to Mirel, by 1982, 39 percent of high school coursework consisted of nonacademic subjects. At the same time, students earned academic credit for participation in extracurricular activities, such as working on student newspapers. Critics charged that the American high school resembled a "shopping mall," in which students could pick and choose courses based on their own interests without a plan for intellectual development.[12]

By the late 1970s, however, the changes in high schools provoked a backlash. Alarmed by perceptions of academic decline—best evidenced by the well-publicized decline in Scholastic Aptitude Tests from the mid-1960s to the mid-1970s—and anxious over threats to American economic dominance from Japan and other countries, policymakers began to press for a renewed focus on academic achievement. The landmark report of the National Commission on Excellence in Education, *A Nation at Risk*, warned ominously that a "rising tide of mediocrity" threatened American economic competitiveness. The report recommended strengthening academic coursework requirements. In response, nearly every state bolstered its graduation requirements, and the proportion of academic coursework increased substantially.[13]

Yet even as policymakers were responding to the perceived inadequacies in academic achievement, a growing body of research on how people learn and how schools should be structured suggested other possibilities for raising achievement. The findings suggested that students need a broad range of knowledge and skills in order to achieve at high levels, and that simply adding more traditional coursework would not be effective to raise achievement and eliminate achievement gaps. And the research suggested that, in some ways, the dichotomy between "academic" and "nonacademic" coursework might be a false one.

LEARNING AND ACHIEVEMENT

In a major review of the science of learning, a committee of the National Research Council concluded that people who are truly competent in a subject area—experts—differ from novices in significant ways:

- Experts notice features and meaningful patterns of information that are not noticed by novices.
- Experts have acquired a great deal of content knowledge that is organized in ways that reflect a deep understanding of their subject matter.
- Experts' knowledge cannot be reduced to sets of isolated facts or propositions but instead reflects contexts of applicability; that is, the knowledge is "conditionalized" on a set of circumstances.
- Experts are able to flexibly receive important aspects of their knowledge with little attentional effort.[14]

These findings suggest strongly that developing expertise among young people is not a matter of simply adding more instruction; it involves teaching in different ways. For example, the report notes, expanding students' breadth of knowledge might be ineffective because students would not be able to organize the vast storehouse of knowledge in meaningful ways. In addition, learning facts and formulas out of the context in which they are used does not help students learn; such knowledge remains "inert."

Other research examined the learning environments that produced high levels of achievement for all students. In their five-year study of schools in twenty-two districts, Newmann and Associates defined "authentic achievement" as consisting of the following criteria:

- Construction of knowledge, including the ability to organize knowledge and consider alternatives
- Disciplined inquiry, including content, process, and elaborated written communication
- Value beyond school, including connecting problems to the real world and engaging audiences beyond schools

Like the cognitive researchers, the researchers who examined restructured schools found that learning environments that produced high levels of achievement engaged students intellectually and provided opportunities for students to organize their knowledge effectively and to relate what they were learning to the world outside the classroom. They found that schools that operated in this way produced high—and equitable—levels of achievement. And they concluded that achieving high levels of intellectual ability is essential for all young people. According to Newmann and Associates:

> The complexities of contemporary society demand that citizens be problem solvers and lifelong learners capable of adapting to changing economic and social conditions. Whether trying to make a living, manage personal affairs, or participate in civic life, citizens are increasingly called on to exercise the kinds of intellectual capacities reflected in authentic achievement. Schools that fail to help students face these challenges deny them opportunities for security, productivity, and fulfillment.[15]

A third body of research looked at the workplace and examined the skills that entry-level workers needed in order to succeed in an increasingly technological economy. Like the cognitive and school-restructuring studies, these workplace studies found that all students needed a broader range of knowledge and skills than most schools tended to address, and that the development

FIGURE 1
The SCANS Workplace "Know-How"

The know-how identified by SCANS is made up of five competencies and a three-part foundation of skills and personal qualities that are needed for solid job performance. These include:

COMPETENCIES—effective workers can productively use:
- **Resources**—allocating time, money, materials, space, and staff
- **Interpersonal skills**—working on teams, teaching others, serving customers, leading, negotiating, and working well with people from culturally diverse backgrounds
- **Information**—acquiring and evaluating data, organizing and maintaining files, interpreting and communicating, and using computers to process information
- **Systems**—understanding social, organizational, and technological systems, monitoring and correcting performance, and designing or improving systems
- **Technology**—selecting equipment and tools, applying technology to specific tasks, and maintaining and troubleshooting technologies

THE FOUNDATION—competence requires:
- **Basic skills**—reading, writing, arithmetic and mathematics, speaking, and listening
- **Thinking skills**—thinking creatively, making decisions, solving problems, seeing things in the mind's eye, knowing how to learn, and reasoning
- **Personal qualities**—individual responsibility, self-esteem, sociability, self-management, and integrity

Source: The Secretary's Commission on Achieving Necessary Skills, 1991

of such abilities would require qualitatively different approaches, not just additional coursework. These studies were particularly influential because much of the push for higher levels of academic achievement came from business leaders concerned that too few students would graduate with the abilities necessary for the workplace.

One such study was conducted by a panel appointed by Lynn M. Martin, secretary of labor in George H. W. Bush's administration. The Secretary's Commission on Achieving Necessary Skills (SCANS) identified the "know-how" that all young people should possess, whether they intended to go to college, the workplace, or the armed service. Furthermore, the study suggested that only half of all high school students had these abilities at the time (see figure 1).

The three bodies of research—those that focused on cognitive science, school restructuring, or workplace competencies—pointed in similar directions. They all suggested that all young people are capable of high levels of intellectual development, but they defined intellectual development more broadly than traditional notions of subject-matter knowledge. They further suggested that enabling students to attain high levels of intellectual development required not simply adding more mandated courses, but adopting a fundamentally different way of teaching and organizing learning.

In many ways, the research harkened back to the ideas of John Dewey and to those of school leaders he championed, like William A. Wirt. By engaging students in work activities, those early-twentieth century reformers were not diverting students from intellectual development; rather they were enhancing their intellectual development.

APPLYING THE RESEARCH

Applying these lines of research, educators in the late 1980s and early 1990s began to develop new forms of curriculum, instruction, assessment, and school organization that were explicitly aimed at developing a broad range of student abilities, and they did so for all students, not just a few. These efforts also informed the national and state standards for student performance that were developed at the same time.

One of the most ambitious of the reform efforts was the New Standards Project (later New Standards), a joint effort of the National Center on Education and the Economy (NCEE) and the Learning Research and Development Center (LRDC) at the University of Pittsburgh. Launched in partnership with seventeen states and six large urban school districts, New Standards aimed to develop a set of standards for all students in core subjects and a related system of assessments that would measure student performance against the standards. These standards and assessments were intended to drive changes in classroom practice.[16]

Significantly, New Standards defined intellectual ability in much the same way as did the cognitive, restructuring, and workforce researchers: the possession of knowledge *and* the ability to apply knowledge in real-world situations. Students who met the standards had to demonstrate their abilities by some kind of performance, such as writing an essay or completing a project. The examinations relied heavily on performance-based assessment, which required students to compose their own responses rather than choose from among a prese-lected set of answers.

Marc S. Tucker, the president of NCEE, and Judy B. Codding, NCEE's vice president, explained that the goal was to meld the best of academic and voca-tional education:

> The disciplines are very much present . . . , and the need to master the struc-tures of knowledge they represent is greater than ever. But they are not to be inert knowledge, mastered for its own sake. They are to achieve their ultimate justification in their active use, which has been up to now the domain of vo-cational education. These standards, then, are the standards for useful educa-tion. They marry head and hand.[17]

A number of states and districts in the 1990s moved to incorporate perfor-mance assessments into their assessment systems, and to measure a wide range of student abilities. Maryland's state assessment, for example, included tasks that would be completed by groups of students. The purpose of this move was to encourage classrooms to engage students in collaborative work.

In addition, many of the comprehensive school-reform designs supported by the New American Schools Development Corporation engaged students in long-term projects, often taking them outside of classrooms to conduct research and present findings to public audiences. These designs were adopted by hundreds of schools around the country.[18]

BACK TO THE FUTURE

However, in an echo of the early-twentieth-century debates about the Gary Plan, many of the efforts made in the 1990s proved hotly controversial, and many were dropped. Maryland's performance assessment was replaced by a more con-ventional test, for example, as was the New Standards Reference Examination, which had been used in Rhode Island and Vermont.

Some of these efforts were abandoned for logistical reasons. Performance as-sessments, which must be scored by individuals who read student responses or observe their presentations, cost considerably more than multiple-choice tests, which can be scored by machine. Similarly, assessments that rely on human judgment are less technically reliable than traditional tests. In Vermont, for ex-ample, an evaluation of that state's pioneering assessment, which measured student knowledge and skills by examining portfolios of their work conducted throughout the year, found that the reliability was too low to allow for individ-ual student scores, at least at first.[19]

But performance assessments and projects have also come under fire from critics who contend that they are less rigorous academically than more traditional forms of instruction, and that they measure students' values and attitudes, rather than their academic abilities. In Pennsylvania, for example, a plan to require students to demonstrate a broad set of outcomes in addition to traditional academic content—including information and thinking skills, the ability to learn independently and collaboratively, adaptability to change, and self-worth—met heated objections, and most of the nonacademic outcomes were eliminated.[20]

Some of the resistance to broadening the opportunities and outcomes for learning reflected the growing concern with the achievement gap. For some policymakers and educators, the gap—as measured by standardized tests—can be closed by a focus on the basic academic skills that the tests measure. As Abigail Thernstrom, coauthor of *No Excuses: Closing the Racial Gap in Learning*, put it, schools that succeed in closing the achievement gap "focus relentlessly on the core academic subjects. They insist that their students learn the times tables, basic historical facts, spelling, punctuation, the rules of grammar, and the meaning of unfamiliar words."[21]

The No Child Left Behind Act reflects this view. As noted earlier, one of the main purposes of the law is to attempt to close the achievement gap, and it does so by requiring states to test all students in grades 3 through 8 each year in reading and mathematics and holding schools accountable for ensuring "adequate yearly progress" for all students and groups of students.

NCLB has had an enormous influence on school practice since its enactment, and in some ways it has expanded educational opportunities for students. For example, there is evidence that the accountability for subgroups of students—African Americans, Hispanics, children with disabilities, English-language learners—has led schools to focus on students who might have been "left behind" in the past.[22]

On the other hand, there is evidence that the law has restricted opportunities as well. Many schools have reported that they have cut back on instruction in the arts and other subjects that are not required by NCLB.[23] And the requirement for annual testing has led states to cut back on their more ambitious assessments that encourage an expanded vision of learning and opportunity. Linda Darling Hammond writes that

> NCLB regulations are pushing states back to the lowest common denominator in testing, undoing progress that has been made to improve the quality of assessments and delaying the move from antiquated norm-referenced, multiple-choice tests to criterion-referenced assessment systems that measure and

help develop important kinds of performance and learning. This not only re- duces the chances that schools will be able to focus on helping students ac- quire critical thinking, research, writing, and production abilities; it will also reduce opportunities for students who learn in different ways and have differ- ent talents to show what they have learned. . . . [There is a] strong possibility that these efforts will actually reduce access to education for the most vulner- able students, rather than increasing it.[24]

Moreover, by holding schools alone accountable for raising achievement and closing achievement gaps, NCLB ignores the critical importance of institutions outside school that contribute to student learning. As Gordon and Bridglall note, high achieving students not only perform well in school, but they also have ac- cess to a wide range of resources—"supplementary education"—that are not available to lower-achieving students.[25] Attempting to close the achievement gap will not succeed as long as the gaps in learning outside school remain large.

AN OPPORTUNITY GAP

The achievement gap is really a gap in learning opportunities. There is consid- erable research to confirm the intuitive idea that students learn what they have been taught. Much of the research comes from international studies, which show that differences in achievement among countries is related to the content stu- dents have opportunities to learn. Studies in this country have also documented the link between the content and depth of instruction and achievement.[26]

Not surprisingly, poor students and students of color, who tend to be on the low end of the achievement gap, also are on the low end of the opportunity gap. Such students have less access to high-quality facilities and teachers, and fewer opportunities to take higher-level courses. Moreover, low-income students are also more likely to receive rote instruction aimed at basic skills.[27] In other words, poor students and students of color have fewer opportunities to engage in the type of learning environments that the cognitive, school-restructuring, and workplace researchers have found are essential to high achievement.

Learning opportunities outside school are also inequitably distributed.[28] These opportunity gaps exacerbate those within schools and make it more dif- ficult to ensure that all students have the opportunity to achieve at high levels. Closing the achievement gap, then, demands attention to children's opportuni- ties to learn both inside and outside school.

In the early days of the standards movement, reformers argued that standards for student achievement should be accompanied by standards for opportunity to learn. Advocates charged that it was unfair to expect students to reach high standards of achievement without assurances that they had the resources necessary for high achievement. Reformers further argued that states should be accountable for providing the opportunities for all students to achieve.[29]

These standards, sometimes called "delivery standards," proved hotly controversial. Critics argued that they measured inputs, not outcomes, and that they could prove costly if states were sued for failing to provide adequate resources. In the end, the legislation that authorized the creation of standards and tests did not mandate opportunity-to-learn standards.

Nevertheless, these opportunities remain critical if the real achievement gap is to close. More importantly, they are necessary *at scale*. Many individual schools have created broad arrays of learning opportunities, and these have benefited the students who have taken advantage of them. But the persistence and scope of the achievement gap suggests that much more is needed to provide opportunities for many more students in many more schools. Moreover, the ad hoc partnerships that individual schools create to provide broader opportunities are difficult to sustain.

Closing the opportunity gap, and thus the achievement gap, takes a city. Cities have the resources and the power to make broad learning opportunities available on a large scale. But few cities have taken stock of the opportunities that exist, much less made them equitably available. The following chapter will examine the rich educational resources that cities possess and the ways that young people can expand their opportunities to learn.

CITY KIDS, CITY FAMILIES:
CITY COMMITMENTS

Dennie Palmer Wolf and Heather A. Harding

There are two persistent images of cities as places in which to grow up. The first is that of an urban childhood, which is often shorthand for a life endangered by substandard housing, street crime, and poverty. In this image, the city is one continuous lesson in hopelessness, deviance, and alienation. It is a place of overcrowded ghettos filled with single-parent households where there is never enough money to pay the bills, few adults engaged in the formal job market, and others lacking the desire and motivation to become so. Viewed through this lens, urban childhoods are criminal breeding grounds where the drug trade is a way of life, and only a few escape via routes of success in school or entry into the worlds of entertainment or professional sports.[1]

A contrasting image is that of the urbane childhood. In this case, cities are cultural hubs loaded with resources for living, learning, and thriving; places where families can access the glamour of an upper-class lifestyle through theaters, libraries, museums, and plazas. It is an image redolent of the yuppie phenomenon of the 1980s and kept alive in the ongoing gentrification of many cities, in which young, white professionals live luxuriously in rehabilitated urban neighborhoods like Brooklyn's Park Slope and the traditionally black sections of Chicago south of the Loop. Part of this image is a young life that includes wearing city fashions, choosing from a menu, playing in city parks, having city playgrounds as personal gardens, and learning about diversity (in class and power) from the day labor of a Caribbean nanny. It is a lifestyle that teaches the ways in which social and financial capital can knit a city's disparate amenities into a way of life. The child who learns these lessons grows up cosmopolitan and sophisticated.

While these two images color public perceptions of childhood in the city, there is also a third—much less dramatic and rarely articulated—view of growing up in a metropolis. This image of a city offers families and their children the diverse, eclectic, and dynamic experiences necessary to produce savvy, risk-taking, and thoughtful citizens who understand both the benefits and the responsibilities of urban living. Consider the perspective of one city mother, talking about bringing up her son in a city:

> We want him growing up in a city for the same reasons we want him in public schools. He is going to be far more educated about the good and the bad of living with lots of different people. He's going to have a full range of experiences. In his neighborhood, he's in an advantaged white majority. At school, he's still advantaged, but he is in the minority. In the afternoons, at the Rec Center, he is the only white kid in the place, and the advantages he usually has don't count for so much when they play basketball or computer games. There he's the cultural outsider. Me, too, I stuck out as the white mom coming to check the place out. I didn't know the black citizen for whom the place was named. I saw the two windowless rooms with the broken-down equipment and it brought all my assumptions that it would be chaotic, or unsupervised, when it was a relaxed, orderly place. He adores it; he rushes out of school to get down there with his friends. So much so that he forgot his homework two days in a row. He wanted me to write him an excuse. I told him he has to stay tight with his responsibilities even though he's learning to move between worlds. That's part of it.

City living can make for a distinctive young adulthood with many opportunities. Bernice, a black sophomore at Brown University, grew up in Boston and was part of a group of student activists who produced a short film comparing urban and suburban schools. When she thinks of urban, she says, she thinks of exposure: "I think of vibrancy, fast-paced and having to be on top of things. Exposure—whether that be too much too soon, I'm not sure." Bernice distinguishes urban people from rural and suburban folks based on their ability to maneuver and have a "ready for action" attitude. "You aren't just waiting for stuff to happen. You're more apt to take responsibility for things. It's about being more efficient, being able to ask questions," she says. Bernice recognizes that there is a negative side to an urban identity; this is its association with poverty, but she emphasizes the knowledge and creativity her peers developed. She cites their potential in business because "they know what the people want, they know how to address problems." In explaining her notion of "street smarts," Bernice doubles back to say the city has a lot to offer its residents in the way of resources, but not everyone "knows how to make use of them."

The kind of experience Bernice describes may make for a special kind of young adult, citizen, and worker. For example, a highly successful white teacher of urban black students, Jennifer Black, claims an urban identity as one of the major keys to her success. She herself grew up in a city that was racially and economically diverse, where the vast majority of students were served by one public high school. She describes her educational experiences as rigorous, diverse, and dynamic, but acknowledges that, for her, urban often meant an eclectic mix of people all listening to hip-hop music at school dances. Ultimately, Black says that being a "city girl" shaped her motivations for teaching urban black students in a way that fosters academic excellence. Her assertion of an urban identity is an explicit way of sharing a commitment to social justice across racial and class lines and a form of cultural capital that allows her access to the lives of her black students.[2] The urban identity provides her with an authentic connection to the lives of "city" kids; what she shares with them surpasses their differences.

The testimonies of this young family, university student, and teacher reveal an understanding of urban education that includes schools, but extends beyond them by highlighting sports, recreation centers, social networks, and the daily experiences of city living. Furthermore, these testimonies underscore that this kind of urban education exerts a powerful draw for families and young people. It does this by offering: (1) opportunities to develop complex personal identities that cross racial, religious, and class boundaries; (2) important cultural and civic dispositions; and (3) expressive and critical power rarely available to young people. Bounded by geography, city dwellers share a collective experience despite the many forms of stratification. This urban identity connotes a particular place-based experience suggestive of both exotic and commonplace elements. If the world understands urban to be synonymous with a cross between cosmopolitan sophistication and edgy, popular culture, then being urban provides a passport across multiple contexts.

In many respects, this chapter is an exploration of whether and how this kind of urban education can take place. We do this in several steps. First, we examine current thinking about what constitutes a city and, correspondingly, what constitutes urban education. Then, because we believe that smart education systems will have to be built in real and particular places, we turn our attention to a particular city, Providence, Rhode Island. Using citywide and neighborhood data, as well as interviews of long- and short-term Providence residents, we then examine a set of "city habits" that keep Providence—like many other cities—from functioning as smart education systems. Subsequently, we look at a set of "city promises." These are ways of doing business that could turn Providence steadily toward becoming a smart education system, that is, a source of opportunity for children regardless of their address. Finally, we forecast a set of next steps to be discussed in detail in this book's final chapter.

REDEFINING CITY, QUALITY OF LIFE, AND URBAN EDUCATION

The dictionary definition of "city" has everything to do with geography and governance: A city is "an incorporated urban center in the United States that has self-government, boundaries and legal rights established by state charter."[3]

But recent thinking about cities suggests a multifaceted dimension to the notion of city. In this book, a city is not only a geographical entity; it is also the experience of living, working, viewing, and being viewed in that particular place. In this respect, a city is not a single place. For example, a native-born European youth and the second-generation North African Muslim youth in Paris live very different lives and inhabit different identities as Parisians. The first is a citizen in good standing free to move throughout the city; the second is only technically a citizen who is immediately suspect outside of housing projects at the rim of the city. In this more dynamic view, cities—whether Paris or New York—are not just the literal geography where children grow up; they are active forces in how they grow up.

Cities directly affect young people's health, mobility, safety, and quality of schooling. They also shape identity.[4] High-status young people experience their city as a network of advantages: they receive the best child care, have the strongest teachers, enroll in places like a downtown arts center, take Saturday excursions to libraries or festivals, and land jobs and internships even while still in high school.

Low-status youths experience a radically different city. A young woman may see her mother work three shifts, while her father searches for a living wage or goes unemployed. A young man is likely to live in a racially segregated neighborhood where his street isn't plowed in a major snowstorm. In addition, he may well be hassled by the police. In this sense, the city of upper- and middle-class children is not the same city inhabited by lower-class children whose families struggle to keep them safe, fed and going to school. Even though these classes of children technically share the same mayor and city council, streets, library, park, and school systems, they live in starkly different ecologies with different neighbors, routes, pleasures, dangers, and opportunities. These different kinds of cities are active forces shaping opportunity and development for youths in sharply different ways.

The differing perspectives on a city suggest that traditional ways of measuring quality of life—average incomes or the availability of amenities not equitably shared—are inadequate. Instead, we propose redefining quality of life to measure indicators that all residents share: basic guarantees regarding safety, health, and nutrition; frequent and respectful interactions among inhabitants; equitable investments of public resources and services in the development and learning of young people, independent of race, class, first language, or address; and an active role for youth in planning the policies that affect their lives.[5]

This redefinition of the quality of life suggests that we also need to rethink urban education. Typically, urban education is thought of as synonymous with the buildings, staff, funding, and practices that go with the school district. While this definition is absolutely correct from a governance point of view, it is insufficient when we think of cities as ecologies for development. A wider definition of urban education, which includes schools and the district that runs them, contains a number of additional and critical ingredients that affect learning:

- Opportunities to participate in activities like a drama club, sports team, band, and choir around and outside school
- Opportunities for free time and informal learning in activities like spending time on the Internet or engaging in pick-up basketball games
- Ability to participate in the adult worlds of work, decisionmaking, and policy-making
- Lessons that a city teaches its youth about their value and the value of people like them

Such a definition encompasses the kind of education to which advantaged children typically have access, and the kind that less-advantaged children could experience if opportunities were more equitably distributed.

URBAN EDUCATION IN PROVIDENCE, RHODE ISLAND

Providence, a city of 175,000, is at least three cities in one. The city's East Side contains the largest surviving stand of pre–Civil War houses in the United States, where the average price for a single-family dwelling is over $500,000. The East Side hosts an Ivy League university, numerous private day schools, and almost no students who attend the Providence public schools. It is an enclave of gardens, Volvos, and high-end food markets. In this "glade," there is virtually no child poverty, no evidence of lead-paint poisoning, and a very low crime rate. As one mother from across the city commented, "We go over there to walk around. It's like being in a park—a really safe, really beautiful one."

There is a second Providence, located in the South and West Ends, that ranks among the ten poorest cities with more than one hundred thousand inhabitants in the United States. This city houses second- and third-generation immigrant families and continues to draw newcomers from Africa, Latin America, and Southeast Asia. In many of these neighborhoods, the battle to stay ahead of rent and bills is tough. Since the decline of manufacturing following World War II, the economy of the city has stagnated, leaving only low-paying day labor and service industries for those without high school and college credentials. Far from the leafy brick houses of the East Side, in neighborhoods like Olneyville and Elmwood, child poverty is high, because even more fundamentally, adult poverty is high, and opportunity to earn and advance is low. As a single mother earning just above the poverty line explains, "It takes sacrificing time; you have to be very involved, even to make sure that they get what they should. I had to work to find the teachers who match what each of my kids needs." This mother effectively maintains two jobs: her wage-earning position and the equally demanding job of piecing together decent public education for her children.

Though it has no specific geography, in scattered places there is a third Providence. It is the city where long-term and immigrant families bring multiple languages, cultural values, and global perspectives to what matters in family, neighborhood, and city life. It is a community that supports an annual Dominican festival, the Black Repertory Theater, and radio stations that play salsa, Texana, gospel, rap, and classical music. It is a place where identities are compound, where there is mutuality and community, and where families have found opportunities for their children that could produce a first generation of college graduates.

Providence's Three School Systems

In terms of schooling, there are at least three parallel school systems available in Providence. In the East Side, most children attend a network of high-end independent schools with their own playing fields, athletic leagues, dances, and field trips. In high school, some students cross over to the public schools to attend Classical, the city's one exam school, established in the nineteenth century as a Latin School. To this day, Classical boasts many more Advanced Placement classes than any other school in the city and is the only high school that is rated "proficient" in the district.

For residents of South Providence and the West End, the public schools are, on average, poor. Families with little knowledge about education or choice in the matter are likely to find their elementary-age sons and daughters bringing home pages and pages of routine work. The state recently declared every middle school "in need of improvement," and the superintendent reassigned or moved all eleven middle school principals. Many of the schools are in need of repair—as one mother put it, "with Plexiglas over the windows that is so old it has turned dark yellow." The churn of students moving in and out of the system is so great that only a seventh of an entering first grade class remains at twelfth grade because of mobility, retention, and dropping out.

But there is a third school system that determined families—even poor and immigrant ones—create by investing hours and every ounce of social capital they can to learn where to enroll each of their children. These parents enter every possible lottery and use every available application process. A young adult remembers how his mother "built" this education system for him and his three sisters:

> Almost as soon as we settled here my mom first started her job as a teaching assistant at the Asa Messer School. She really refined her English and worked at getting an internal view of the Providence Public School System so she learned all the kinks, where to go and who to talk to. Even now I ask her "What if you never had that job there?" First she put us in Providence Head Start. While she worked my grandmother took care of me and I had an uncle who came later who picked me up. My mom really started to know what was really going on, so she put us in St. Mary's because they had a full day of kindergarten, not half day like every other school. Right after that she pulled us right out and threw us into the gifted resource program at E. W. Flynn. I don't know if she worried about it being safe since it's not in the best area, but she figured out it did have a gifted resource program and that's what she wanted for us. So for sixth-grade through eighth-grade we went to Nathaniel Greene because it had the transitional gifted resource program my mom was really interested in. After Nathaniel Greene, we went to Classical, the exam school in Providence. The whole time, my mom especially was proactive about getting us the best. You couldn't ask for help at home because my parents only did high school and both of them were always working. Because they are immigrants they couldn't really play that role. But every single day my mom would ask me, "What are you getting for your grades?" or "How are you doing in school?" She only had high school but she always pushed me to do better, always told me I could do better.

This cobbled system of school experiences relies on individual agency and familial resources to identify and access the best of what the formal educational

institutions have to offer. The effort expended does result in a high-quality product, but it also reinforces a system of winners and losers. A superstructure that
coordinated services and assumed accountability for quality education would
all but eliminate the disparate experiences described above.[6]

Providence's Three Education Systems

Schools are only part of Providence's urban education system. Snapshots of the
athletic opportunities of three young boys' make this clear:

> Nine-year-old Henry is white and of the middle class. On Monday evenings,
> he has hockey league—an almost all-white affair where white-collar dads, re-
> membering their own leagues, all coach from the sideline as if each game is a
> major tournament. On Thursdays, Henry has soccer in a city park where the
> kids and families are largely Cape Verdean, Guatemalan, and Dominican and
> steeped in soccer as it is played and understood in Africa and Latin America.
> After school he goes to the rec center, where he is the one white student.
>
> Four blocks down the hill, Henry's friends from school, Justice and Jabril,
> live in a long-standing African American neighborhood that is a mix of projects,
> worn single-family homes, and "three deckers," some of which are boarded
> up. The two boys go to the free Rec Center attached to the Y after school. It is
> two windowless rooms with outdated-sports and computer equipment. Once
> they have finished their homework, the boys play pick-up basketball. In their
> free time, Justice and Jabril have invented an athletic contest of their own: a
> bike trail that snakes through empty lots, up and down invented ramps, and
> into an abandoned garage.
>
> Half a mile away, in the extremely privileged East Side, lives Camden, who
> is also nine and white. He attends a private school where he plays on the ele-
> mentary soccer team, which is a part of an intramural sports league with other
> independent schools throughout the region. The team regularly has "away"
> games with other private schools to which they travel in the school's vans.
> Outside school, in summer, Camden takes private tennis lessons. He has also
> learned to swim at newly built Y on the city's East Side.

The added experiences that Camden and Henry have are as much a part of
their education as the formal classrooms where they spend the school day. Camden's sports learning is bolstered by excellent in-school team sports instruction, and Camden's family uses its considerable income to purchase excellent
equipment and tickets to professional sporting events. Henry's family, though
not wealthy, has two incomes and sufficient funds for the dues of a hockey
league and gas for their car that transports him to away games. What's more,

his parents have flexible work schedules that make it possible to drive to evening practices.

But the added experiences that Camden and Henry have are not available to Henry's friends down the hill. Although Justice and Jabril are just as energetic, talented, and determined as Henry or Camden, they have a very different set of opportunities to learn and play sports beyond their gym classes at school. They have time, but very little access to training. Their daredevil bike path, fantastic as it is, is not going to bring them to the notice of a coach, another father, or a scout. Though it is challenging to build and use, the path doesn't build their intellectual or social capital as the mainstream/hegemonic adult world conceives of these resources.

Athletics are just one slice of the differences in the city's wider education systems. Similar patterns exist in art centers and afterschool jobs. Families know how these inequalities magnify the differences in what their children are learning. One Providence working mother remarks:

> I work, no choice about that, and I have four kids still in school. I have to have care from eight to five, no question about that either. I want it to be good. I wish there was money for lessons in this and lessons in that. And a way to get them back and forth. But I am stuck with the afterschool that's right there. Or what the Y can offer. Different years I know it was only babysitting for one or more of them. They are safe, that's about all I can say. Sometimes, especially for my youngest, that is all it was. He needs structure and it was wild in there with kids running all around for three hours. So he was getting in trouble. The most he learned from there was that he was "bad." It is not a bargain I would make if I had a choice.

As a city, Providence has the resources for a more holistic education system with plentiful and diverse opportunities for learning and development. From the foundation of the local school district, a system could emerge from the myriad formal and informal providers of learning across the metropolitan area. Unfortunately, these resources remain largely undiscovered or uncoordinated. A family or a young person must have far-reaching social networks to locate these opportunities and the social capital to access them. Doing so often requires deft scheduling maneuvers and complex transportation arrangements. Putting all the pieces together requires enormous personal agency.

Consider the experience of Eli, an immigrant student from the Dominican Republic. Eli has recently been recruited to the planning committee for his new math/science-focused small high school. A self-described motivated student, Eli is involved in several activities that enhance his education. He rates studying Japanese on the bus after school and time spent at local community centers as the most valuable parts of his day:

> Right now I have all these activities in my life. So on a Friday I go to welding and wrestling and then to the Broad Street Studio to get help on my Japanese. . . . I'm at Broad Street Studio because I make it in time to, like, sign up for them and I get one of the few spots, which is kind of selfish on my part but I think it's just that a lot of students don't have that kind of opportunity. I just think it's just a lucky few. There's not that many programs that are available in the city, so me, personally, I'm pretty lucky I got in a lot of programs. It's sad but it's just about word of mouth. I'd see a lot of my friends from wrestling freshman year around the Plaza and they told me I should go to the Davis Community Center and, like, go practice over there. That's how I found out about wrestling. I found out about welding because a friend of mine, she told me about the program. She told me that there were a couple of spots empty, that if I hurried up I might be able to make it in time. So that's how I signed up for that and Broad Street Studio was through the welding program that I got involved with them. But before that I didn't even know that was an actual workshop. At my high schools before this you didn't find out anything about the clubs or the activities outside of school.

Access to high-functioning education systems that include but exceed classroom learning is more than a nicety. A growing body of research suggests that this kind of complementary or supplementary learning is as necessary as in-school academics for closing the stubborn achievement gaps that plague American education.[7]

Clearly, an effective partnership between in- and out-of-school learning is critical to the future of a city like Providence. To recover from the economic downturn of the 1960s–1980s, the city will need a next generation who can afford housing, who can stabilize the school population, who can start small and midsized businesses, and who can raise children with early learning skills and high aspirations of their own. The city needs an educated citizenry.

CITY HABITS

Providence, like many cities, has an underlying set of habits that perpetuate the unevenness of learning opportunities throughout the city. It is important to examine four of the most fundamental of these—segregation, inaccessibility, fragmentation of opportunity, and failure to involve the families and youth in substantial ways—so that the city can develop a fully functioning and equitable education system.

Habit 1: Segregation of Opportunity

In contrast to the traditional view of segregation as division by race, today's urban segregation is threefold: it divides along lines of income, race/ethnicity, and language. Income inequity is at an all-time high in U.S. cities.[8] Census data show that middle-class neighborhoods have virtually disappeared in cities, creating more polarized neighborhoods comprised of all high- or all low-income families. Gentrification exacerbates this trend and adds to the segregation by ethnicity. Downtown areas that were once middle-income, racially and ethnically diverse neighborhoods are turning into higher-income, largely white neighborhoods.

The Hispanic population boom has resulted in greater segregation by language. Latino students, the fastest growing group of students in U.S. schools, are the most likely to attend segregated schools. The average Latino attends a school that is 55 percent Latino.[9]

Providence, like many other cities, has perpetuated these trends through housing policies that failed to value, stabilize, or create mixed-income, mixed-race neighborhoods or affordable housing. And the divisions along class, racial and ethnic, and language lines invariably produce unequal opportunities, particularly educational opportunities. As a parent in South Providence reveals her feelings on this subject:

> I was listening to that other mother talking about the after school program where her kid goes. I'm thinking, "Wish my kids had stuff like chess club. Where they go it's a holding pen. They don't sit down and do the homework like they say they do. They believe the kids when they say they don't have any. The people in the program are always talking about 'these urban kids.'"

Habit 2: Inaccessible Opportunity

In Providence, as in many cities, there are actually many opportunities for learning and development; however, they are, in large part, unorganized and implicit. The system works largely by word of mouth. For example, the programs of many small arts organizations are ostensibly open and available to all. But, if enrollment is limited, and if public transportation from modest and low-income neighborhoods involves two buses and walking, then the programs are functionally inaccessible to large numbers of students and families. If the chance to attend advanced classes in a studio, or to step up into an internship or assistant teacher role in the same place, depends on social networking with the staff there, then the benefits of participating in opportunities offered by the studio reach a small and replicating population of students.

Cities often build programs but not the infrastructure to support them. This means that while urban centers may have debate, wrestling, or mentoring programs located throughout the city, it is hard to get to them. For instance, high school students in Providence are entitled to a bus pass only if they live more than three miles from the school they attend. While this may be fiscally responsible at one level, it makes it a student's responsibility to pay the bus fare for his or her activities. This creates one more barrier to accessing the opportunities that are "on the books," as expressed in the voice of a youth worker:

> I would say the biggest obstacle is what I'll call the bootstrap mentality: this idea that if kids want something it is there for them. So often it is said without any compassion for the struggle with the actual dimensions of the work of being a kid growing up in this city: the responsibilities for other kids in the family, or for older members of the family, for translating, for being a co-income earner, dealing with the snarl and slowness of public transportation. So often people are just inflexible around this belief. "Kids should just do it." They rarely ask how can the institutions be supportive of kids' success. That is what we have to change.

And in the voice of a parent:

> I don't know what they are thinking when they put programs in place. They think they've laid out this big banquet in front of you. There's this and this, and over on the other side of town, there's this and this. But it's like there are no forks on the table. No way an ordinary family with several kids, one car, and only just so much money, can pick up what's offered. It's like you have to be rich to use what's supposed to be for free.

Habit 3: The Fragmentation of Opportunity

Even if a youth manages to avail herself of a learning opportunity, there are few clear pathways to enable her to pursue her interest or develop a talent over time. Through a school or community program, a Providence student may develop an interest in chess, drumming, or debate. But frequently, there is no program that directly follows the original one. This means that a student has to give up on her interest or search outside the system to find a continuation of the program. Added to this is the money needed for transportation and often dollars to support the interest. One parent cites the costs of negotiating the pathways to enable her daughter to pursue dance:

> In elementary school they had this dancer for a while as part of the gym program. She really got into it, but then it was over. And there wasn't money for

dance lessons. So her teacher suggested that maybe she would want to try out for cheerleading, that it had a lot of the same moves in it. She said they practiced right there at the school and there was a late bus. So I thought "Okay." It worked out real well until the season actually started and she had to get to games on time, across the city. I had to put my other two in the car, grab them something to eat. She wanted to keep it going, but it was costing the other three of us something terrible.

Habit 4: Opportunities Designed for, Not with, Families and Youth

Advocates for children's rights and youth development describe young people as "excluded" from cities where they live.[10] At one level, this phrase refers to the fact that few city spaces and institutions are designed or run with children—and especially older youth—in mind. But at a second level, this description refers to the lack of young people's voice in the designs, policies, or programs that are meant to serve them. Consider the Rhode Island Department of Education's high school graduation policy. Under state requirements, each school district must come up with its own measures to determine whether students demonstrate mastery of high school coursework. These regulations are rooted in a commitment to using multiple measures of student proficiency, as well as a determination to ensure that high school diplomas throughout Rhode Island are meaningful. Yet the rules were developed without any input from families and students. This is a stunning example of design for "their own good" that has not, to date, involved the people best informed to think about such issues

PROVIDENCE'S PROMISE

At face value, Providence—like other small to midsize cities—has the potential to use its substantial resources effectively to meet the challenge of providing a high quality education to all its children. For a small city, Providence has a great deal of intellectual, human, and organizational resources. If marshaled, these could provide the force needed to address its characteristic city habits. Then, Providence could create a public education system that worked for all children the way the system works for the affluent children of the East Side.

In each of the previous sections, young people and families have identified opportunities, programs, and schools that could, with some help from the city, serve their educational needs. Their testimony points to the tremendous potential of American cities, particularly Providence. What Providence needs now is a *system* that links resources across sectors, and is responsive to the diverse socioeconomic and cultural needs of city dwellers. The following two examples from Providence illustrate the degree of collaboration, information sharing, and widening participation needed for building such a system.

Data for Social Change: Building Equitable Systems of Out-of-School Learning

The Providence Plan is a nonprofit organization dedicated to using data to create powerful social change. Over the last several years, it has sponsored "Ready-to-Learn Providence," a project that has resulted in neighborhood-by-neighborhood maps and addresses of early-child-care providers. These maps accomplish two important ends: (1) they create an undeniable, readily understandable image of how early childhood education is distributed throughout the city; and (2) they create a communication system that enables child-care providers to engage in high quality professional development, whether the provider is a large center or an individual mother caring for a few neighborhood children.

What a difference it would make if the same system were used to publicize out-of-school learning opportunities throughout the city for students aged five through eighteen. Under the leadership of Mayor David N. Cicilline, the city has established a public-private initiative known as the Providence After School Alliance (PASA), designed to serve the city's middle school students. PASA has established a set of afterschool zones that offer program supports, resources, and transportation tailored to a particular neighborhood's needs. If PASA and the Providence Plan coordinated their efforts, accomplishments would be significant. Any resident could enter any branch library throughout the city and log onto a citywide website that mapped and described the programs available not only in his own neighborhood but throughout the city. With funding from the mayor's office, both experienced family members and youth could act as mentors demonstrating how to use the system and sharing their on-the-ground knowledge about opportunities every Saturday throughout the year. Another powerful mentoring experience could be that of selected mothers sharing their knowledge about turning the city's resources into coordinated and affordable sets of opportunities.

Pathways at the High School Level

As this book shows, Providence is the home of a set of separate efforts that, if coordinated, could create pathways through high school and beyond, to college and substantial employment for its youth. The district and its partners have created a number of new high schools in the last five years and divided up some of the large comprehensive high schools as well. The city is also home to The Met, a nationally recognized model for restructured high school education that combines in- and out-of-school opportunities for learning and achievement. In part because of its strong advisory program, it has a track record of engaging and graduating students whom other schools in the district and surrounding districts would have lost to dropout statistics. Some practices of these new and proven high schools could be used to assess the new graduation requirements. And Providence's already established citywide student government could take on a year-long project to work with the district and the state to design and field test the local version of the new requirements for graduation from high school. Perhaps there could be an elective course in research methods for students working on piloting, observing, interviewing, and analyzing data for this project.

As a next step, a citywide campaign could radically reorganize the school volunteer program to provide trained advisors for students who would remain with them throughout high school. These advisors would use a plan indicating requirements in high school and beyond if a given student is to achieve his career goals. The plan would include not only courses and exams; it would also include activities and programs taking place after school and during the summer. Such an option would enable students and schools to develop creative ways to meet the state's new graduation requirements. It would also engage businesses and higher-education institutions as partners who would provide employees and students as mentors and advisors.

CONCLUSION: CITY HOPES

In many ways cities are on the upswing. Many researchers are encouraged by the drops in concentrated poverty in America's inner-city neighborhoods over the course of the last decade.[11] While there remains a call for continued focus on the spatial distribution of poverty and patterns of housing segregation,[12] many U.S. cities appear stronger and more vital. Neighborhoods once characterized as filled with a discouraging permanent underclass[13] now seem more hopeful in regard to their population. The policies of the 1990s have been partially successful in alleviating conditions of concentrated poverty and urban blight once considered intractable. Welfare reform has had some success, and urban development projects continue to fuel revitalization efforts in central city neighborhoods.

Immigration and diversity have also helped revive cities. The fastest growing cities have attracted residents from all racial/ethnic populations, suggesting that cities hoping to achieve growth must offer attractive conditions to families with various backgrounds. According the Brookings Institution, as of 2004, cities with growing, multiethnic populations, such as Austin and Phoenix, had lower than average child-poverty rates, largely due to their higher rates of parental work and lower rates of single parenthood.[14] Thus, racially and ethnically diverse environments seem to be good for children. Similarly, within cities, mixed-race and mixed-income neighborhoods are often vital for the support of early education, arts, and faith-based organizations. This network of institutions often draws and holds families, creating a stable group of adults who advocate for crossing guards, stop signs, safe parks and playgrounds, and who create the demand for higher-quality public education and out-of-school learning.[15] These adults pass along their knowledge and advocacy skills to their neighbors, to younger families, and to their own children. Such neighborhoods also give rise to multiracial schools where the student body may be comprised of three or more historically excluded minority groups, as well as white or Asian students. These are schools in which new patterns of achievement, different from the familiar white/Asian versus black/brown gaps, could arise.

Providence—and other cities—could leverage these trends to build stable and deepening opportunities for children and youth. It could build systems that help families understand, demand, and support learning both in and out of school. There are individuals and organizations poised to help, and there are efforts underway. But it will take data, coordination, and shared civic impatience with traditional habits that provide benefits and resources for some but not for all.

We would like to acknowledge the help of a number of residents of Providence and other cities, whose insights allowed us to include the perspectives of stakeholders often absent from discussions about life in the city: children, youth, and their families. We especially want to thank Tyanne Carter, Amy Rittenhouse, Elvis Pena, and Bernice Fedestin.

PART II

DISTRICTS AND SCHOOLS
IN SMART EDUCATION SYSTEMS

SMART DISTRICTS AS THE ENTRY POINT
TO SMART EDUCATION SYSTEMS

Marla Ucelli, Ellen Foley, and Jacob Mishook

I f the modern era of school reform is considered to have begun with the publication of *A Nation at Risk* in 1983, it's fair to say that the reform spotlight was rarely cast on school districts until after the turn of the twenty-first century. When the light was shone, it was to highlight districts' potential to do harm. The reform focus was on incentives and authority to spur improvement. Standards-based education reform emanated from the state level, largely bypassing districts. Whole-school reform methods and the legislation that put federal resources behind them targeted action at individual schools.

There were good reasons for bypassing school districts. Although they successfully serve some societal functions (such as employment for adults, contracts with businesses and service industries, and vehicles for local democratic participation), most large districts are not adequate educational institutions, especially for poor and minority students in our urban centers.

Because so many districts are failing in their central purpose, they are easy targets for critics who contend that their isolation from schools and communities and their outdated and ineffective infrastructure impede, rather than enable, improvements. Increasingly, though, even school district detractors acknowledge that incentives, authority, and one-school-at-a-time approaches are not up to the challenge of closing the gap and raising the bar for literally millions of students in urban schools.

WHY DISTRICTS MATTER

In recent years, the need to speed the often slow pace of improvement, to meet the requirements of the No Child Left Behind Act (NCLB), and to see the plight of urban public education as a high-profile problem of both policy and politics has led to a different focus on districts. In a number of large American cities, mayoral involvement and outright control of public school systems has become the overarching reform strategy of choice (see chapter 9). Mayoral involvement is also drawing greater attention to alternative methods of school governance and operation, such as private and nonprofit management of groups of schools within a city (see chapter 5).

The growing body of knowledge about the potential and success of these approaches in places such as Boston, Chicago, New York, and Philadelphia is not our focus here.[1] But it does raise a fundamental point that we believe brings us back to the district and central office as a leverage point for change: By themselves, the governance changes that typically occur when mayors play stronger roles in education may have an immediate impact on organizational efficiency, but they don't necessarily promote long-term improvements in the instructional core.

Mayor-led district reforms have been more successful in decreasing corruption, improving business practices, and devolving authority and resources to schools than they have been in enhancing the quality and efficacy of instruction across all schools. Put simply, shifts in district governance and leadership have more to do with the locus of authority and the distribution of resources than with how both are used to affect teaching and learning. Creating whole cities of successful schools is a technical, professional, and relational/cultural challenge that cannot be won through politics and governance alone.

The Annenberg Institute for School Reform's task force on the future of urban districts, known as School Communities that Work, convened leaders from the education, civic, business, and nonprofit communities to help imagine what high-achieving school communities would look like and how to create them—school communities that do, in fact, work for all children. It was obvious that to do so would require that districts take on new roles and perform others far more effectively. The focus on the district central office is bolstered by a series of recent studies that have documented some of the expectations, habits, policies, and strategies in school districts that ultimately have an impact on school- and student-level outcomes.[2]

RESULTS + EQUITY + COMMUNITY = SMART DISTRICTS

The task force—having in mind the technology-industry notion of "smart," meaning nimble, adaptive, and efficient, that Warren Simmons outlines in chapter 12—described this new kind of district as a "smart district." A smart district focuses on the three themes: results, equity, and community.

Results

The current imperative to improve results requires both high-quality instructional supports and high-quality data on student and school performance. Early intervention and support have been shown to produce huge rewards in the case of students; the same kind of monitoring, diagnosis, and support might make sense when dealing with schools in "turn-around" conditions. Again, these interventions must be calibrated to the unique needs of each school. The remedy should be appropriate to the situation—not based on a one-size-fits-all policy prescription—and should be accompanied by the support necessary to produce results.

Sound data on the implementation and outcomes of such activities is also needed to improve results. Districts already collect a wealth of data, but the information is often inadequate and relies heavily on narrow measures like test scores and graduation and promotion rates. Such indicators are important, but they don't tell the whole story. They do not provide information about other aspects of youth development, such as health or well-being, or a community's supports for children and families; they seldom show growth over time; and they usually arrive too late to help individual children or schools who are struggling.

By focusing on results, smart districts build instructional capacity, and monitor performance, make decisions, and hold themselves accountable with data. Smart districts not only collect data, but also incorporate the serious and regular examination of data into the normal operating procedures for schools and districts.

Equity

Educators and policymakers increasingly recognize that results and equity are not mutually exclusive; they go hand in hand. The goal of ensuring that all students reach proficiency recognizes the interrelatedness of results and equity. Yet achieving equitable results requires a different approach to supporting schools than school districts typically employ. It means that smart districts tailor and distribute resources—from professional development to curriculum guides to distribution of teaching talent—to fit the specific needs and assets of each school's faculty, students, and community. Strategic variation in resource distribution requires close collaboration between central office and school staff, among units of the central office, and with teacher unions and other key partners. It yields more targeted supports for schools and minimizes variations that are the result of politics, inertia, or happenstance.

Community

Many districts lack the capacity and sometimes the desire for serious partnerships with civic and community-based organizations. This not only limits opportunities for parents, students, and community members to influence district policies; it also leaves districts out of the distribution of other community resources that might support education. Smart districts communicate and collaborate both within the official system and with and among key external partners. By focusing on community, smart districts expand the notion of who is a district leader. Many different individuals and organizations—including schools, parents and families, civic groups, research groups, unions, community and faith-based organizations, private-sector companies, and city agencies—already work together to support and sustain the healthy learning and development of children and youth. But a smart district deepens the level of connection with the community so that the relationship goes beyond support and advocacy to one of mutual accountability. This can only be achieved through a change in a district's organizational culture—a change to value collaboration.

The Annenberg Institute for School Reform over the past several years has conducted a variety of research activities to describe the practices of districts that are getting smarter. This work includes the Central Office Review for Results and Equity (CORRE), a process of analyzing the effectiveness of district support for schools; a cross-site analysis of data from CORRE reviews in six sites; a case study of instructional improvement in the Boston Public Schools, jointly conducted with the Aspen Institute; and a study of eight districts using data-warehousing technology. These districts varied in their success at improving results for students; however, they all had the common interest of a willingness to work with the Annenberg Institute in an effort to improve those results or to help other districts learn from their experiences.

PRACTICES OF A SMART DISTRICT

As noted above, school districts that are getting smarter focus on three themes: results, equity, and community. In practice, a focus on these three themes means performing a limited set of functions effectively: supports and interventions for schools; equitable distribution of resources; use of data for accountability; and engagement with partners. A smart district that effectively promotes these practices—within an organizational culture that promotes collaboration—can serve as an entry point to the development of a Smart Education System. What, then, are we learning from districts that are improving in these critical functions, and what are the implications for other districts that are trying to "get smart"?

Results

Districts that are getting smarter focus on results by building instructional capacity and carefully reviewing data about the implementation and outcome of such efforts.

Timely Supports and Interventions

The central offices of most school districts typically provide professional development, curriculum guides, and other materials to some schools, but such supports are often applied haphazardly, without regard to schools' improvement needs. And districts often wait to intervene in schools only in extreme circumstances, when it is most difficult to turn the situation around. Before districts act, students languish.

From our work and research, we've learned that a smart district provides timely supports and interventions to schools by

- having a strong theory of change that drives professional development supports, and
- providing differentiated supports and interventions based on school needs.

Smart districts have a theory of change that drives professional development (PD) supports. A smart district has a well-defined and communicated theory of action that drives teaching and learning, and supports these theories of action with strong supports and interventions for targeted professional development. In Newport, Rhode Island, for example, the theory of change centered on improving literacy. To this end, literacy coordinators provided professional development for teachers, "particularly in aligning curriculum and assessments with standards," according to one elementary coordinator. The district set aside significant time for this type of professional development. A member of the School Committee, which helps to set Newport district policy and represents the community, said that the literacy training was "the best investment we've made." He added later that although the district does "a lot of PD . . . as a system, it's a lifetime process." Building instructional capacity, then, is a long-term investment, not a short-lived initiative.

Similarly, in Boston there was a strong commitment from the district to its educators. Here, the district partnered with the Boston Plan for Excellence, a local education fund, to develop the Collaborative Coaching and Learning (CCL) program in Effective Practice (EP) schools. An evaluation of the CCL program found that it "showed great promise for the improvement of teaching and learning and for the further development of high-quality, instructionally focused cultures in the EP schools."[3] Boston's model for timely supports and interventions differed somewhat from Newport's in that CCL was administered by a partner, rather than by the district itself. This highlights the importance of external partnerships within a smart education system, something that will be discussed in more detail below.

Smart districts provide differentiated supports and interventions based on school needs. Timely supports and interventions from a smart district can identify low-performing schools and provide individualized, tailored support to improve teaching and learning. In Hamilton County, Tennessee, the Public Education Foundation received $9 million in funding from the Benwood Foundation to partner with the district to provide students at nine low-performing, Title I urban elementary schools with extra academic help, including before- and after-school tutoring, with a particular focus on reading. Teachers received intensive professional development. As a result, Benwood schools made significant gains in all subject areas on state testing. The proportion of students proficient in reading jumped from 53.1 percent in 2003 to 74.4 percent in 2005. Teacher turnover also declined significantly.[4]

Smart districts make decisions by using indicators of school and district performance and practices. Most school districts collect plenty of data. But their ability to analyze what the data mean or to use the data to inform decisionmaking is limited. School districts are often saddled with antiquated technology systems that produce fragmented and inaccurate data. Many potential users lack access to the data, or the data arrive too late to have an impact on what happens in the classroom.

From our work, we've learned that smart districts

- provide access to data and make it user friendly;
- offer support and professional development so staff understand and know how to use data to inform decisions;
- collect data about the performance of the central office.

Smart districts provide access to data and make it user friendly. In most cases, providing access to data involves investing in technology that provides accurate, up-to-date information to central office- and school-based staff, as well as other leaders, such as board and community members. We studied eight districts using "data-warehousing" systems—in which data from different computers in different locations and in different formats can be accessed seamlessly, usually through a Web-based interface—and found that making data available to more people, more quickly, and more easily, was a major goal of the investment in such technology.

Access to the data warehouse was usually provided to staff focused on system goals and business needs. These typically included the superintendent, chief financial officer, and divisions of accountability and testing, research and evaluation, instructional technology, and information technology. Most school districts also had secure Web-based portals for principals to access teacher, student, and school information. Secretaries often could input data, download information, and print reports on request. Teachers, parents, and students were less likely to have direct access to the data warehouse, though providing broader access was a key part of the future implementation plan for all the districts we studied.

Districts that were getting smarter also sought ways to make using and understanding data easier. The eight districts in our data-warehousing study reported that this task is time-consuming and ongoing, but well worth the trouble. A director of research told us:

> I had an epiphany around this time. For years I supported schools by providing them with reports and I was still not seeing data used the way I wanted it to be. It hit me then that if [analyzing and reorganizing data was] what they really wanted to do, they would work in this office! It was a primal issue. I recognized that we needed to make this very simple for teachers or they will just not do it. An ATM, like one provided by a bank, was our driving model. We had to make sure the interface to users was easy to access.

Districts that did not have the resources to invest in new technology still sought to make data easier to use and understand. Sacramento, one of our CORRE sites, drew from a statewide database called Just for the Kids-California developed by the National Center for Educational Accountability. Sacramento's leadership made the data available to principals who could then use it to develop data-informed action plans for their schools.

Smart districts provide support and professional development so staff understand and know how to use data to inform decisions. As we learned from the eight districts we studied that implemented data-warehousing technology, districts face challenges in providing adequate support to schools for using data to inform decisions. These challenges include both technical issues—staff members' comfort level using a computer and accessing websites varied—as well as analytical issues—once you know that 20 percent of your third graders are scoring below the basic level in reading comprehension, what do you do about it? Many educators are not accustomed to asking powerful questions about instructional outcomes.

In many ways, the desire to foster use of the data forced central office departments (including information technology, research and evaluation, and curriculum and instruction) to work together in ways they never had before. In Boston, for example, the information technology division worked in conjunction with the research office to integrate training on how to use the technology as well as how to interpret the data generated. Both groups worked closely with instructional staff, especially school-based coaches and other professional development providers. The coaches would then convert their learning into professional development or in-service opportunities for teachers to discuss findings and act on data. The Boston Plan for Excellence, the district's local education fund, has been a key support in such efforts and continues to publish newsletters, provide professional development for coaches and other teacher trainers, and communicate the advantages of using data to teachers and principals.

Smart districts collect data about the performance of the central office. Every school district in the country must now collect academic performance data about its schools and students. But few districts understand whether the supports the central office provides actually contribute to improving student performance. Smart districts seek out this information informally through direct discussion and feedback, and formally, through districtwide surveys and feedback loops.

Several of the districts in our data-warehousing study had established users groups to collect regular feedback about warehouse functioning, supports, and training. In Boston, the superintendent developed a "community cabinet" that advised him on reform efforts and both central office and school performance. And Sacramento annually surveyed principals and other school staff on the level of customer service provided by central office departments.

Equity

Our research has shown that most districts distribute fiscal and human resources unevenly among schools and types of students. Many inequities are buried in complicated accounting procedures, antiquated staff-based budgeting policies, and multiple funding streams for programs such as bilingual or special education. Some differences make sense, such as additional dollars for disabled children, but others are not systematic and may even conflict with the district's stated goals.

From our work, we've learned that smart districts

- distribute resources to schools based on the characteristics of the students;
- alter human resources policies so that they are more streamlined and more flexible;
- prioritize the development of educators, not just their hiring and placement.

Smart districts distribute resources to schools based on the characteristics of the students. Most school districts use staff-based budgeting formulas to allocate resources in the form of full-time-equivalent staff to each school. Based on the number of students, additional staff or programs are added on a school-by-school basis. Assignment of teachers is driven almost exclusively by seniority rules and teacher preferences. And expenditures for teachers are quantified by using an average teacher salary (not the actual salary of the teachers assigned to the school), which masks variations in teacher costs from school to school. Our research has shown that such policies result in large differences in budgets from school to school within the same district.

Smart districts have devised ways to address these potential sources of inequity. Some districts, such as Cincinnati and Houston, have moved to student-based budgeting policies, which incorporate not only the number of students in a school, but also address the students' characteristics. Students who are English-language learners or who require nonacute special education services, for example, receive a weighted allocation that reflects the additional resources needed to support their learning. Other districts have used grants and funds from special programs to target schools with large proportions of such students.

Smart districts alter human resources policies so that they are more streamlined and more flexible. Because education is inherently a labor-intensive endeavor, a school district's human resources practices exert tremendous influence over each school's ability to succeed. In most districts, human resources policies offer only one set of employment terms, limit the way performance is evaluated, adhere to seniority-based salary advancement and disconnect professional development from human-resources development. The hiring process is also often slow and cumbersome, limiting the pool of educators available to work in the district's schools.

Smart districts have worked closely with teachers' and principals' unions to alter human-resources policies so that they serve both the needs of the professionals and of the students. In Boston, contractual changes were made that helped speed up the filling of teacher vacancies and limited the impact of "bumping," a process where tenured teachers were allowed to force junior teachers out of a particular school or position.

Smart districts prioritize the development of educators, not just their hiring and placement. In many school districts, the human resources department serves primarily as an employment office, advertising positions, processing forms, and placing successful applicants. In several of our CORRE sites, the department was seen as unnecessarily bureaucratic and slow to support the needs of schools.

In smart districts, the importance of developing human resources is understood throughout the district and is the task of everyone, not just the human-resources department. This requires coordination of various departments that offer specialized training, such as training for people working with students in special education or with English-language learners. In Newport, Rhode Island, at the time of our analysis, principals and teachers had been taking part in learning walks, where they observe classrooms and discuss standards and expectations for instruction and student work. In Boston, Readers' and Writers' Workshop is the primary pedagogical approach in classrooms throughout the district, and every teacher is involved in professional development designed to support that work. The district has also developed its own teacher and principal academies so that they can "home grow" educators whose pedagogy is compatible with the district's.

Community

Typically, districts develop only rudimentary partnerships with external partners. These partners usually are not integrated with one another in any meaningful way, and often cannot identify the district's primary goals for student learning. Additionally, communication with stakeholders, especially parents, is haphazard, top-down, and one-way. Looking across our own work, we identified several themes that characterized "smart" community and partner engagement by districts.

From our work, we've learned that smart districts

- cultivate strong, integrated partnerships;
- develop routine, two-way communication with stakeholders;
- share decisionmaking with partners;

- build a shared understanding with external partners about district goals, and communicate those goals outside the central office;
- communicate data-informed decisions to partners and the general public.

Smart districts cultivate strong, integrated partnerships and back them up with significant investment, both monetary and institutional. In many school districts, external partners receive a very small percentage of district funds, and private funding is not aggressively sought. Furthermore, partners are often isolated from one another, and are not aware of what other external partners are doing. In smart districts, however, integrated partnerships are strongly supported by the district through substantial funding and institutional buy-in from the district.

For example, the Boston Public Schools have received large amounts of outside funding, totaling approximately $100 million between 1995 and 2005. Beyond fundraising, however, the district, under the leadership of former superintendent Thomas W. Payzant, was able to unify the funding strategies toward well-defined district goals. According to the district's chief financial officer, "That resulted in an Annenberg Challenge grant and it was structured within [the Boston Plan for Excellence], and it served as the umbrella to bring all the folks together. [Our efforts to get] resources that were available from the private sector—that has been hugely successful."[5] Similarly, in Hamilton County, Tennessee, the district has been successful at developing strong outside partnerships and funding. The latter includes funding from Carnegie Corporation of New York for high school redesign and the Benwood Foundation for urban schools, as well as funds from the local Public Education Foundation. Hamilton County also received the largest grant ever from the NEA Foundation.

Smart districts develop routine and strong two-way communication with stakeholders, and especially parents. Communication is a universal concern among the districts we have studied. Most districts treat communication with stakeholders as a one-way process: from the central office outward. However, at least two districts have made some progress towards involving stakeholders in two-way communication. In Newport, the district was aware of the importance of communicating with partners and the broader community. Outside stakeholders did report that school and district personnel were accessible, though there was inconsistency from teachers and schools in communicating with parents. And in Boston, in response to community concerns, the district created a position of deputy superintendent for family and community engagement. Although the superintendent acknowledged that there had been difficulty in getting the right person for this role, the current deputy superintendent is there "for the long haul."

The superintendent also acknowledged that the central office needs to give parents information about their children that is "not threatening or condescending. . . . And you've just got to get out in the communities. It takes a lot of time."

Smart districts share decisionmaking with partners, but ultimate ownership and accountability still lies at the central office. The power to make decisions, especially about teaching and student learning, is closely held by most districts. Decisions, if explained at all, are still often completed without consultation from outside partners or the community. However, smart districts realize that including external partners and the community in some aspects of decisionmaking develops a sense of shared responsibility and accountability for the entire community. Additionally, by sharing decisionmaking, smart districts can actually help develop capacity by tapping the resources and expertise of external partners. In Boston, the High School Renewal Group, made up of representatives of the district's major external partners—the Boston Plan for Excellence, Jobs for the Future, and the Center for Collaborative Education—are involved in key decisionmaking roles. According to the director of Education Matters, the Boston Plan for Excellence functions as the research-and-development arm of the district. "They have the capacity, they can work quicker, focus on an area, in many ways that a district can't do."[6] In this sense, capacity for positive educational change has been developed outside the central office. The next step for a smart district is to move beyond formal, organized partners like the Boston Plan for Excellence to include less powerful, more diffuse stakeholders in decisionmaking—parents, students, and the community at large.

Smart districts are effective at building a shared understanding with external partners about district goals, and communicating those goals outside the central office. Many districts either have no explicit goals for achieving improvements in student learning, or they have goals that are not widely shared with external partners and the broader community. Clear goals, however, can build strong partnerships because partners are able to align their goals with those of the district. In Boston, even during a period of unsettlement while the city searched for a new superintendent, there was still a consensus around the educational goals of the district. As the school board chair put it, "There has been an incredible sense of consensus that the [district's] educational agenda, as it's been translated throughout community, within schools, in political and funding sectors, and with the general public, is the right kind of reform agenda." She goes on to say that "there is trust and credibility that has been built over time by the superintendent, mayor, and school committee with the general public. . . . It's quite an accomplishment."[7]

Smart districts communicate data-informed decisions with their partners and the public at large. Ambiguity about decisionmaking results in difficulty in reaching consensus in the community on issues of student learning, and ambiguity can create distrust between the district and its partners. As we have learned through our CORRE work, perceptions are powerful but often inaccurate. Smart districts develop explicit district goals for student learning and share them with the community. Smart districts also back up decisions up with data and share the information both internally, with other educators and leaders, and externally, with the general public, to "show the real picture of what's going on."

One example of a district becoming smarter in communicating data-informed decisionmaking to the public is Hamilton County. Throughout the CORRE process, principals, teachers, and community partners praised the central office for providing access to data about student outcomes. Such efforts are challenging in a politically charged environment. As a Hamilton County official noted, using data for decisionmaking processes "is frustrating to the political environment. [Politicians want] it to become 'believe or don't believe the messenger, not the evidence.'"

CHANGING PRACTICE, CHANGING CULTURE

As the preceding examples show, districts that are getting smarter engage in a number of activities—from providing differentiated supports to schools, to using data for decisionmaking, to integrating their work with the work of partners. But actions alone are not enough; without efforts also to change the organizational culture of school districts—what Burney describes as the "nature of the work"—even smart activities will feel hollow to school-based staff and other potential partners.

How district leaders go about their work is as important as *what* they do. Typically, central-office leaders have had what Burch and Spillane describe as an authoritative orientation, and have seen school-based staff "primarily as targets and beneficiaries of their own and others' expertise."[8] From our own research, we conclude that many central office leaders also apply this approach with partners outside the district. Communication flows in one direction, out from the central office, with school-based staff and partners having little chance for input or feedback on the district's actions.

Smart districts have what Burch and Spillane call a collaborative orientation. Central office leaders with a collaborative approach view themselves as servant-leaders, providing guidance, direction, support, and expertise to school personnel. They also broker the expertise that exists beyond the central office in schools and among community partners and they seek input from these same groups.

Building a smart district is an iterative, not linear, process; that is, it involves both strong technical solutions as well as explicit attention to how those solutions are implemented. This is true especially in terms of how partners both inside and outside the district are incorporated into reform. But, it is not as if the organizational culture is completely transformed first, and then technical solutions are implemented. Rather, both technical and cultural changes are sought simultaneously and complement and reinforce each other.

THE FUTURE: FROM SMART DISTRICTS
TO SMART EDUCATION SYSTEMS

Districts get smarter by doing two things: (1) engaging in activities designed to improve results, equity, and community, and (2) purposefully altering their organizational culture to be more collaborative.

Both are easier said than done, but taken together they help the district become a vital community institution that is positioned to expand its reach and capacity. As such, smart districts are a key potential entry point for building smart education systems.

Smart districts are similar to smart education systems in many ways. A collaborative orientation is essential to both smart districts and smart education systems, and an emphasis on the importance of educating the whole child is part of both, as well. But smart districts alone move only part of the way to the overall vision of a smart education system.

A smart education system is a system of systems, involving the district, but also engaging a wide variety of partners in accountability for outcomes for children. In a smart district, the district remains the leader and is often the only institution that is held accountable for outcomes, which are typically limited to the academic achievement scores of students. In a smart education system, the district is not solely accountable, nor is it the leader in determining the appropriate approaches to improving outcomes. Instead, both control and accountability are distributed among a number of partners, including the district. And the outcomes themselves will be broader, including, but not limited to, academic achievement.

Furthermore, a smart education system is defined partly by the broader range of citywide services or "web of supports" beyond classroom and extracurricular learning that it provides. Addressing the equity gap outside schools—in accessing cultural and enrichment opportunities, in working alongside adult mentors and applying learning to real-world situations, in understanding basic health and social service availability—is even more daunting than addressing the gaps within schools.

This transition from smart district to smart education system requires another set of adjustments—in both organizational culture and technical approaches to problems—by central office, school and community leaders. But a truly smart district's balance of results, equity, and community may be the most essential building block for achieving the vision of a smart education system.

TEACHING AND LEARNING
IN URBAN DISTRICTS

Deanna Burney and Kenneth Klau

S chools and districts throughout the United States operate under the now-familiar mantle of standards-based reform. From a policy perspective, the premise of standards-based reform is relatively simple: if states promulgate high standards, devise an accountability system to gauge student performance against these standards, and provide educators with some flexibility in attaining their goals, then students will achieve at high levels.[1] As expectations for performance have risen over the past decade, school and district accountability for student performance has also increased.

Public school districts, particularly large urban systems, are uniquely poised to face the challenge of helping all students reach proficiency. Most urban districts have the "economy of scale" necessary to provide human, material, and fiscal supports to many schools, tasks beyond the reach of smaller systems and not well-suited to larger state departments of education alone, which may lack the proximity and capacity to efficiently concentrate adequate resources and expertise on a wide array of districts. This focus on the district's role is, therefore, timely and appropriate. But with this increased attention to districts has come a growing realization among educators, parents, and policymakers that if urban school systems are to become one of the central change agents affecting the life outcomes of urban children, then these districts must better understand how they conduct their core function: teaching and learning. They must scrutinize what students are actually taught in classrooms (the enacted curriculum), and evaluate the quality of teaching and learning within and between classrooms in order to ascertain the actions and supports that might be needed to improve student performance.

A close examination of a district's performance is critical if it is to become "smart." Such studies provide important indicators that help determine whether schools are on track to achieve the desired results. They also help ensure that districts are equitable by providing resources where needed. And, when done effectively, they engage community members. Only by enlisting community partners to take part in the examination of teaching and learning can districts provide the support that schools and students need.

This chapter considers some themes that are emerging as districts tackle the difficult problem of teaching so that all students achieve at high levels. Among the emerging themes or issues are the following:

- Attainment versus performance
- Aptitude versus effort
- Alignment versus coherence
- Internal versus external accountability
- Technical versus adaptive work

To illustrate the challenges that districts face in addressing these issues, we consider data from two large, complex urban districts that have undertaken reviews of teaching and learning.

TEACHING AND LEARNING REVIEWS

Like all urban school districts, the Baltimore City, Maryland, and Portland, Oregon, public school systems struggle with the complex task of meeting the needs of a large and diverse student population. In recent years, both Baltimore and Portland sought to better understand and improve teaching and learning in their schools—to build capacity and meet the challenge of helping all students reach proficiency. Toward that end, they each partnered with the Annenberg Institute for School Reform (AISR) and participated in the Annenberg Institute Teaching and Learning Review (hereafter called the Review). AISR describes the Review as "a collaborative process that brings district and school staff together with community partners, supported by staff members of the Annenberg Institute, to investigate three key questions":

1. Where is effective teaching and learning occurring? How can that work be acknowledged, supported, and built upon?

2. Where is there a need for added investments and improvement?
3. What immediate and longer-term actions can the central office, educators, families, students, and community members take to strengthen the quality of teaching and learning experienced by all students?[2]

The purpose of the Review is first, to promote a frank and informed discussion among a full range of stakeholders; and second, to use the discussion as a basis for thoughtful recommendations for urgent, intermediate, and longer-term actions to improve both teaching and learning throughout the system. These discussions, and the action plans emerging from them, are continuing.

The Cities

Baltimore. For almost three decades, the Baltimore City Public Schools had been in crisis. The city had lost 90,000 manufacturing jobs in the 1970s and 1980s, and with that loss came the attendant characteristics of high poverty and low employment.[3] Its school leaders recognized the slow erosion of the city's economic and cultural base, setting the conditions by which "Baltimore's poor and working-poor families rely heavily on the city's public schools to convey the knowledge and skills their children need to succeed in higher education and the workforce."[4]

Unfortunately, the unprecedented dependence of the community on the system to deliver high outcomes for students coincided negatively with the accountability demands of federal and state policies. The requirement that states annually test students revealed just how critical the crisis had become. In 2003, 60.9 percent of the city's third graders scored at the Basic level in literacy—the lowest performance level on Maryland State Assessment—while just 37.6 percent scored at the Proficient level and 1.5 percent at the Advanced level. In grades 5, 8, and 10, the percentages of students scoring at the Basic level were 55.6, 67.2, and 71.5 percent, respectively, and math scores were similarly low.[5]

Because of low levels of student achievement and allegations of fiscal mismanagement, the district had been partly taken over by the state of Maryland in 1996. Yet since that time, flat or declining test scores, fiscal mismanagement by school administrators, and the shadow of a longstanding court battle over inadequate funding and services threatened to throw the district into an even deeper crisis. In 2003, Nancy Grasmick, Maryland's chief state school officer, ordered a comprehensive review of the system's management and operations, with a focus on professional development and the quality of literacy and mathematics instruction. She charged Education Resource Strategies—a nonprofit organization based in Wayland, Massachusetts, that works with school systems to improve the strategic management of resources to enhance performance—to conduct an audit of the district's professional development spending, and the Annenberg Institute to lead the investigation in classrooms. For several months, researchers conducted document reviews, observed classrooms, and interviewed school and central office personnel. The results of the study, entitled "Becoming a Capable and Accountable System," were published in September 2004.

Portland. Historically, Portland has had to cope with issues of racial imbalance in its schools, and more recently, a decline in student enrollment. Until recently, however, these issues—particularly those dealing with race, class, and power— were masked by improving test results. As compared to Baltimore's results on the Maryland State Assessment, Portland scored more favorably on the Oregon State Assessment in 2003. Only 16 percent of Portland students performed at the lowest level on the state assessment in reading.

The Portland Public Schools entered into partnership with Annenberg in the summer of 2003. At that time, the school board and community had developed a long-range strategic plan for the district and were seeking a superintendent to carry out the plan. The district and a local education fund, the Portland Schools Foundation, asked Annenberg to lead a Central Office Review for Results and Equity (CORRE) to assess the quality of support that the central office provided to schools and to make recommendations that might guide the new superintendent (see chapter 3).

Following the release of that report, the newly hired superintendent, Vicki Phillips, asked Annenberg to conduct a Teaching and Learning Review, similar to the one undertaken in Baltimore, to ensure that the district would continue to build capacity to meet the needs of students and their families. Together, the perceptions of key stakeholders in the CORRE review and the classroom observations of the Teaching and Learning Review provide a portrait of instruction and student support in the district.

While both Baltimore and Portland partnered with the Annenberg Institute to engage in this Review process, the studies differ in several significant ways. In Baltimore, the study was ordered by the chief state school officer; it did not involve community input in the review process; and it carried the implicit threat of sanctions. By contrast, the Portland Review was initiated by the district; it engaged community partners from the outset; and there were no consequences associated with the results. But the findings from these two districts indicate that they are both grappling with several of the salient themes that are, or should be, front and center in any consideration of urban school reform.

CONTRASTING THEMES

The Slow Shift from Attainment to Performance in American Schooling

The American K–12 educational experience has changed over the past several decades. For example, thirty years ago the Carnegie unit took precedence in American schooling. It drove course development and grouping, and it served as a yardstick by which every high school student could gauge his or her progress toward earning a diploma.[6] It was also a method by which students could be conveniently and efficiently sorted into vocational, career (noncollege), and college-preparatory tracks. The reliance on the seat time and tracking might be described as the "attainment model" of schooling because, according to this theory, attainment of the requisite number of Carnegie units in a given track would place students in the postsecondary field most appropriate to their skills and abilities.

The nation's shift away from this sorting model and toward a focus on setting high standards for all students—especially, historically disadvantaged children (children with disabilities or children from low-income families)—has changed the "business" of schooling and drawn enormous sums of money into the system. Now, classrooms are more likely to be heterogeneous, not only in terms of students' knowledge and skills, but in terms of their language, race, and ethnicity as well.

Another major change that has occurred over the past twenty to thirty years is an increased national focus on student performance, as embodied by the standards-based reform movement. In many states, students must demonstrate specified levels of proficiency on state tests to be eligible for a high school diploma. And teachers and school administrators are increasingly held accountable for student performance; schools that do not make adequate progress in student performance face sanctions.

Even though the demands of the twenty-first-century economy—combined with the advent of standards-based reform—have shifted the programmatic focus from attainment to performance, the attainment culture of Carnegie units and seat time lives on. Even when systems are no longer structurally intended to sort students according to their perceived abilities as measured by attainment, tracking persists, albeit more subtly. One explanation for this is the current disparity between the cultural, demographic, and economic characteristics of teachers and their students in many of the classrooms of city schools. While it is true that schools are less likely to manage classrooms along specific career, vocational, or college tracks, teachers are still likely to hold different expectations for different groups of students—particularly if they do not share the same skin color or socioeconomic status as their students.[7] Moreover, while students now require the sort of knowledge and skills needed for the United States to compete in the global economy,[8] many urban systems are struggling to make the transition from being mere sorting mechanisms to organizations that must produce fundamentally better educational outcomes for the majority of students.

In America's large cities, school systems face an added crisis, and not simply because they serve large numbers of culturally, ethnically, and economically diverse students and their families. Schools and districts are just one piece of the fabric that supports families with young children. Social-service agencies, faith-based organizations, and other community-based resources also are intended to provide needed supports; however, most of these agencies tend to be under-funded and lack significant resources. As a result, since schools are the one arm of the public service sector that nearly every urban family encounters, schools have taken on the burden of meeting students' emotional, behavioral, and social needs in addition to their academic development. These added responsibilities have taxed schools' abilities to carry out their primary mission of educating students.

How have Baltimore and Portland responded to the new emphasis on performance, while reconciling issues of race and class? The early indications from Annenberg's reviews have not been heartening. In Baltimore, researchers found that, for the most part, teachers in the schools studied tended to emphasize compliance: they "teach the curriculum," rather than foster students' competence. The researchers found little evidence that Baltimore's teachers and administrators were grappling with the central issue of instructional practice as it relates to performance or competence. Because Baltimore's review teams did not involve people from the community, as was the case in Portland, issues about race and class did not emerge. The implications of this omission for Baltimore's chances for sustainable improvement are discussed later in this chapter.

In Portland, the teachers who were studied tended to emphasize the delivery of instruction without always considering their students' individual backgrounds and needs—students arrived at school each day, received the curriculum, and went home. There was little evidence that the district successfully engaged parents and community members to fulfill the social service component of students' learning. Annenberg's review teams found a "lack of diversity and cultural competency among district staff at all levels. . . . [This] leads to disconnections among staff, students, and community, in addition to negative impacts on students' experience of school."[9] These disconnections likely hamper teachers' abilities to know and understand students—what they bring, and what they don't bring, to the teaching and learning relationship.

Effort Begets Aptitude: Toward a Theory of Action

Historically, school districts have handled the operational features of the system: transportation, meals, busing, human resources, physical plant, and supplies. Effectively, carrying out these functions was guided not by theory, but by the tried-and-true business practice of ticking off easily measurable inputs (funding, books, desks) and outputs (Carnegie units, seat time, course credits, and so on). And, for many decades under the attainment system, school districts functioned more or less according to the requirements of the model: educators enrolled students with promising aptitude on intelligence tests into the college courses; and they placed students with less demonstrable abilities into tracks that emphasized practical, work-ready skills.[10] "After all," a school administrator from the early part of the century might have argued, "effort has its limits."

One of the bedrock principles underlying standards-based reform, however, is that *all* students are capable of achieving at high levels if they are held to the same challenging academic standards. This idea, based on emerging findings from cognitive science, has created a new paradigm for educators, one that forcefully confronts the tenet of the attainment system that students have certain limits to their aptitude to learn. The notion, then, that effort might *create* aptitude emerged concomitantly with the advent of standards-based reform and is perhaps best articulated by Resnick in her work, *From Aptitude to Effort:*

> Early in this century, we built an education system around the assumption that aptitude is paramount in learning and that it is largely hereditary. The system was oriented toward selection, distinguishing the naturally able from the less able and providing students with programs thought suitable to their talents. . . . In the absence of publicly defined standards, our inherited aptitude assumptions lead us to hold out lower expectations for some children than for others. . . . The best remedy, the equitable solution, is to set clear, public standards that establish very high minimum expectations for everyone, providing a solid foundation for effort by students and teachers alike.[11]

These and other assertions underlined policymakers' commitment to equity and excellence for all students. But the implications for district implementation of these reforms were less clear. Educational researchers looking at the effectiveness of systemic reform typically focus their analysis on the organization's "theory of action," which articulates how available resources—people, time, materials, money—are marshaled strategically toward achieving continuous improvements in teaching and learning.

But in many districts, Baltimore and Portland among them, the theory of action is unclear because these cities use what we might call the "variability paradigm"; that is, they tend to devolve accountability for student learning and use of resources to individual schools. As a result, these districts have made it more difficult to ensure that all students achieve at high levels. The Baltimore City Public Schools used federal funds to implement a planned variation scheme through the adoption of "comprehensive school reform" models that prescribed very specific approaches to curriculum, instruction, and assessment. Portland had a similar history of school variation, in that principals exercised considerable discretion in how they used their resources to support improved student achievement.[12] Variation there was more the legacy of a central office that lacked the capacity, need, or political will to impose consistency. Indeed, Annenberg's interviews and focus groups revealed conflicting perceptions as to whether variety was a strength or a weakness of the Portland system, despite the unequal distribution of resources.

The Annenberg review found that variation in both cities diluted the central offices' ability to support their schools effectively. Moreover, the variation created even more fragmentation in programs and achievement. The largest studies of curriculum implementation at scale suggest that there is greater variability within schools than between schools; in other words, the difference in student performance is likely to be greater between Classroom A and Classroom B than between School C and School D.[13] This means that the planned variation among schools, combined with the variation in implementation within schools, resulted in a kaleidoscopic mix of curricula and achievement levels across the districts.

This wide variety was evident in Baltimore:

> Schools employ a wide range of curricular programs, depending on the training and beliefs of their leadership and staff . . . [and] in turn, possess a wide range of curriculum materials intended to be aligned to the instructional "philosophies" inherent in the different programs. [School leaders] . . . were concerned that many teachers lacked the ability to articulate a theory or understanding of "good instruction." At the higher grades, a wide range of variability was present in the design, intellectual rigor, and delivery of . . . courses.[14]

Moreover, evidence gathered from classroom observations found that "students were not typically expressing student voice or agency, where their experience, funds of cultural knowledge, or points of view mattered in a substantial way."[15]

In Portland, curriculum and testing regimes were intended to bring consistency to the instructional experiences of students from different neighborhoods, and to address the equity concerns of parents and community members. But the implementation of such policies did not preclude "issues of race, culture, power, and insider/outsider status [that] feed negative interpersonal relationships and divisions in central office." And while the CORRE review found that "many in central office, schools, and community shared concerns about respect for diversity of all kinds," they discovered "no forum for addressing issues of race and culture openly or productively."[16]

The degree to which teachers and administrators have the cultural competency to work with diverse students is a function of the professional development strategy utilized by the district. And although infusing cultural competency into the programs is critical, it is not just the content of the training that is important. For example, to some extent, teachers in Baltimore and Portland have received at least some exposure to the issue. Given scarce resources, it is also crucial that the central office deploy the training in a way that fits the achievement levels of each school and the learning needs of the adults (teachers and principals) working in those schools.

Annenberg's findings of the overall professional development programs in both Baltimore and Portland revealed that these districts employed piecemeal approaches to professional development. In Baltimore, the researchers found that available resources for professional development were not allocated "strategically or equitably across schools and among teachers . . . [nor did they] support a coherent district strategy for instructional improvement." Furthermore, the professional development "investment varies widely across schools and programs in ways that do not dependably match the varying needs of students, teachers, coaches, principals, schools . . . or other recipients."[17]

In Portland, the Annenberg review teams observed from interviews and focus groups that the "provision of professional development is said to be weak, inconsistent, and fragmented. This fragmentation contributes to confusion about accountability and responsibility for professional development in central office." Moreover, "there are very few centrally provided curricular supports. Several school-based staff noted this absence and expressed concerns about the consistency of what is taught and how teaching is supported."[18]

In both Baltimore and Portland, "silos" were used as a metaphor to describe how schools perceived the functions of central office staff in relationship to its schools. In Baltimore, Annenberg found that "the current infrastructure continues to impede the district's capability: it is still characterized by variable expertise, work that occurs in uncoordinated silos, and a lack of clear lines of accountability and benchmarks for steady improvement in the performance of educators."[19] In Portland, "Collaboration and communication across units and departments within central office are weak; many people inside and outside central office described central office staff as working in silos."[20]

The conclusion many districts are reaching—and which the Annenberg reviews recommend for Baltimore and Portland—is that a single theory of action must govern the system and encompass all decisions about resource allocation, curriculum, and professional development; and this single theory of action must be responsive to the community in addressing issues of race, class, equity, and culture. This does not imply that every school must approach curriculum implementation in the same way. It does mean, however, that school leaders and teachers must reach consensus on the best approaches to teaching and learning within their individual schools, and that these approaches must remain consistent with the overall achievement goals set by the district. If teachers across very large districts were to develop learning experiences for students that embraced this theory, then it follows that groups of teachers could work together to refine their efforts using a common language. This would mean drawing from a common knowledge base about how best to bridge the gap between aptitude and effort.

Alignment versus Coherence

A major focus of the Annenberg studies was to "form a concise picture of how stated policies are translated at the district, school, and classroom level."[21] In education, a system is considered to be "aligned" when the teaching level of the system—state, district, school, and classroom—communicates consistent, high expectations for student performance. The written and unwritten demands made of all actors in the system must also be in alignment. These demands should be communicated through formal documents, such state standards, curriculum guides, and textbooks. Expectations for student performance should also be communicated informally—in what a principal looks for in evaluating a teacher's practice, for example, or what teachers expect of individual students in their classrooms.

If large systems can achieve a measure of vertical alignment, they must also achieve coherence. In a school where coherence is lacking, within-grade variations in classroom instructional practice occur. Coherence is strengthened when teachers develop common approaches for students, hold all students to the same high expectations for performance, and ensure that students who learn differently have the supports they need to be successful. Because teachers probably will depend on materials indefinitely, the way in which they interpret and use curricula plays an important role in determining whether students have access to quality learning experiences.[22] And, the extent to which this interpretation and usage varies from teacher to teacher negatively affects coherence.

The following chart shows the dimensions of a curriculum.

CURRICULUM DIMENSIONS[23]

Intended Curriculum	Written and/or stated expectations for what students should know and do as promulgated by states, districts, and schools through academic standards, curriculum guides, scopes and sequences, and textbooks
Enacted Curriculum	What actually gets taught in classrooms, or the instructional decisions teachers make that are based on, and/or mediated by, their internalization of the intended curriculum; the available time in which teachers have to teach; their comfort level with their own pedagogical skills and content knowledge; and their perceptions of, or expectations for, the kind of academic work that students in their classroom can perform
Learned Curriculum	What students believe they are capable of learning and thus actually learn in the enacted curriculum
Assessed Curriculum	The knowledge and skills assessed on tests, including high-stakes tests

The methodology used by Annenberg in the Baltimore and Portland reviews sought to identify the degree of alignment and coherence at each level of the system. These reviews gave particular attention to the enacted curriculum—what students were actually taught in classrooms. A textbook or curriculum guide that sits on a shelf might be described as being "in neutral" until it is put to use. The enacted curriculum is typically anything but neutral; it is mediated by people with built-in biases or theories about what their students are able to learn and therefore do learn. The reviews thus answer the question, "What gets taught to whom?"

Written nearly a decade before the standards movement entered the consciousness of U.S. educators, Brophy's analysis of classroom instructional practice found that teachers charged with educating low-ability students were concerned less with the material they covered or what students actually learned under the conditions of instruction than they were with keeping students occupied. He found such students received "qualitatively less effective instruction from the teacher."[24]

In Baltimore, Annenberg found that

historically, tools developed by the central office for use in the schools—particularly curriculum guides—have been "disconnected, lacking in alignment" with state and national standards, and unrealistic in their pacing for content coverage. . . . [They] also differed "philosophically" from the curriculum-in-use in the schools, therefore sending mixed messages to teachers.

At the classroom level, Annenberg researchers found that, in all but the most advanced courses (taught to a very small minority of students), students "encounter a steady diet of routinized, basic-skills instruction that is rarely rigorous or motivating. . . . The same skills are practiced across as many as four grades; and there is uncertain articulation across grades or levels of schooling."[25] In Baltimore classrooms

students struggle to read the materials intended to form the backbone of classroom instruction. As a result, many teachers often invent their instructional materials, which vary from thoughtful adaptations of texts . . . to serial photocopying out of "activity books" that bear no resemblance to the standards-based curriculum. . . . [These practices are] most prevalent in the poorest schools.[26]

Similarly, in Portland, the CORRE review found a widespread perception that "students of color, low-income students (particularly where concentrated in certain neighborhoods), and English-language learners" were underserved.[27]

Where, then, is the locus for improvement? If accountability is ideally viewed as a reciprocal relationship between the district and the school, and if district expectations for improved student outcomes carry a concomitant expectation that the district and its partners will provide the necessary resources and support, then one natural locus for improvement is at the level of the central office. If this were the case, resources could be distributed more equitably. The expectations of the entire community for student achievement could be communicated to schools. Teachers could receive training and guidance on working with students from diverse backgrounds. And administrators could certainly look at the cognitive demand of curriculum materials and the ways in which teachers translate them to students in the expectations they embody for students' work. But accountability exists within schools as well, and in the ways schools and the district involve the broader community in holding high expectations for students.

Internal versus External Accountability

Only recently have reformers taken into account the fact that schools are deeply social organizations. Its members have very specific conceptions of accountability, of what passes for acceptable student performance, and of the methods and processes by which the organization might reach its goals.[28]

Although the alignment of curricular expectations is important, decreasing the level of variability within schools requires more than better coordination of instructional programs and testing, and more than additional monitoring. The ways in which school districts respond to the accountability question must be explicitly linked to the work of teachers in the system; in other words, accountability must occur from the "inside out."

Even the most pressing accountability demands of district, state, or federal policy will not translate into sustainable student performance gains unless there is within schools a consensus on the instructional goals of the organization and on the best way to reach these goals.[29] Consensus can be achieved through structures that foster communication, collaboration, and shared accountability for student outcomes.[30]

In particular, networks that foster collaborative, professional exchange between teachers are increasingly the method used by districts at the school level to foster greater internal accountability for student performance.[31] Such exchanges employ student work and other data that provide opportunities for students to demonstrate and apply special skills and knowledge.

There must be shared accountability outside schools as well. If a district and community lack a common understanding of expectations for student performance and their role in contributing to improvement, improvement is not likely to happen. Schools will receive mixed messages, and the impact of any support that a district and its partners can provide is likely to be muted.

In Baltimore, there is evidence of fragmented accountability. Many factors from outside the system—external partners, professional development providers, or consultants—were placing conflicting demands on teachers. This led to "a chaotic or ineffectual implementation of district messages and a failure to meet the state's high standards for student performance."[32]

In Portland, teachers commented that, other than school-based coaches, there were "very few centrally provided curricular supports." As a result, they expressed concern about "the consistency of what is taught and how teaching is supported."[33]

However, the Teaching and Learning Review in Portland itself was aimed at helping the district reverse this situation and develop a community consensus about the expectations for student performance. By involving community partners in the review, district leaders and their partners sought to build the capacity of the community to understand teaching and learning and the means they provide to support it. In addition, the district made a concerted effort to bring the Annenberg reviewers together with other reform-support organizations who provide instructional assistance to the district. In that way, all the organizations could try to achieve some synergy in their efforts.

Technical versus Adaptive Work:
The Real Challenge Appears When the Obvious Work Is Done

Heifetz and Linsky developed the dichotomy of technical versus adaptive work to illustrate that some forms of change can be achieved through the application of clear, proven solutions, while deep and lasting change in organizations—such as maintaining high levels of teaching and learning over time—require more transformative work. This kind of work involves changing deeply held perceptions, beliefs, values, or rituals.[34]

What might be surprising to some is that the solutions to many of the previously described problems are, in fact, technical solutions. Ways exist, for example, to create strong lines of communication in districts, to better fund schools based on academic need, or to provide teachers with time and expertise to collaborate and thus improve their practice. But technical changes alone will only put into place structures with the potential for facilitating improvement. The nature of the work that goes on *within* those structures is much more important. Equally critical is the degree to which the education system's theory of action embraces not only the core realm of instruction but also the wider circle of the community.

Historically, school districts have focused on moving students through the system as efficiently as possible. Standards-based reform has changed this orientation. Yet, ten years after its inception, school systems speak the standards-based language, but continue to grapple with making it meaningful in practice, and this is the reason that finding evidence of deep, systemic improvement is difficult.

There is a critical, but often missing, element in standards-based reform, and this is community engagement. The degree to which communities are engaged has direct implications for the extent to which they decide that the local school district is worth its support and advocacy. This means that actors from the larger context in which school districts exist—parents, policymakers, and the public— must understand how the system operates, why it makes the decisions it does, and why it needs certain resources or assistance

Just as the beliefs and values held by the staff of an organization influence the work that it does, so do the beliefs and values of the community that the organization serves; therefore, community engagement in the change process is essential to the adaptive part of this equation. In more practical terms, the ways in which local school districts allocate and set priorities regarding scarce monetary, material, and human resources are, in fact, reflections of their theory about how best to move all children toward the goals that the districts set. These include not only students who are proficient in reading and math, but citizens who will someday be heads of families, and productive contributors to the economic, civic, and cultural lifeblood of the community. What the district communicates, implicitly or otherwise, about how it perceives its students, their abilities, and life trajectories affects the district's credibility within the community, and thereby affects its prospects for deep-seated transformative change.

CONCLUSION

The focus of this chapter has been on Baltimore and Portland, but it could as easily have been any urban district in the country. While the historical, cultural, and political context of school systems may differ, the issues with which they struggle are often variations on very similar themes. Schools are expected, at this stage in the life of standards-based reform, to be "on board" with the idea that all students can achieve at high levels. And, there are likely few educators who can't speak this language. However, what we see at the classroom level— what is taught, how it is taught, including the variability in both from classroom to classroom—suggests that some of the contrasting themes described here are deeply rooted and continue to exert a strong influence on practice.

For example, while changes in policy can handily do away with mechanisms of the attainment model, the vestiges of "sorting" are slower to disappear, particularly in schools where teachers don't live near, look like, or culturally relate to their students. The review of Portland provided clear evidence of this disconnection, or lack of cultural competence, and its effect on the expectations for and achievement of historically disadvantaged students. A promising caveat to the Portland case, however, is the fact that the district was aware of this problem when it sought the review, and it also engaged community stakeholders in the study from the very beginning.

Given the social nature of schools as organizations, it is essential that they reach consensus within and between levels of the system on defining and reaching instructional goals. This means that internal and external accountability structures must be coordinated so that they don't wind up at cross purposes, as was noted in Baltimore. Professional development must be similarly deliberate and transparent in its purpose. In both Baltimore and Portland, professional development was found to be inconsistent and, therefore, confusing and ineffective. What the findings from the Review demonstrate is that resources for and delivery of professional development must be strategic, equitable, and tailored to the capacity of each school. This responsibility falls squarely on the district and requires that the central office know its schools at the classroom level. In that respect, the Teaching and Learning Reviews offer a promising start toward improvement.

EXPANDING THE POSSIBILITIES: THE DIVERSE-PROVIDER MODEL IN LARGE URBAN SCHOOL DISTRICTS

Kenneth K. Wong and David Wishnick

Since 1992, when the nation's first charter school opened in Minneapolis, large urban districts have gradually opened the public school sector to include diverse providers. In contrast to the past, when schools were exclusively district-run, schools now are operated by teachers, community groups, universities, and national organizations. These providers enable districts to provide the kinds of learning opportunities and connections to the community that are not widely available in conventional districts. At the same time the practice of enlisting diverse providers also fits with the notion of smart districts as nimble, adaptable organizations that focus on results, equity, and community. Employing diverse providers enable districts to hold schools accountable for results, to devote resources (the expertise of community and outside organizations) where they are most needed, and to engage community assets in support of education.

But the practice of employing diverse providers has also attracted some controversy. Perhaps the most heated arguments have arisen over the role of for-profit companies, which endeavor to earn profits for their shareholders as they operate schools. According to Arizona State University's Education Policy Research Unit, there are over thirty major for-profit companies that manage almost 400 traditionally public and charter schools in two dozen states.[1] Edison

Schools, the nation's largest for-profit organization, manages both contracted and charter schools that educate some 330,000 students in twenty-five states.

In many cases, the diverse providers operate charter schools, which are independently run public schools that operate under charters granted by the school board or another entity. But districts themselves have also turned to diverse providers to run schools, as a way of expanding their own capacity for school management and introducing innovation into the system. And mayors are looking to diverse providers to expand options for students and families and, ultimately, raise student performance. Mayor Bart Peterson of Indianapolis, for example, the only mayor in the nation with the authority to create charter schools, has sought out a range of providers to operate such schools in that city. Other mayors have attempted to attract national organizations to their cities, such as Edison and KIPP (Knowledge Is Power Program), a network of schools based in San Francisco.

This chapter examines the key features of the service-provider arrangement in large urban districts. Following an examination of the promise and the limitations of the model, we discuss the reform efforts that are underway in Philadelphia and Chicago. Lessons learned from these two cases will have broad implications for the future of urban school reform.

THE DIVERSE-PROVIDER MODEL
AS A REFORM STRATEGY

The diverse-provider model aims to attract and develop innovative ideas that will raise student performance and enrich the educational experience by empowering organizations outside the district to implement their plans while holding them accountable for meeting certain measurable outcomes within a given time frame.[2] In this governance arrangement, the contracted service providers are expected to "do the job better, or cheaper, with no fewer positive effects and no more negative ones than the public alternative."[3]

The increased use of the diverse-provider model can be attributed to five factors: "a history of outsourcing for special education services, growth in accountability policies, increasing use of school choice programs, greater use of school district outsourcing, and increases in the number of charter schools."[4] The last factor is particularly significant. In the 2006–07 school year, there are 3,977 charter schools enrolling an estimated 1.15 million students in forty states and the District of Columbia. The total number of charter schools represents an 11 percent increase over the previous year, and that year's total represents a 13 percent increase over the total from the year before.[5] In Arizona, California, and

Michigan, charter enrollment constitutes a substantial percentage of the public school population. In Dayton, Ohio, about one-fourth of the public school students enroll in charter schools.

There is much debate over the effects of the diverse-provider model on school systems and communities. Proponents of the model argue that diverse providers will promote innovation and raise performance without additional financial cost to the district. A policy brief from the Cato Institute, for example, suggests that competition from diverse providers would "likely result in decreased tuition costs."[6] Others maintain that the competitive pressure from outside providers can create incentives for district-run schools to operate more effectively.[7]

Proponents of the model also state that locally operated schools can enhance community-based involvement and ownership of schools. Community-based providers have in some cases gained significant support; the Bill & Melinda Gates Foundation, for example, allocated to Green Dot, a service provider that manages several charter schools in low-income communities in Los Angeles, more grant dollars than it gave to the district in 2006.

Skeptics of the model remain concerned about treating public education as a market good and are unconvinced of the effects of competition on schools.[8] Moreover, some contend that the addition of diverse providers introduces instability into a system, particularly when the providers leave or change hands. One of the biggest concerns among critics is the role of for-profit companies. The National Education Association has been particularly vocal in opposing the involvement of for-profit organizations in operating schools, contending that such firms tend to give a greater priority to their profit margin than to the education of children.[9]

The effect of diverse providers on community values has been a particularly contentious issue. In some cities, such as Baltimore, outside providers have attracted opposition when they failed to raise student performance. Yet even where providers have improved academic performance, there have been concerns that they failed to address broader community concerns about school quality.[10] For example, community members and teachers have resisted what they see as attempts to impose a generic model that does not match a particular school's context.[11] Likewise, local politics can constrain the type of services the providers can offer. For example, in Philadelphia, political factors rather than educational issues set limits on the role of Edison Schools (see below).[12] To the extent that political barriers do get in the way, the diverse providers might be less likely to take risks in pushing for innovative reform.

With regard to the effects of the diverse-provider model on student achievement, the research findings remain mixed. Not surprisingly, the service providers themselves claim that they are supporting students to achieve academic gains. In their Annual Report on Student Performance, for example, Edison Schools states that their "record is a strong one." Their report presents a number of positive indicators, but the analysis does not include a comparison with other service providers.

Studies that have carried out more thorough analysis remain mixed about the effects of diverse providers. A 2002 Government Accountability Office (GAO) synthesis of studies of Edison, Mosaica, and Chancellor Beacon found that "little is known about the effectiveness of these companies' programs on student achievement, parental satisfaction, parental involvement, or school climate because few rigorous studies have been conducted."[13] A year later, the GAO carried out its own achievement study, but found that "analyses of test scores in six cities yielded mixed results."[14] From a comparative perspective, looking at the United Kingdom experience in conjunction with that of the United States, Fitz and Beers concluded that diverse providers "have not experienced the success that was expected of them when they launched into the field of public education."[15]

IMPLEMENTATION OF THE DIVERSE-PROVIDER MODEL: CHICAGO AND PHILADELPHIA

While the evidence on student achievement remains inconclusive, some large urban districts have been ready to launch the diverse-provider model as a strategy to raise student performance. Philadelphia and Chicago offer two such examples. In this section, we will highlight the key features of these two initiatives in terms of design, implementation, and politics.

Diverse Providers in Chicago: The Renaissance 2010 Plan

Under Chief Executive Officer Arne Duncan, the Chicago Public Schools (CPS) have focused on the strategy of bringing school diversity to Chicago's large urban school system. Though the "school diversity"[16] reform agenda does not represent all of the "smart" reforms taking place at CPS under Duncan,[17] it does involve an innovative and wide-reaching implementation of a diverse-provider model, including charter schools and contract schools. The most public manifestation of this strategy is the "Renaissance 2010" plan.

Design of Renaissance 2010

In 2004, Duncan announced that he wanted "to make Chicago the Mecca for people with an educational vision."[18] To carry out the plan, Duncan and Mayor

Richard M. Daley unveiled Renaissance 2010 to much applause from the business community and much resistance from the Chicago Teachers Union (CTU) and other community groups.

The plan consisted of the creation of charter schools, contract schools, and new CPS performance schools to replace existing neighborhood schools that would be closed due to low academic performance and declining enrollments. All three types of schools would be public schools, in that they were to be funded on a per-pupil basis by CPS. However, the three types of schools would operate with significantly different degrees of autonomy. Only the charter and contract schools were to be operated by diverse providers. These would be administered by their own autonomous school boards or by outside educational management organizations. Performance schools, on the other hand, would be run by CPS and would operate under the same restrictions as other schools.

CPS Charter schools have autonomy in curriculum design and teacher and principal hiring and compensation. Their curricula must meet state standards, and the curricula must be specified in the charter plan. CPS Contract schools have autonomy in curriculum design, but they must hire only certified teachers. Contract school curricula must meet state and CPS standards, and the curricula must be specified in the Performance Agreement signed with CPS. Importantly, the collective bargaining agreements between CPS and the CTU do not apply to charter and contract teachers, although they do apply to performance-school teachers.[19] While applicants for charters must all be nonprofit organizations, some of these nonprofit organizations can contract out the management of the school to for-profit companies.[20]

The idea of the plan was to create a nimble district, opening innovative new schools and closing failing old ones. Part of the goal was to enhance the responsiveness of the central office and to make it leaner and more efficient. The plan would also check the power of the CTU, a key factor in that union's opposition.

At the beginning of the 2006–07 school year, CPS was home to forty-seven charter schools and one Renaissance contract school.[21] Organizations involved in the program include community-based nonprofits, groups of longtime CPS teachers, national educational-management organizations, and the CTU. At the same time, partly as a result of Renaissance 2010, at least eleven schools closed or were reconstituted for academic reasons between 2004 and 2006. But meeting the initial goal of opening one hundred new schools and closing sixty failing schools might prove to be too ambitious.

From the outset, there were to be four central benefits to school quality driven by Renaissance 2010:

- *The development of improved school models.* This would be achieved through the experimentation encouraged by a competition-based system that gives educational service providers much decisionmaking authority with which to craft their school models.
- *The development of schools with diverse missions.* The availability of diverse schools is intended to give families more educational options—ones that more closely fit their interests—than they would have had access to under a single-provider system of the centralized district (barring the choice of a private school). Some critics question this claim because they believe that more choice within a school system reduces civic capacity by shifting decisions from the political arena to the new education marketplace.

  From an all-girls school to a school with an African-themed curriculum to other kinds of specially crafted schools, these plans allow for diversity within the system and create a fuller set of options for families choosing schools for their children. They allow a school to create a unique identity within the large system and to offer to more students options usually available only to more privileged youth.
- *More intimate knowledge of a school community by the service provider.* Independent educational-service providers are in charge of only a few schools—often only one in Chicago—so they can be intimately aware of community circumstances, needs, and interests; but central district officials are more removed from the individual community and so have less knowledge of it. In the centralized district model, the principals and CPS's twelve Area Instructional Officers and Local School Council officials—elected parents and community members—are the "on-the-ground" administrators. In the diverse-provider model of Renaissance 2010, however, the educational service providers, as a whole, are supposed to be smaller organizations with more at stake in their relationship with individual communities.
- *Greater support from the business community.* At the announcement of the Renaissance 2010 plan, businesses in Chicago pledged to raise $50 million to support it. Both business leaders and civic nonprofit organizations planned to support the start-up process of the one hundred schools throughout Chicago.

Politics and Implementation

Renaissance 2010, when it was first announced, struck many as quite ambitious. The plan called for involving diverse city organizations, from the business leaders who had first championed the idea at the Commercial Club of Chicago (authors of the influential study, "Left Behind"[22]) to cultural organizations and universities. According to Arne Duncan, one of the most important features of Renaissance 2010 was the breadth of its coalition: "For years, no one cared . . . everyone sat on the sidelines and let someone else worry about it. . . . Now everyone wants to get involved, and I think that will be the salvation of public education."[23] Indeed, the Daley-Duncan civic leaders regime announced Renaissance 2010 with much fanfare and a pledge of $50 million from private philanthropic donors.[24]

But Renaissance 2010 had serious opponents from the start. The opposition of the CTU, which had previously fought Daley over pay raises, was natural since the program opened the door for nonunionized teaching jobs in the schools.[25] Renaissance 2010 also provoked community protests from myriad groups who claimed that the program was a top-down reform dictated by the business community without any input from the wider community. The character of the plan, which called for market-based reforms, combined with the sponsorship of the business community, caused some opponents to claim that Renaissance 2010 was "part of a 'much bigger plan' to move poor minority families out of 'prime real estate areas'" to pave the way for gentrification.[26] In at least one limited way—insofar as the plan did result in the reduction in neighborhood schools (schools with student populations coming from within specified attendance boundaries) and the growth of schools of choice—this claim is not without merit.

While CPS declared a desire to find charter operators who would take over neighborhood schools, it could find no applicants for neighborhood schools for the fall of 2006.[27] So, while CPS pledged to guarantee students displaced from neighborhood schools a spot in a revamped school if their age fell within the age group served by the new school,[28] residents could not bank on that possibility. And though students who moved into receiving schools actually fared just a little bit better academically than they did at their previous schools, that little improvement was not enough to quell the fears of families who wanted their children to stay in their neighborhood schools.[29]

How well has the implementation of Renaissance 2010 adhered to the theory of the diverse-provider model? In some respects, very well. As the model predicts, the process of opening school operations to a wide range of organizations did, in fact, foster new ideas and competition. For the 2007–08 school year, CPS received thirty applications for Renaissance 2010 schools from a wide variety of organizations, some of which had applied before and some which applied for the first time.[30] This allowed CPS to select the most promising applicants and encouraged them to develop strong plans for the schools. Additionally, Renaissance 2010 gives CPS the right to revoke the charters and contracts they issue, so the holders of both contracts and charters are compelled to perform well in order to maintain their relationship with CPS. For the 2006–07 school year, forty-seven charter schools operated by twenty-seven different organizations provide educational-management services for CPS.[31]

Another great boon to the Chicago Public School System following the announcement of the Renaissance 2010 plan has been the infusion of significant philanthropic dollars to the district. As of October 2006, the *Chicago Tribune* reported, more than $33 million had been donated to the Renaissance 2010 schools from various sources, both civic and business, and from large nonprofits dealing with education such as the Gates and MacArthur foundations.[32] These organizations presumably see value in the development both of innovative school programs and a new class of strong leaders within the school system. And it is the autonomy of the Renaissance plan and charter program that makes the development of these new leaders possible.

However, the philanthropic dollars have not completely lived up to the promises of the Commercial Club of Chicago. As it stands now, the chairman of the fundraising committee states that he "think[s] there's a reasonably good likelihood that we'll get it [achieve the fundraising goals]."[33] But nine million of those dollars have been donated to nine specific schools; the funds tend to support exciting startups, while other aspects of Renaissance 2010 do not receive similar financial attention.[34] This means that CPS cannot close some low-performing schools because the money does not exist to house students in new schools.

In addition, it is too soon to determine the effects of Renaissance 2010 on educational outcomes. Anecdotal reports and initial test scores are mixed, but there simply has not been enough time since the opening of the Renaissance schools to determine the impact of the plan on educational quality. Moreover, a serious analysis of the effects of Renaissance 2010 would have to assess the political effects, as well as the educational changes.

The Philadelphia Case

The reforms in the School District of Philadelphia are the most high-profile efforts to implement the diverse-provider approach in the nation. Public education watchers are particularly interested in results of the involvement of for-profit companies in the large urban school district of Philadelphia. Service provider contracts and charter contracts in Philadelphia combine in a system that is structured to include a high amount of private-sector involvement.

This system was born out of political turmoil that tempered the full realization of the theoretical diverse-provider model. While some of the facets of the model that are already visible in Chicago are also seen in Philadelphia, Philadelphia's diverse-provider model was shaped by district centralization in a way that Chicago's was not.

The Politics of Reform Design

Philadelphia's contract system for school operation grew out of an organizational and political situation that was fairly typical of major urban districts: Schools throughout the city had continually failed to produce successful test results, and school funding had been in crisis for many years. Additionally, state lawmakers were not interested in coming to the aid of what they considered to be an ineffectively run school system.

By the end of the 1990s, the situation between the city government of Philadelphia and the state of Pennsylvania was dire, and the state was poised to take over the Philadelphia School District. When Edison Schools, Inc., completed a review of the Philadelphia School District (funded by a $2.7 million contract from the state government), Governor Tom Ridge, a strong proponent of market-based education reforms, advanced plans in October 2000 for a state takeover of the Philadelphia schools. Struggling to maintain control of his city's schools, Philadelphia mayor John Street attempted to forge a bargain by gaining significant dollars from the state for the school district in exchange for accepting the takeover as "friendly."[35] Then, in December 2001, Street negotiated an additional agreement with Ridge's successor, Governor Mark Schweiker. This agreement gave Street the ability to appoint two members of the School Reform Commission, the five-person committee that would lead the reform in place of the old school board.

The School Reform Commission hoped to see changes in the following areas:

- Private involvement in the school district, something advocated by Edison in its review reports
- Development of competition via market-based reform
- Elimination of the monopoly held by the Philadelphia School District

The city leaders, on the other hand, wanted to reduce the involvement of Edison, Inc., in the reform initiative, and they also desired to garner more dollars from the state to help alleviate continual budget shortfalls. Finally, a bargain was struck where seven service providers were contracted to manage Philadelphia schools for the 2002–03 school year. These seven providers would operate a total of forty-six schools. Edison would operate only twenty schools, far fewer than the company had expected to run; two other for-profit companies, Victory Schools, Inc., and Chancellor Beacon Academies, Inc., would operate five schools each; two local nonprofits, Foundations, Inc., and Universal Companies, would operate five schools and three schools respectively; and two local universities, Temple University and the University of Pennsylvania, would operate five schools and three schools, respectively. These seven service providers would operate alongside twenty-one schools designated for restructuring by the School Reform Commission under the jurisdiction of the newly created Office of Restructured Schools.

Trade-Offs between Standardization and Diversity

Concurrent with the implementation of the School Reform Commission (SRC) agenda was the hiring (by the SRC) of Paul Vallas as chief executive officer of the School District of Philadelphia. Vallas, known as the strong-but-tough leader of the Chicago reform in its early years, made good on his reputation almost immediately by rejecting Edison's additional organizational review project that would have cost the district $18 million.

While Chicago's implementation of a diverse-provider model followed several phases of school reform, the implementation of Philadelphia's diverse-provider model followed a period of intense political struggle for control of the school district. Indeed, it was during this political back-and-forth that Philadelphia's diverse-provider strategy was forged. In contrast, Chicago's diverse-provider model is attributed largely to the work of a regime of major civic leaders.

The diverse-provider model implemented in Philadelphia was not so much an innovative experiment in school diversity as it was a political deal to align the efforts of the state and the city toward school reform. The Research For Action report, "Privatization 'Philly Style': What Can Be Learned from Philadelphia's Diverse-Provider Model of School Management?" notes that, while the goals of school diversity, competitive fostering of quality, and choice for families are the central theoretical tenets of the diverse-provider model, "the . . . model that has evolved in Philadelphia is quite different than the model anticipated by this literature."[36] The authors contend that the political context in which the diverse-provider model has been implemented in Philadelphia has prevented the development of competitive forces within the diverse-provider contract system (as separate from the charter system). These authors further report that the result is something more like a centralized district that benefits from the assistance of some private-sector organizations instead of a district that manages a competitive marketplace.[37]

Moreover, Philadelphia did not create the kind of "thin" bureaucracy envisioned by the theory of the diverse-provider model; it did not, in effect, break the centralized monopoly of an urban school district.[38] Instead, the district mandated a number of reforms that were intended to be implemented citywide.

For example, the central office maintained control over crucial areas such as human resources and hiring. Furthermore, in 2003–04, the district led the development of a core curriculum and a benchmark assessment system modeled on the system used by Edison. Thus, as the Research for Action report notes, Philadelphia represents what Henig and his associates call a "public/private hybrid system," in which private providers implement district practices, rather than their own models.[39] On the other hand, the citywide use of the Edison-style assessment system suggests that Philadelphia has been able to tap the ideas of its private partners for use on a large scale.

Additionally, some reforms did fit the theoretical view of the diverse-provider model. For instance, the Philadelphia school district did cancel the contract with Chancellor Beacon for the second year because of students' poor performance on tests. This action made it clear that the district would use its power to eliminate poor performers, and this action lent a stronger sense of competition to the system.

CONCLUSION

Urban districts are moving forward with their vision of diverse providers. Our comparison of Chicago and Philadelphia suggests that local context matters. While Chicago's Renaissance 2010 involves the creation of charter schools, contract schools, and district-managed schools, Philadelphia's reform focuses on a districtwide instructional and assessment policy that is in part stimulated by management practices among diverse vendors, including universities and Edison Schools. Although, the experiences of Philadelphia and Chicago differ in relation to school reform, the challenge for both is to sustain citywide processes of evaluation and learning that build on the successes of their service providers. Local politics, as the two cases suggest, will remain a key mediating factor in shaping the future of the diverse service provider model.

In the broader perspective, even if service innovators show measurable progress, a key challenge is the feasibility of enlarging the scale of successful pilot projects. This means that practitioners at all levels of the policy system need to be empowered with the tools and methods for ongoing self-assessment so that they can "fine tune" their innovative practices. In the context of accountability and transparency, the scope of self-assessment must be systemic, including proactive analyses that would form the basis for renewing the innovative vision in the future. In considering strategies to improve school quality, for example, service providers need to pay attention to both formal and informal constraints, such as an inadequate "pipeline" of innovative leaders, complacent governing boards, and the inertia of "risk-averse" decisionmaking behaviors. These problems can hinder a nongovernmental service provider just as they can hinder large urban districts themselves. Clearly, research and development on these kinds of issues will be critical to the ongoing efforts toward a "smart system."

PART III

COMMUNITIES IN
SMART EDUCATION SYSTEMS

THE ROLE OF COMMUNITY ENGAGEMENT IN A SMART EDUCATION SYSTEM

Richard Gray and Lamson Lam

This book envisions smart education systems that would support children's learning and development inside and outside their city schools. While legislative and administrative changes are essential in creating such systems, the effort to build these systems cannot stop at the schoolhouse or statehouse door. School reform literature clearly recognizes the integral role of families and communities in creating and sustaining school improvement.[1]

In this chapter, we will define and position community engagement with schools and school districts as an essential "cog" in the engine of citywide redesign for student success. We will also analyze some of the barriers that have historically prevented districts from realizing their potential for engagement. We will then outline our recommendations for planning and implementing a comprehensive strategy for community engagement.

WHAT IS COMMUNITY ENGAGEMENT?

A crucial and challenging part of transforming school districts and their city partners into smart education systems is knowing how to build the public will and the power necessary to improve the quality of public schools and other educational supports in low-income urban communities. To enable city agencies and institutions to coordinate the resources and policies of the variety of systems serving youth and families, there must be a consistent process to ensure that the stakeholders within those systems are committed to a set of shared goals and outcomes at similar levels of understanding, depth, and intensity. Within the framework of a smart educational system, this process itself can be considered "community engagement."

More broadly, we define community engagement as the collaboration of constituency groups and the mobilization of specific constituencies into active and accountable relationships. Furthermore, these constituencies should aim to accomplish a common mission, goal, or purpose, one that improves schools and increases student achievement.[2] A smart system can consistently create ongoing opportunities for a range of stakeholders and constituency groupings to debate, negotiate, and articulate the education goals or purposes they share, and to build relationships and structures that link the capacity of those various players to the pursuit of common purposes.

Clearly, community, in its broadest sense, can include all individuals in a given setting. However, since the focus of this chapter is on the connection between communities and education systems and networks, our definition of community will concentrate on constituencies organized into groups and represented by leadership.[3] Though our definition includes elite sectors as well as the local civic/cultural infrastructure, we will focus primarily on the critical role of grassroots, community-based organizations.

BARRIERS TO SCHOOL-COMMUNITY PARTNERSHIPS

Despite convincing evidence of the positive impact of family and community involvement, schools and school districts have historically lacked the vision, the means, and, too often, the desire to integrate the resources and capital of community and city organizations into the public school system. As a result, the opportunity for a productive exchange of ideas, information, and resources between school systems and their nested communities is lost to barriers of culture, perceptions, and communication.

Cultural mismatches can easily divide schools and communities. A culture of bureaucratic professionalism has historically pervaded district and school administration. And this culture has created a relationship in which schools and educators supposedly possess all the necessary expertise, and parents and the community play only a passive supporting role. This limited perception of the potential contributions of parents and community, coupled with the wide racial and socioeconomic discrepancies between most urban school teachers and the families they serve, has led to massive breakdowns in trust between teachers and family members.[4]

Because of these issues of perception and culture, schools and school systems have not taken advantage of genuine offers of resources and support from parents and community organizations and institutions. Groups offering support in areas such as afterschool programming, art, and literacy have experienced "difficulty in engaging district or school administrators and maintaining access to schools to conduct their programs."[5] Many of these organizations felt like outsiders to the school system and were kept at arm's length by the schools whose students they were trying to serve. Even people within the system who are open to offers of help from the community have found themselves operating in a school culture that provides little time, resources, or professional development for them to take full advantage of the significant resources outside the school community.

When community groups develop parent- and community-led campaigns to improve poorly performing schools, they are often seen as unwanted competition for school-based parent associations.[6] Parents who express concern about their children's education and their desire to support school improvement by using a community group as their base of power are often told that the school's parent association is the only legitimate body to represent parents. Additionally, what masquerades as parent involvement in many low-income urban schools at best amounts to pro forma representation, and at worst becomes a system of marginalization and exclusion. As a result, such forms of parent involvement seldom represent the broader school community and often "mirror the larger dysfunctional school culture."[7]

Howard Baum of the Urban Education Community Service Program noted, "There is a high degree of paranoia in the school system."[8] In the late 1990s, Baum worked with the Southeast Education Taskforce (SET) in Baltimore, Maryland. SET emerged from a community-based planning process to focus existing community assets and attract outside resources to improve the quality of life in Southeast Baltimore. Staff from the university helped SET collect and analyze data on the problems in the community's schools, and also craft an agenda for school improvement. The SET education agenda concentrated on building a new culture of respect and collaboration between schools and communities to support significant change within the SET schools.

By working through the existing parent-involvement channels, such as the PTA and school improvement team (SIT), and by focusing only on issues pre-approved by the principal, SET specifically aimed to minimize any threat to the school staff. But in spite of SET's deference to principals and its desire to establish a new culture of partnership, conflicts between parents and principals surfaced anyway. Many parents believed principals and staff were not interested in addressing the issues they identified. In some schools, parents began meeting separately from the SIT and the PTA. Although a few principals welcomed this extra parent and SET involvement, most principals complained to the SET committee about its staff creating "another parent group to deal with" and also for giving support to "rabble-rouser" parents. According to Baum, "School culture treats even the most benign outsider as the enemy."

While it would be easy to dismiss dysfunctional school-community relations as the result of incompetent or uncaring educators, we must acknowledge that a highly pressurized school culture creates a tense and distrustful environment for educators and fosters a school climate of "intensification."[9] School staff have very little time, few resources, and very little if any professional development or support in building collaborations with organizations outside the school setting. In this pressurized atmosphere, educators tend to rely on those people they already know and trust; such a closed circle rarely includes parents, community members, or community-based groups. Engaging the community and parents, while seen as commendable by some in the school system, is not seen as the "real" work of educators. Even when community and parent engagement is a stated district and school priority, there is hardly any professional guidance or support given to enact these priorities, nor are there consequences when they are not acted upon. Educators who want to develop real partnerships with parents and community groups must do so on their own time. This results in teachers shutting out the community at the exact time when inviting them in could help most.[10]

BUILDING COMMUNITY ENGAGEMENT IN
A SMART EDUCATION SYSTEM

How can educators and community members break down these barriers and enable community engagement to play its critical role in a smart education system? One way is to tap the potential power of grassroots organizations. Although there is a vast array of organized constituency organizations, community-based grassroots organizations[11] are untapped potential partners with whom smart education systems could collaborate. Using these organizations as another power base would help produce educational improvement and equity.

By grassroots we mean those organizations and institutions whose

- offices, work, and relationships are housed within the community; and

- constituencies have had direct contact and experience with community public schools that have traditionally underserved them.

Why the community-based organization? The persistently low quality of schooling in certain neighborhoods, particularly low-income communities and communities of color, is partly due to the limited political power and social capital of those communities. Simply stated, many schools in low-income and working-class communities have been allowed to fail because there are few consequences for the continued provision of poor educational services and resources to those communities (see chapter 8). However, many grassroots organizations have demonstrated their experience and capacity to build and support community power to address the needs of the communities they serve. By "demonstrated experience and capacity" we mean groups that have a successful track record using approaches that include the following key characteristics:

- Parents and residents, including youth, are viewed as a constituency to which the organization is accountable.
- Community problems are addressed through collective-action strategies, making the process as transparent and participatory as possible.
- Internal democratic decisionmaking processes are developed so that constituent concerns drive group activities.

Improvement in the quality of services and resources in low-income communities happens when the residents, organizations, and institutions in those communities demand it. This type of change can be supported when resources are invested in building and expanding the existing infrastructure and power base within those communities to produce, direct, and support their own agendas for change.[12]

Over the past ten years, a growing number of community-based organizations—with paid (often professional and trained) staff and independent funding—have provided the infrastructure and leadership for parent/community engagement and organization that could improve their schools.[13] These efforts have created vehicles for leadership development and direct action for parents, young people, and neighborhood residents who have a direct stake in effective, accessible, and accountable neighborhood schools. Despite these efforts, districts and schools still tend to place the role and responsibility for community engagement on the shoulders of individuals with limited experience, resources, and relationships in the communities they are trying to serve.

The following examples illustrate how district alliances with community-based organizations can make school renewal and improvement a reality.

The Community Collaborative

In 2001, New York University's Institute for Education and Social Policy and New Settlement Apartments (NSA), a neighborhood association in the South Bronx, decided to reach out to five other South Bronx community-based organizations—ACORN, Citizens Advice Bureau, Highbridge Community Life Center, Mid-Bronx Council, and the Northwest Bronx Community and Clergy Coalition—to form a new partnership called the Community Collaborative for District 9 (CC9) to organize for education reform in the district's chronically underserved and under-performing schools.

The members of CC9 decided that in order to affect teaching and learning inside the schools, they had to find a way to create something other than an adversarial relationship with educators. In the past, groups had started school-improvement campaigns committed to offering support to school and district staff. However, parent concerns and offers of help were often met with disrespectful and dismissive responses from school staff and administrators. Thus, offers of partnership were turned into difficult conflicts.

The collaborative decided to explore a new approach by creating a meaningful relationship with the United Federation of Teachers and with the New York City Department of Education. After several months of conversation and negotiation, these partners announced the pilot of a one-year instructional plan in District 9.[14] The program itself was a promising and innovative approach that sought to improve teacher quality by implementing a "lead teacher program," in which selected master teachers would become responsible for mentoring less-experienced colleagues in some lowest-performing schools in the South Bronx. A first-year evaluation found the lead teacher program had produced a higher teacher retention rate and contributed to increases in student performance. The leadership role played by the community collaborative was cited as a significant factor in the success of the program. The program has been expanded to include two hundred new lead teachers throughout the city.

The success of CC9 triggered the formation of a new alliance between educators and the community in New York City. In 2003, ACORN, United Federation of Teachers (UFT), Cypress Hills Advocates for Education, the 1199/SEIU Employer Child Care Fund, and the Community Involvement Program of NYU's Institute for Education and Social Policy came together to form the Brooklyn Education Collaborative (BEC). BEC began with staff and leaders from the groups discussing ways to organize and improve local schools in East Brooklyn. For more than five months, groups of parent and teachers met, talked, and studied together to come up with a shared vision of better schools. Those discussions resulted in

BEC's "K–12 Platform for Change," approved in the summer of 2004. The platform included a call for rigorous, engaging, and nurturing schools built to meet the academic, social, and emotional needs of all students, and with high expectations for all. Additionally, the platform demanded supports for teachers, principals, and other school administrators to ensure that they get the resources necessary to meet student needs.

BEC chose to focus their efforts on the middle grades by calling for the establishment of a "BEC Learning Zone" aimed at strengthening middle-grade education in Brooklyn's Districts 18, 19, and 23. Seven out of ten eighth graders read below grade level in the districts, which serve the communities of East New York, Brownsville, Cypress Hills, Canarsie, and East Flatbush. BEC wanted the New York City Department of Education to put into action changes such as smaller class sizes and more guidance counselors.[15] BEC kicked off its Learning Zone campaign with a rally attended by more than three hundred people in the fall of 2004. UFT president Randi Weingarten and 1199/SEIU secretary-treasurer George Gresham were there to pledge their support. A petition drive asking for public support for the Learning Zone collected more than eight thousand signatures.

CC9 and BEC both have taken on the task of changing the culture of mutual distrust and animosity that has often tainted the communication between educators and parents. Both collaboratives have created opportunities for parents, community members, and educators to talk openly and honestly with each other, learn about what they have in common, and plan how they can work together toward a common goal of improving schools. To this end, parents and teachers participate in one-on-one conversations to break down fears and misconceptions about each other. Educators and community members also work side by side in study sessions and school visits to review information on instruction and curriculum. As a result, the collaboratives have cultivated new forms of interaction and practices—all grounded in conversation, study, collaboration, and action—among educators, parents, unions, district staff, and community groups.

Additionally, the collaboratives stress mutual investment and accountability, rather than blame, between schools and community. Each participating group is clear about the time and resources it is prepared to invest to enable the collaborative to achieve its goals. Member groups dedicate staff to conduct the work of the collaborative, raise funds, and mobilize their organization's constituency for collaborative meetings and events.

The move by community organizations to a collaborative structure also has a practical side. Community groups have limited resources that put them at a disadvantage in their struggles to change large institutions that have greater resources. When these organizations link their individual resources and constituencies around a shared agenda, they create their own "power bloc" that enables them to take "an equal seat at the table" when negotiating or working with the school system.

Getting to Parents

When schools and districts do attempt to reach out to the community, their most common concern is that "We just can't get people to come." This statement is often followed by the criticism that parents and community members are apathetic about the education of their children, and so they do not show up for meetings or school events. However, there are reasons why parents and community members decide not to show up for school-led meetings. One explanation is that these meetings lean heavily toward "informing" the community about an existing or already developed school agenda. When this kind of attitude exists, the response of parents and communities is often only lukewarm. They find very little compelling in processes that provide little opportunity for them to understand and help create the kinds of schools and schooling they want for their children.

The Harwood Institute for Public Innovation identified two important factors that move people from a focus on their private lives to engagement in public concerns. First, people seek public relationships and information to help them to make sense of the world and to understand their place in it. Second, while people may start by speaking out on a public issue because of frustration and anger, they ultimately are looking for hope and a sense of possibility.[16]

These same principles apply to parents and community members when they try to navigate from their private lives to a relationship with public schools. Most people have very little contact with what goes on in schools and, in many cases, the language and culture is alien to them. Therefore, when parents and community members come to schools, they are seeking relationships, settings, and information that will help them understand the world inside the schools, and allow them to become active participants in defining their place there. Also, the anger that gets people inspired enough to speak out about schools often flows from a desire for a better educational environment for their children.

Most importantly, the many parents and community members who do not come to school meetings and events, nonetheless, have meaningful conversations about school issues—but with friends and family members, not with educators. As the Harwood Institute notes, "talk about concerns are embedded in everyday life."[17] This means that it makes sense to shift engagement efforts to the places where these conversations are already taking place. Doing so would help integrate school improvement into the everyday lives of parents and community members.

Sacramento ACT, a member of the PICO network in California, took the idea of educators going the places where parents already are—their homes—and turned it into a joint school-community venture. The idea began when persistently low academic performance and high levels of suspensions in the Sacramento Unified School District, led Sacramento ACT to invite parents, teachers, and principals to a listening campaign in 1997. The campaign revealed that many parents felt unwelcome in schools, but they did want an opportunity to express their concerns about the education of their children. These parents indicated that they would be more comfortable meeting with teachers at home. Continued conversations between parents, teachers, and administrators led to a proposal for a teacher home-visit program.

Sacramento ACT met with representatives from the teachers' union to discuss their the proposal. The union and ACT agreed that teachers in the program should be compensated for home visits, and that participation by teachers would not be mandatory. After getting the approval and funding from the school board, a pilot of the home-visit program was initiated in eight schools during the 1998–99 school year. Teachers taking part in the program were paid based on the highest district stipend rates. Sacramento ACT's parents and staff provided the training and monitored the impact of the program.

In the first year of the pilot program, teachers conducted visits in pairs and made at least two visits to each family, with a total of three thousand home visits. These visits focused on building lines of communication between the family and the teacher and providing parents with information and materials they could use to work with their children at home.

After the program's first year, evaluators found improvements in standardized-test scores, classroom behavior, parents' and students' attitudes toward school, and homework-completion rates. By 2000, thirty-nine districts were participating in the program and ACT had trained close to eight hundred teachers who made more than seven thousand home visits. Today, more than five hundred schools have started teacher home-visit programs, and Sacramento ACT has provided training in the program throughout the country.

Access to and Use of Data

Community groups have used both quantitative and qualitative data collected by the school system, or through independent studies, to help give context and clarity to the educational experiences of their community's children and to define the direction needed for school change. In addition, community groups have used visits to high-performing or greatly improved schools so that parents and community members involved in improvement campaigns can more clearly envision what achievement and learning looks like in effective classrooms. For many parents in communities with low-performing schools, examples of good instruction and learning are difficult to find. Therefore, the data collected through observation gives parents the language and images that support the possibility of change in their own communities.

An example from New York City shows how data can be a powerful tool for school improvement. When and the staff of New Settlement Apartments became concerned about reading skills of the children in their afterschool program, they asked the NYU Community Involvement Program (CIP) to create a workshop for staff and parents to help identify the right questions to ask about the problem. Together, they chose to analyze school-level data for PS 64, because it was the school closest to NSA, and the school demographics were similar to those of the community: 80 percent of the students were Latino and 18 percent were African American, and 93 percent were eligible for free lunches.

In the summer of 1997, CIP staff designed and facilitated a four-week training series to help parents and staff review demographic and outcome data on PS 64 from the Annual School Report, the Board of Education's school "report card." During the training, parents were shocked to discover that only 17 percent of the children at PS 64 were reading at grade level and that the school ranked 657th out of 674 city elementary schools based on scores on the citywide reading test. Learning about this data helped galvanize a campaign by the NSA Parent Action Committee (PAC) to demand improvements at PS 64.

The outcome data on reading persuaded the parents that something needed to be done at PS 64. But because there were few examples of successful schools in their neighborhood, PAC, with the assistance of CIP, arranged a series of visits to schools that had produced significant improvements in student performance. The parents and NSA staff observed active classrooms with engaged students in inviting and comfortable facilities. The schools visited were the kinds of places they wanted for their children. Armed with this new information, PAC led a campaign that resulted in a change in leadership at PS 64. and became a major force in the creation of CC9.

Research and Strategic Support

Transforming failing schools is enormously difficult. It requires knowledge about effective instructional practices as well as successful organizational development and strategies for change. While many community organizations have demonstrated the capacity to carry out a broad range of community development and revitalization initiatives, these organizations have less access to and experience in leading school-improvement campaigns. To address this lack, many groups have established positive and productive relationships with university-based or nonprofit partners to help support their organizing work.[18] These groups help perform technical tasks, such as data analysis or policy research, or to help the community organizations with strategic planning. In each case, the university partners do not attempt to define the problems for the group. Instead, they apply their expertise to help groups understand issues identified by the groups themselves. The university partners' commitment to community control over the content of the work likely stems from their previous experience with community-organizing efforts.

A case in point is the Community Involvement Program of the Annenberg Institute for School Reform. It provides intensive technical and strategic support to the Community Collaborative for the Bronx-CCB (formerly known as CC9) and BEC. CIP produces custom data analyses (based on school- and district-level data), policy research, and exploratory research, all of which assist collaboratives improve public schools in their neighborhoods.

Similarly, the Bay Area Coalition for Equitable Schools provided data and research support to Oakland Community Organizations in their highly successful small-schools campaign. These relationships are most effective when the support organization acknowledge that locally based organizations and individuals are the final arbiters of the content and direction of the work to be done.

CONCLUSION

As we attempt to envision a smart education system with an interactive network of structures that cut across and include a variety of sectors and stakeholders, we must also face the challenge that what we are trying to envision flies in the face of the prevailing culture of schools and districts. As the smart system strives for new forms of collaboration and leadership that will deliver higher-quality education to students, it should revise the roles that educators, parents, community members, and community groups play in the new education process.

What makes this process even more difficult is the fact that creation of the new means removal of the old. This effort involves changing not only systems, but also attitudes about and attachments to those systems. And, in education, attitudes and attachments change slowly, if they change at all.

The creation of a smart education system is not a reformation process, but rather a transformation effort. This effort is not only about making improvements in the existing system; it is also about changing the character, nature, and conditions of the system. Relationships between public school stakeholders and policymakers, must become mutually accountable relationships. And these relationships must link all groups to the pursuit of a common goal: improving educational opportunities and outcomes for all children.

LEVERAGING REFORM:
YOUTH POWER IN A
SMART EDUCATION SYSTEM

Kavitha Mediratta, Amy Cohen, and Seema Shah

They say they need scanners to detect
We say we need justice and respect!

Members of the Urban Youth Collaborative Student Union gathered on the steps of Tweed Courthouse Thursday evening to protest so-called safety efforts—scanners, police, actions of security guards—that they say detract from learning and show a lack of respect for young people.

Charging that such security moves make students feel like criminals, the young people delivered thousands of postcards addressed to city officials and signed by kids in [270] public schools protesting the safety measures. The message urge[d] the Department of Education to "include youth voice and experience" in formulating security policies. "We hope the chancellor and mayor will see how important this is to us and how they should include youth in decisionmaking," Elisabeth Ortega, a student at DeWitt Clinton High School in the Bronx, said.

The students brought the cards, stuffed in several large plastic bags, to the top of Tweed's imposing stairs. Neither Mayor Michael Bloomberg nor Chancellor Joel Klein came to accept delivery.[1]

Across the country, high school students are increasingly engaged in planning and carrying out sophisticated campaigns to improve schooling outcomes in their communities. In Los Angeles, for example, high school students were part of a coalition of parents, other advocates, and policy researchers that forced the school district to make a college-preparatory curriculum mandatory for all the district's high school students. In Philadelphia, high school students led a campaign for a radical reform of high school education, and partnered in the redesign of several large high school campuses into small schools.

Because youth organizing for education reform is so new and expanding so rapidly, it is difficult to assess the actual number of existing groups. But research conducted in 2002 identified at least forty such groups in the San Francisco Bay Area, and suggested that many more are active throughout the country.[2]

This chapter examines the emergence of youth organizing as a strategy for education reform, and argues that youth power is an essential component of smart education systems. First, we situate youth organizing within the wide array of student leadership and youth-voice initiatives in schools and districts. Then, drawing on a study of school-reform organizing led by researchers at the Annenberg Institute for School Reform, we describe the basic characteristics of youth-organizing groups and report the impact of youth organizing on district policies, school practices, and, most importantly, on student learning and persistence in the educational arena. Finally, we return to the concept of a smart education system and identify the necessary shifts in practice if school systems are to engage young people fully in schools and in education reform.

STUDENT LEADERSHIP AND VOICE
IN A SMART EDUCATION SYSTEM

The vision of a smart education system presented in this book is one that is nimble, adaptive, and efficient in function; focused on educational services; and aligned with community needs and priorities. The district role within a smart education system is to provide schools, students, and teachers with support and interventions; ensure that schools have sufficient power and resources to make good decisions; and make decisions and hold people throughout the system accountable by using indicators of school and district performance and practices (see chapter 3).

Though a smart education system implies a transformation in the way districts function, the concept is potentially far more encompassing. In smart education systems, schools and districts exist in a dynamic relationship with the communities they serve. Students, families, and other community constituencies possess power, access, and legitimacy, and they participate fully in defining and creating learning opportunities and experiences. Importantly, smart education systems acknowledge youth as critical stakeholders in schooling success, and foster a climate in which young people can hold adults accountable for educating them well.

If a smart education system offers a vision for the seamless union of school and community capacities in the service of children's positive academic, social, and emotional development, what are the levers for moving schools, districts, and communities closer to that vision? Though promising examples of some components of a smart education system exist, no urban district has managed to construct the necessary dynamic relationship—based on accountability and partnerships—with its least powerful community constituencies that a smart system demands. Instead, as the following quotes from high school students suggest, urban youth of color today encounter a very different reality in their schools:

> I went through life in high school just like the youth in my neighborhood, planning to fail.
>
> I am a student who is being criminalized in school.
>
> I slowly became less interested in school.
>
> I see a cycle repeating itself.
>
> While I'm talking right now, I'm dying inside, because—come on—it's not fair that we are being treated like animals when all we want is an education to be successful in college and life.[3]

In a smart education system in which students have authentic voice, young people's despair over their educational experiences and their demands for improvement in the quality of education in their schools would be acknowledged as calls to action and transformation. In today's education system, though, educators' responses to young people's voice and leadership are all too often shaped by race- and class-based assumptions about student limitations. A Latino high school student recounts his experience advocating for college-preparatory curricula for himself and his peers:

> There was a bill that we were trying to pass where they'd make legislation so the [college-prep courses] are given to you [as] the [mandated] curriculum. And we went to talk to legislators about it. Some were supportive. Some were like, "No, it's too hard for students to go through. They're not going to be able to graduate if we give them these classes. They're not smart enough." And one lady, I remember her saying, "If everyone's going to college, who's going to fix my car?"[4]

In contexts in which educators' behaviors are shaped by deeply held assumptions that the young people they serve have limited capabilities and aspirations, authentic student engagement is essential to create genuine opportunities for young people's academic achievement and leadership in education reform. Indeed, substantial research demonstrates the benefits of student engagement in schools.[5] Such engagement enhances student learning, prepares students for life after high school, and helps educators define priorities for increasing school effectiveness.[6] Yet in most urban districts serving low-income communities of color, student engagement is not only minimal and episodic, but also actively undermined by the low expectations of adults.

The Dominant Paradigm of Student Leadership and Voice in Schools

Youth leadership in schools is commonly understood as participation in school-based groups and voluntary clubs focused on planning and promoting school-based extracurricular activities. Student involvement in school governance generally occurs through representative government groups to which students are elected by their peers. Through these student government groups, students plan social events and, when the school's administration is receptive, offer feedback on school policies.

If student governments provide a structural route for student participation in schools, the opportunity for such participation is differentially distributed across schools and among students. Most student governments restrict student participation to the most academically successful students. In many poorly performing schools, student governments rarely meet, and when they do, they provide only limited opportunities for student-directed activity.

During the past decade, another form of student engagement in schools has emerged, one that is driven in part by increased opportunities for community-based organizations to work in partnership with schools. Though the concept of youth voice is not new, its popularity has escalated through these emerging partnerships.

A wide variety of community-based organizations, using a range of approaches and philosophies, engage young people in programs designed to support their social and emotional development. Some of these programs also integrate civic engagement into the school curriculum, often through service learning and political education. Originating in an emphasis on reducing and preventing harm, youth development focuses on cultivating the individual capacity (skills and competencies) of young people to avoid risk-taking behaviors.

Advocates of positive youth development emphasize the concept of young people as community assets and as individuals who act from strengths rather than deficits.[7] The concept of youth voice embodies a view of young people as resources rather than problems or recipients of services, and implies an expanded role for young people in defining the activities they undertake. Proponents of youth voice argue that "when young people participate in decision making (as equals) with adults, mobilize and create or change public policy, and take influential leadership roles in organizations and institutions, the benefits accrue to adults, organizations and communities as well as contributing to the positive development of young people themselves."[8]

In the early 1990s, efforts like the Beacon initiative in New York City enabled scores of community-based organizations to initiate programs for students and families on school sites during and after school. As the 1990s progressed, this trend was facilitated by efforts to increase student access to school-based afterschool programs, which were promoted by funding from the Open Society Institute and the Clinton administration's Twenty-First Century Community Learning Center initiative. The resulting expansion of school-based services and afterschool programming injected the principles of positive youth development, which had evolved within the arena of community-based organizations (CBOs), into the world of schooling.

But on many sites, schools and community-based activities shared a location and little else. Educators and CBO staff continued to function independently, and created few opportunities to integrate the principles of youth voice developed by community groups into the culture and practices of everyday schooling.

The nationwide emphasis on creating small high schools that began at the turn of the century with funding support from Carnegie Corporation of New York, the Bill & Melinda Gates Foundation, and the federal government's Smaller Learning Communities grants program, encouraged deeper partnerships between schools and external organizations. These partnerships are bringing the principles of positive youth development directly into school practices through expanded curricular offerings, including community-service projects, and more experience-based pedagogy. For example, at the South Brooklyn Community High School, which serves students identified as "at risk" of dropping out, classes engage students in experiential projects with real-world applications. Advisors help students problem-solve the issues that may have impeded their past academic success, support students in making plans for life after graduation, and also in developing a range of job-related skills.[9]

Participation in youth development activities can provide formative leadership experiences for students as well as create opportunities for student engagement focused on enhancing school effectiveness. Even in their most expansive form, however, school-based youth-development activities are, at their core, paternal; they conceptualize a set of options and experiences that schools provide to youth to spur their positive development, rather than a set of opportunities for engagement through which youth can seize and shape or reshape their settings.[10] Though students can exercise a range of choices within these activities, the parameters for their efforts—including even whether they can actually come together as a group—are established by the expectations and priorities of the adults in the school. Service notions further limit the effectiveness of many youth development initiatives, defining them as "doing for" rather than "doing with" young people.[11] Thus, youth development programs rarely create settings in which youth can learn with, and through, each other rather than from adults; and, because this is the case, the programs mainly fail to challenge the dominant paradigm of school-based leadership.

Confronting the Dynamics of Race and Class

In *From Governance to Accountability: Building Relationships that Make Schools Work*, Mediratta and Fruchter frame organizing in low-income communities as an organic response to the exclusion in schools faced by low-income families of color. Mediratta and Fruchter assert that organizing develops the potential to build the power equivalent to that held by middle-class, white communities. We believe the development of such a power base is even more necessary among low-income youth of color, who experience the added disadvantage of adult paternalism at a critical point in their adolescent social/emotional development.[12]

From Governance to Accountability elucidates the role that differential access to cultural capital among public school parents plays in defining the relationships that low-income families develop with educators. Annette Lareau and other researchers have demonstrated that, because of their class status, middle-class parents are able to transmit a kind of cultural capital to their children. This capital takes the form of attitudes, preferences, behaviors, and credentials that facilitate inclusion, successful participation, and upward mobility in schools and other social institutions.[13] Drawing on Lareau's framework, we argue that a similar dynamic occurs among students; that is, middle-class students are more likely than working-class or poor students to understand school expectations and to bring with them the cultural knowledge and resources necessary to succeed in school, regardless of their long-term educational aspirations and goals.

In affluent communities, accountability relationships develop organically between educators and parents, and these expectations are passed on to students. Educators expect students to engage with them, and students can do so without feeling intimidated because they have had sufficient experience communicating with adults. White, middle-class students' relationships with educators start from their earliest encounters with schools and their experience of their parents' access to educators. These experiences shape an implicit—and sometimes explicit—sense of power and self-efficacy among students that ensures schools' receptivity to their input.

When students in poorly performing schools challenge educators—without the power that their middle-class counterparts can employ—school practitioners and district administrators often react by criticizing and dismissing the students, sometimes even disciplining them or defining them as threats to school safety. Students who challenge or protest are frequently admonished for not working through the established structures and mechanisms of the school, regardless of how dysfunctional these structures may be. In such environments, student government, school clubs, and other educator-directed youth-development efforts are often used by school and district officials as instruments for silencing student leadership and marginalizing nonconforming students. A high school student from California explains this dynamic:

> [My principal] came in my homeroom one day to talk about the exit exam. So he walks in, he looks pretty calm. Then he makes eye contact with me and he starts getting all nervous looking and stuff. I think they're like petrified of us or something, just because we can put them out there and tell everybody that they're not doing what they're supposed to be doing, which they aren't.[14]

In contrast to school-based forms of student leadership and voice, community-based youth organizing seeks to build power among urban, low-income youth of color to challenge institutionalized norms and relationships that create and maintain poorly performing schools in their neighborhoods. In schools where assumptions of student capacity and aspirations are low and defined by stereotypes and prejudice, students gain authentic voice in their schools by mobilizing large numbers of students, by articulating a positive vision for change based on their analysis of the dynamics that shape local conditions, and by building strategic alliances with influential allies (see figure 1).

Like youth development, youth organizing focuses on building the individual skills and capacities of young people. Many youth organizing groups provide homework tutoring, link students to supportive services, and support students through the college application process. But youth organizing aspires to a larger goal: it seeks to develop the capacity of young people to act collectively to confront injustice and transform the institutions that shape their lives.[15]

Youth leadership does not mean that adults are absent. Most youth organizations are staffed by adults whose job is to maintain what Camino and Zeldin call "facilitative processes and structures," defined by young people and through which they can exercise control over their work.[16] In neighborhoods and schools disadvantaged by years of political, social, and economic marginalization, such efforts to build genuine youth voice inherently involve demands for social justice.

Youth-organizing groups generally share the following characteristics:

- They are nonprofit community-based organizations with histories of working to improve their communities in a variety of arenas such as environmental conditions, juvenile justice, and employment.
- They are committed to developing the capacity of young people to lead campaigns that challenge the status quo, and raise demands for improved educational conditions and expanded youth opportunities.
- They work with the dual objective of achieving broad structural changes and winning specific school improvements.
- They work independently of schools and school systems, though some groups develop relationships with schools through service or youth development activities.

An Expanding Field

Youth organizing has long been critical to social-justice activism in this country. Young people have played critical roles in almost every social movement of the twentieth century, including the antiwar and civil rights movements of the 1960s. But the number of youth organizing groups has increased exponentially during the past two decades. As Daniel Hosang explains, youth organizing

> [arose] in many ways in response to the austere days of the Reagan, Bush, and Clinton eras, both because of the assault launched against youth "citizenship" and because the federal government itself retreated from encouraging young people to become politically engaged in their communities. The War on Poverty dictum of "maximum feasible participation" of the poor was anathema to programs like Clinton's AmeriCorps, which largely forbids its cadre of youth leaders from joining community organizing efforts. Like the first President Bush's "Thousand Points of Light," these programs promoted a politically indifferent volunteerism, encouraging youth participants to eschew issues like police brutality, toxic pollution, and educational discrimination in favor of community crime watches, neighborhood clean-ups, and afterschool tutoring.[17]

Yet several key trends within the arena of public education also supported the expansion of youth organizing.[18] In the late 1980s, following a rise in juvenile crime, school districts across the country began developing "zero-tolerance"

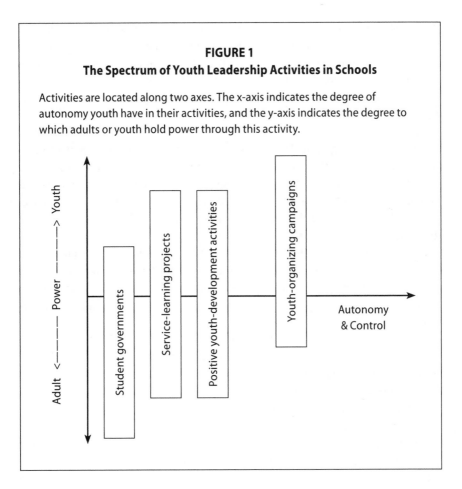

FIGURE 1
The Spectrum of Youth Leadership Activities in Schools

Activities are located along two axes. The x-axis indicates the degree of autonomy youth have in their activities, and the y-axis indicates the degree to which adults or youth hold power through this activity.

policies to reduce the threat of youth violence. Though predictions of a crime wave among urban adolescents later proved incorrect, zero tolerance as a school disciplinary strategy expanded across urban districts during the 1990s. The resulting increase in school expulsion rates sparked a wave of youth protests in urban districts against school practices that pushed them out of school.[19]

For example, "Generation Y," a youth organization in Chicago, surveyed 350 students from different high schools about their school's zero-tolerance policies, and collected data on student suspension rates. Its report, "Suspended Education," documented a rise in the number of student suspensions for minor offenses, such as tardiness and skipping classes, and it advocated for alternative disciplinary policies that keep young people in school.[20] By the end of the 1990s, young people in California and Mississippi were also developing campaigns to challenge not only the racially charged application of zero-tolerance policies in urban districts, but also the stark disparity between rapidly rising expenditures for prisons and stagnant or declining funds for schools.[21]

During this period, school districts were undergoing transformations in curriculum, assessment, and governance that increasingly emphasized test-score preparation and performance, and narrowed the scope of student learning in schools.[22] Beginning in the late 1980s, states began to develop content and performance standards to specify the critical skills and knowledge necessary for high school graduation, and to link these new standards to more rigorous and standardized exit exams. Successive reauthorizations of the Elementary and Secondary Education Act, culminating in the No Child Left Behind Act (NCLB) of 2001, intensified the pressure on low-performing districts and schools to produce higher test scores. Within five years of NCLB's enactment, a majority of urban districts had introduced or expanded standardized testing, had created new promotion and graduation standards, and had developed new accountability systems dedicated to identifying, rewarding, and sanctioning individual student and school performance.

In some respects, these new accountability measures highlighted the inadequacy of student performance in many schools and facilitated external demands for improvement. But the emphasis on test-based accountability—and particularly on the types of tests that states and districts have tended to use—ended up constricting the ways in which students are taught and the kinds of things students learn in school. In response, youth groups like Sisters in Action for Power in Portland, Oregon, which develops organizing and leadership skills among young women of color, began organizing to challenge the implementation of NCLB in local schools.

At the same time, in the early part of the twenty-first century, the introduction of small high school reform in urban districts became a catalyst for youth-driven oppositional activity to influence reforms in their communities. For example, in Philadelphia, following seven years of school-based organizing to win incremental changes, such as improved curricula, adequate text books, and facility improvements, two youth organizations came together to articulate a sweeping educational agenda. Working as allies, Youth United for Change and the Philadelphia Student Union fought for a transformation of the high schools in their neighborhoods, and participated in selecting the theme-based small schools that were created on these campuses. In New York City, Sistas and Brothas United seized the opportunity afforded by the small high school reforms to design and open their own small school that was based on a youth organizing model of student leadership for social justice. The group also joined with other allies to build a citywide power base of high school students through the Urban Youth Collaborative, to inject youth influence into what they saw as a top-down, insular high school reform process.

In Los Angeles, meanwhile, South Central Youth Empowered thru Action (SCYEA) led a successful campaign to gain equal access to college-preparatory classes. The group, which had started a decade earlier to improve the physical conditions of Los Angeles high schools, gathered data on the low rates of college attendance by inner-city high school graduates and launched protests, work with media, and coalition building to gather support for a policy of greater access to college-preparatory classes. In 2005, the school board adopted a policy that mandates the college-preparatory curriculum as the default curriculum for all Los Angeles high school students.

THE IMPACT OF YOUTH ORGANIZING ON SCHOOLS AND DISTRICTS

What is the impact of youth organizing on school and district capacity? Researchers at the Annenberg Institute for School Reform are in the fifth year of a six-year study to examine that question. Funded by the Charles Stewart Mott Foundation, our study sample includes three established youth organizing groups: Sistas and Brothas United of the Northwest Bronx Community and Clergy Coalition in the Bronx, New York; South Central Youth Empowered thru Action of the Community Coalition in Los Angeles; and Youth United for Change in Philadelphia.

Our research utilizes both qualitative and quantitative data, including survey data from youth leaders; student achievement and school data from publicly available state and district data sets; observations of key organizing activities; and interviews with critical stakeholders, including educators, policymakers, allies, organizers, parents, and youth. Drawing on these qualitative and quantitative data, our impact analysis focuses on three critical questions:

1. Do educational decisionmakers attribute key school reform decisions to the organizing activities of the groups in our study?
2. Are schools showing improvement in the specific areas targeted by each of the groups, and do these improvements contribute to increased school or district capacity?
3. Is there evidence of improved educational outcomes in schools that demonstrate increased capacity?

Early findings from our research suggest that youth-organizing groups have indeed influenced the decisionmaking of school and district administrators and achieved major policy victories. At the same time, these groups have exposed the stratification of educational outcomes, and raised demands for college pathways that include curriculum, expanded college counseling supports, and a range of early academic and social/emotional interventions.

In each study site, school and district interviewees attribute a range of policy decisions and school-level innovations to the work of youth-organizing groups, as shown in figure 2. As one district official notes, the impact of youth organizing on schools is significant:

> They have been largely responsible for the shape that those [two high] schools are taking—the evolutions in those schools are in large part the result of their effort. We've really listened to them, and we've involved them in the process, and we've sometimes deferred to them. They've been very influential in the redesign of those two schools.[23]

Impact on Student Learning and Educational Persistence

Our research suggests that participation in youth organizing for education reform also impacts the lives of young people in significant ways. A survey of 124 youths involved in the core groups of our three high school youth-organizing sites indicates that as a result of their involvement, participants felt more invested and engaged in their educational experience, believed they were more likely to persist in school, and were more focused on longer-term goals for college and work (see figure 3). In the context of a pervasive race-based opportunity and achievement gap, and the resulting dismal college attendance rates for urban low-income youth, these data suggest that youth-organizing initiatives have a very central role to play in education systems that help young people succeed.

Impact on Civic and Political Engagement

When compared to a national sample, youth survey participants demonstrated significantly higher rates of civic and political engagement than youths nationwide, as shown in figure 4. Sixty percent of respondents in our sample indicated that they had participated in community problem-solving in the last year, 58 percent volunteered for a nonelectoral organization, and 75 percent participated in protest activities.

Recent studies on the impact of political engagement on social/emotional development processes among youth of color suggest that the high rate of civic and

FIGURE 2
Educators' Attributions of Impact

The following table shows the key areas of impact attributed to organizing groups by school and district administrators.

Youth-Organizing Group	District-Level Impact (priorities & resources)	School-Level Impact (practice innovations & participation)
Sistas and Brothas United of the Northwest Bronx Community and Clergy Coalition	School facilities and resources Teacher, student, and community relationship	Small school creation/youth designed school Student voice in schools Improved safety procedures Expanded support for campus sharing among small schools
South Central Youth Empowered Thru Action of the Community Coalition for Substance Abuse Prevention and Treatment	College-preparation policy Expanded resources for school facilities	Improved college counseling Student voice in schools
Youth United for Change	Small-schools strategy	Small-school theme Specific school improvements Student voice in schools

political engagement among our survey participants has potentially far-reaching effects.[24] Shawn Ginwright and Roderick Watts link the participation of youth of color in civic and political activism to the development of a critical consciousness, positive self-concept, and sense of agency among marginalized youth of color. This process of "sociopolitical development" among youth of color increases their skills and motivation to fight for more just social and political arrangements in society, and to act in ways that expand the possibilities for their own lives. Consistent with these theories, our data suggest that organizing positively affects the capacity and, potentially, the futures of the young people in-

FIGURE 3
Impact of Involvement on School Motivation and Engagement

The series of graphs below shows survey responses on sets of questions probing student knowledge, school motivation and engagement, and long-term educational aspirations.

Impact of Involvement: Political and Community Engagement

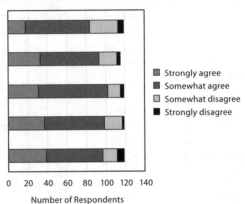

Impact of Involvement: School System Knowledge

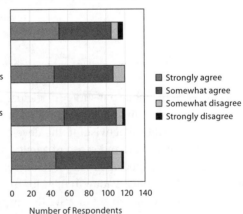

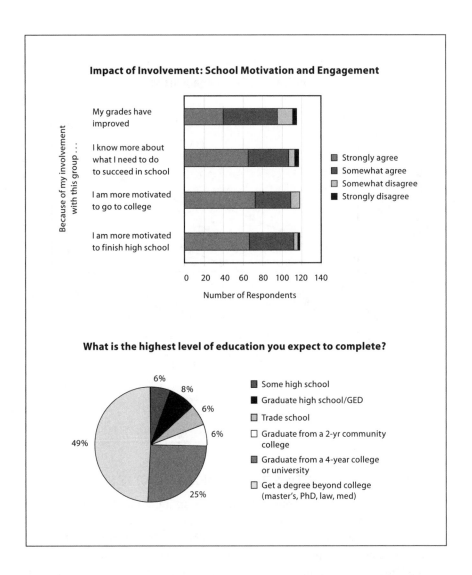

Impact of Involvement: School Motivation and Engagement

What is the highest level of education you expect to complete?

volved in organizing. Young people who are invested in community-school prob-lem solving, who see themselves as active agents of change, are more likely to become key actors not only in pushing districts and schools to move towards more effective practices and policies, but also in expanding the capacities of their communities to create more responsive, effective, and supportive learning experiences for children.

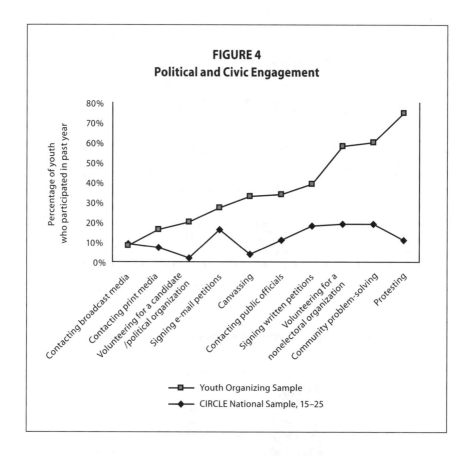

FIGURE 4
Political and Civic Engagement

TOWARD AUTHENTIC STUDENT ENGAGEMENT IN SCHOOLS

Our research suggests that youth organizing is an important lever for creating the will and capacity among school systems, and the knowledge, skills, and power among low-income communities of color, to move from particular components to a comprehensive vision and reality of a smart education system. In this chapter, we have argued that smart education systems must be built on norms of student organizing and must recognize the critical role that authentic student engagement plays in creating and maintaining effective and successful learning experiences.

Youth organizing plays a key leveraging function: Without intense and sustained pressure from young people and their parents and communities, districts are unlikely to achieve the sweeping transformation necessary to deliver a high-quality education to its poorest and most poorly served communities. Such external demands are essential to convincing—and providing the necessary political cover for—educational and political decisionmakers to set priorities and implement improvements that will provide a high-quality education to all students. Youth organizing also plays a function in engaging students, families, and communities in school and school-improvement processes. Such engagement helps create cultures based on trust and high expectations, which can challenge, disrupt, and ultimately transform historic patterns of exclusion, neglect, and contempt that undermine the success of urban youth of color.

In urban school districts, educators' efforts to involve students must move beyond the traditional, adult-controlled forms of student leadership and youth voice, to build relationships with students based on participative forms of governance and accountability. Building such relationships requires a dramatic shift in how educators think about and engage young people in schools. Among the necessary shifts are the following:

- *Acknowledge the legitimacy of youth-organizing groups in educational improvement.* Educators need to affirm young people's rights—as members of the school's community—to raise and act on demands for justice and equity. Administrators should meet with youth-organizing groups on a regular basis and work with these groups to engage student leadership within schools and at the levels of district and city leadership.
- *Confront the pervasive culture of low expectations for students of color.* Schools and districts should involve young people in the professional development provided to teachers, administrators, safety agents, and other key personnel. Doing so would not only surface and challenge deficit-based assumptions about students, but also provide concrete strategies for engaging youth of color effectively. Schools and districts should also create multiple pathways for feedback from students—through annual surveys and focus groups—to assess whether educators are meeting the goal of raising expectations.
- *Expand pathways to youth leadership in schools.* Young people should be substantively involved in defining reform priorities at all levels of educational systems. Pathways should be crafted so that all students, not just the most academically successful, are able to contribute to these important decisions, and to have input into evaluating their results. Administrators should make the functioning of schools transparent, share important data with students, and develop regular forums for engaging all students in conversations about how well the school is meeting its goals and what it needs to do to improve.

CIVIC CAPACITY AND EDUCATION REFORM: THE CASE FOR SCHOOL-COMMUNITY REALIGNMENT

Jeffrey R. Henig and Clarence N. Stone

We have long known, but not always fully appreciated, that schools and families are just one of many interconnected factors that shape academic performance. So, we will start with the premise that education is a community enterprise. Although the individual household is enormously important as a force in academic achievement, it matters greatly how households are clustered. As parents are keenly aware, many factors come into play through such clustering. Tax base, forms of civic engagement, and the nature of peer influences are just a few that affect the quality of education available to their children.

From our opening premise, it follows that education reform cannot confine itself to internal school affairs. Genuine reform calls for attending closely to school-community relations and, where needed, reconfiguring a bundle of relationships of which schools are only one part. After all, local communities are not mere aggregations of individuals, nor are they simply spaces that house disconnected institutions. They are places where challenges call for collective attention. The ability to act on such challenges is what we call civic capacity.

CIVIC CAPACITY

Communities have several collective needs. Whether the issue is maintaining social order and promoting public safety, achieving and sustaining a viable local economy, or educating the young, none of these challenges can be confronted effectively by governmental action alone. Just as education involves more than schools, so the ability to respond to a wide range of community issues rests on more than the institutions of government. As a concept, civic capacity underscores the multisector nature of problem-solving.

Communities differ greatly in their established capacities to respond to the challenges they face. In some cases, where capacity is largely in place and needs only marginal adjustment to meet specific issues as they arise, the matching of civic capacity to challenge requires no special form of mobilization. In other cases, where capacity may be weak on several counts, it is only through explicit intervention and mobilization that capacity can be strengthened. The latter circumstance goes to the heart of urban school reform.

Like other arenas of community engagement, education is part of a total configuration of how people are related to one another, and not a specialized activity unconnected to the rest of community life. It is a process embedded in that life. For this reason, school reform cannot simply be enacted; it has to be part of a wide realignment of how a community operates. A body of relationships has to be reshaped. In order for education reform to take firm hold, low-socio-economic-status (SES) neighborhoods cannot be stereotyped as hopeless, neglected physically, written off as crime infested, staffed by people who are either inexperienced or castoffs from elsewhere, and in general given low priority by government and the nonprofit and private sectors. Changes such as a new pedagogy, a different superintendent, revamped management procedures, or an added reading specialist here and there are insufficient. Although some combination of such changes might make a marginal difference, it would still leave weighty forces in place. This is not simply speculation. While there have been many times and places in which communities have neglected the educational needs of disadvantaged neighborhoods, there have also been innumerable sincere and sometimes well-supported efforts to intervene. So, we can see that indifference and neglect are not the sole explanation for the educational inequalities we can all observe. And the fact that incremental rearrangements have had less positive impact than hoped for gives us evidence that something more, something different, is required.

To talk about academic performance being closely tied to SES is to acknowledge that some configurations of community life are more conducive to academic achievement than others. The implications of that acknowledgement are profound. It means, for one thing, that we cannot go very far in reforming education without altering the environment in which schools operate. Consider two quite different cases of the education challenge, one in an affluent area of Houston, and the other a lower-income neighborhood in Chicago.

Houston

Donald McAdams, a former school board member from Houston, said about parents in his affluent district:

> Most volunteered some time in their neighborhood school. Some . . . were exceptional. I called them the PTO mothers. They were usually wives of professional men with excellent incomes. Some had professional degrees themselves. They had put their concerns on hold to be full-time homemakers. And as their children grew older, some became practically fulltime, unpaid school employees.
>
> The PTO mothers volunteered time to chaperone students on field trips, assisted teachers in the classroom, worked in the office, and managed events like fall concerts, show choirs, carnivals, auctions, Christmas programs, and fundraising walkathons. Some programs attracted nearly 1,000 parents. These PTO mothers (and sometimes fathers) helped raise $30,000, sometimes up to $100,000, per year for teaching materials, computers, stage curtains, or whatever the school needed. And they didn't just serve their own children. If a field trip . . . required money from each student, they raised the money to pay for the children . . . who otherwise would not go.
>
> These PTO mothers made schools successful. They demanded effective teaching, high academic standards, and strong leadership. They were towers of strength to effective principals. But if principals were ineffective or the bureaucracy did not respond to programmatic or facilities needs, they took action. They called their [school board member], took him out to lunch, organized letter-writing campaigns or circulated petitions. They knew how the system worked, and they got results.[1]

Chicago

About a lower-income Chicago community, we have this contrasting view:

> Problems of urban life weigh heavily on parents and children who know about failure firsthand and have come to expect it as "the way things are around here." The life circumstances for children are particularly devastating. Early on, they learn about peers who drop out of school. They see friends who per-

sist to graduation but cannot get jobs. They see cousins and brothers who do not live long enough to drive a car or vote in an election.

Not surprisingly, many minority and low-income parents transmit conflicting signals to their children about education and learning. Although these parents may speak about the importance of going to school and getting an education, much of their behavior actually contradicts this. Overwhelmed at times by feelings of exclusion and low self-esteem, parents can convey a sense of hopelessness to their children.

Such concerns carry over into the interactions of parents and teachers and their perceptions of one another. An atmosphere of distrust and suspicion permeates many of these encounters. Teachers see parents' goals and values as impediments to students' academic accomplishments. As one teacher . . . told . . . reporters: "Give me the parents of these children. Let me show them how to parent and we wouldn't have the problems we have." Parents, in turn, believe that teachers are antagonistic toward them and fail to understand the difficult conditions that shape their children's lives. This misalignment of perspectives and values between home and school seriously undermines the work of urban schools.[2]

The impact of social class is fully evident; in the Houston case, it infuses strength into the community's civic capacity, but in the Chicago case, it weakens the potential.[3] In both cases, class is a pervasive force, affecting material resources, scope of parent involvement, abilities of parents to monitor what is happening in schools and act on their reading of the situation. Political access varies, and so does the availability and utilization of extra school activities and postsecondary opportunities.[4]

In these brief vignettes, much is not covered directly. Most important are the expectations that surround students—what they can look forward to, what receives encouragement materially and psychologically, and what becomes an ingrained part of their everyday lives. In one setting, students understand deep down that they are valued. Their families, the teachers and administrators who willingly choose their schools, friends and neighbors, the broader public they interact with and the stereotypes and assumptions they encounter in the mass media—all these collectively convey a message that, as students, they are important and can look forward to a respected place in society.

In the contrasting setting, that sense of being valued is much more tenuous. Signals may be mixed at best. If a neighborhood is filled with decaying buildings, illegally dumped trash, abandoned cars, and other signs of neglect—all signs that society does not value the people who live there—then students can easily pick up the notion that "they don't count."[5] And this notion becomes an obstacle to be overcome. Sources of dependable support are likely to be scarce, and the media have little positive to offer.

Conditions in one community combine to encourage academic achievement, in the other they hinder achievement. And there is an additional contrast. While the Houston PTO mothers display a strong sense of efficacy, the Chicago neighborhood offers quite a different picture. There resources are scarce, and the inclination to use them collectively is weak. In brief, in the Houston community a capacity to act collectively is at hand, but not in the Chicago community.

In the case of Houston's affluent district, the broad goal of quality education was tacitly understood, and the overall effort on its behalf was also tacitly coordinated. Explicit mobilizations occurred around immediate goals and specific tasks. Hence the collective-action challenge was consistently modest, and because efforts were typically successful, they were also easily reenacted. Class disadvantage, as illustrated in the example of the Chicago neighborhood, poses multiple, interlocked barriers to meeting the education challenge. Such interlocked barriers are the reasons that single targeted solutions cannot succeed. And so, effective intervention is not simply a matter of introducing a potentially effective practice; the policy challenge is too complex.[6]

In lower-income neighborhoods, tacit understandings and tacit cooperation are modest at best and fall far short of the full complexity of the problem-solving task. For that reason, explicit goal setting and explicit mobilization on behalf of those goals are needed to invigorate an otherwise weak capacity and bring new relationships into play. When tacit processes prove inadequate for meeting a challenge, whether it is education or some other policy area, a broadly conceived intervention is in order. A neighborhood organization here and a new principal there are insufficient for achieving sustainable gains. A narrowly conceived initiative might bring about some positive results, but, given multiple interlocked barriers, effectiveness is also bound to be limited. Because of these limited, rather than broadly conceived interventions, many reform efforts fail to take root and spread in lower-income neighborhoods.

Let's digress for a moment to make sure that our assertions here are clear because we do not want to be misunderstood. Discussions of class and race are not easily negotiated against a stormy background that leads some to consider that all generalizations about systematic disadvantages are "blaming the victim" while others see them as "blaming society" for historical and episodic failures that should pose no major obstacle to individuals who are determined to succeed. In linking community capacity and class we are not saying that all affluent neighborhoods are capable collective problem-solvers and all low-income ones are not. There are low-income neighborhoods that heroically mobilize, but this often requires heroism while more advantaged communities require much less. We are not saying that the individuals within high-capacity communities are more talented or resourceful or farsighted than those in low-capacity communities; indeed, we are quite convinced that many successful leaders in affluent neighborhoods would falter and fade away if confronted with the conditions faced by their counterparts in less-advantaged settings. But to say that class does not have to determine outcomes is not to say that it does not have often predictable and consequential effects. To say that individuals can surmount personal disadvantage is not to say that cumulative and spatially concentrated disadvantage can be casually brushed aside. In our eagerness to proclaim that "all children *can* learn," we must take care to understand that the opportunities to do so may yet be fundamentally different, depending on the circumstances into which each child is born.

The logic of this argument is that, while lower-SES communities ought to have additional resources, providing them in a piecemeal fashion has little lasting effect. Provision of services and the ultimate goal of comprehensive resource enrichment must be linked to the building of a collective capacity to act within these communities. Acting collectively does not occur in a vacuum. Generating resources can serve as a medium for building a capacity to act collectively, which, in turn, can serve as the foundation for an ongoing, vigorous, and multifaceted effort to educate a community's youth.

A durable capacity is the key. An unusually talented and responsive principal may improve relationships between the school and community and provide meaningful help to dozens or more families that would otherwise be shunted aside or lost in the shuffle. However, the weight of other pressures on families means many will fail despite this help, and the likelihood that the principal's policies will outlast her or his tenure in that particular school are slim. Choice options provided by No Child Left Behind may give a small number of families the opportunity to move to a better school, but the loss of those parents and children may leave their previous school worse off than it was before.[7] Also, high-stakes testing may spur some schools and some children to try harder and accomplish more, but the increased pressure may lead some children to drop out, and some good teachers to flee to more privileged schools where it is easier to hit the requisite marks.

Effective reform calls for a broad understanding of the problems, and this is why it is necessary to recognize the full scope of social class and its impact on education. Understanding a problem is, however, only a first step. Mobilization of effort needs to measure up to broad understanding. And while understanding and mobilization are conceptually distinct, they are intertwined in practice. Understanding guides mobilization, but mobilization also shapes understanding. Hence understanding is never static but something that is always evolving as it is shaped by concrete effort and enlistment of support.

For education reform, the civic-capacity approach does not begin with the classroom or even issues of governance. It starts with the basic context of social class and how it shapes the challenges that schools face. And, where the challenge is severe, capacity-mindedness makes us ask what might make the challenge more manageable.

ALIGNING SCHOOL AND COMMUNITY

One obstacle to building a more vibrant form of civic capacity in lower-SES areas is the failure to recognize that poor communities can, and indeed must, contribute a great deal to solving community problems. Of course, they cannot do it alone, but they have an important capacity to contribute.[8] Under conditions of concentrated class disadvantage, moving toward positive school-community synergy involves some closely interrelated steps. One is overcoming alienation and cynicism within the community, but accomplishing this depends on resources and extended hands from outside the neighborhood. Reminders of past negative experiences have to be surmounted, and that requires more than vague promises and distant prospects. Constituting the face of the larger society to poor neighborhoods, schools and other organizations are crucial factors. The following text offers some examples of school and community alignment.

Two Mini Cases

One is the Pio Pico Elementary School in Santa Ana, California.[9] Opened to serve a surrounding low-income Latino neighborhood, the school was designated a Spanish Language Arts Demonstration School. Under the principal's leadership, Pio Pico started with a welcoming attitude. To inform parents about the school's program, teachers invited parents to a family night before the school year started. At this meeting, in response to this level of openness, parents talked about safety concerns for their children. Because the school was located on a block dominated by gangs and drug-related activity, some of the parents developed a plan to escort their children to school. And soon after, they organized into the Pio Pico Safety Committee.

This committee met regularly with school staff and enlisted the help of the Santa Ana Police Department to rid the school area of drugs and gangs. The combination of efforts succeeded in reducing crime by 35 percent. With assistance from Pio Pico's principal, the Safety Committee reconstituted itself into a neighborhood association, with representatives from nearby apartments. In partnership with the school, this association, along with school staff and other groups, next moved to organize *Operacion Limpieza* to clean up around the school. Members of the fire department, city council, school board, and the city's Neighborhood Improvement Program joined in, and the clean-up initiative became an annual event. The school then added what became a well-attended program on parenting skills. Cumulatively these activities created a highly positive school climate, with parent-teacher conference participation reaching 99 percent and PTA meetings 85 percent.

The Pio Pico case shows that civic cooperation is possible even in very poor neighborhoods. Welcoming moves by the school were an important catalyst, strengthened by supporting actions from city departments and elected officials. Beyond that, a crucial point in understanding the concept of civic capacity is the important role filled by parents. They identified a problem and acted upon it. What made their action more than a one-time effort is that they organized, and the principal helped them with this. Moreover, the support from the principal was amplified by the cooperation of the police department, and support from others followed as the initial agenda grew.

So, with the neighborhood in an active role, the city became involved and services, such as parenting classes, expanded. School-community synergy sprang from a small beginning, but the Pio Pico case shows that alienation can be put behind, partnerships built, and a positive-sum game can take shape. Synergy came, not from a single intervention, but from a cumulative sequence of steps.

One of the significant features of this example is that the teachers and the principal played a key facilitating part at all stages. The importance of what Lisbeth Schorr calls "the new professionalism" is much in evidence.[10] And "the usual suspects" did not sabotage the process. Thus cross-agency cooperation proved possible. Channeled thinking and turf battles did not stand as insurmountable barriers to schools, police, fire department, city council, and neighborhood working together. And, significantly, professional educators recognized that the neighborhood could make important contributions to the school, the quality of its environment, and the accomplishment of its academic task.

Let's turn now to a second case, this one from Philadelphia.[11] It began with external funding for a community organizer to work with parents at the Watkins

Elementary School (a pseudonym). The funding came from a business source, but was channeled through an intermediary, known as the Alliance Organizing Project (AOP). AOP, in turn, provided a community organizer to work with the school as part of a broader strategy of strengthening lower-income neighborhoods. The school was not performing poorly, but the principal, after some initial reluctance, accepted the idea that parents might provide him, as he put it, "with another level of support." With assistance from the school counselor, the organizer found a small group of parents as a starting base, and then used one-on-one meetings to expand the circle of participants. When these parents talked about their concerns, safety emerged at the top of the list, so restoring some of the crossing guards that had been cut in recent economy moves became the solution they settled on and toward which they worked with parent groups at other schools. A few teachers joined the "public action" as well. (Note that the parents did not achieve their success without conflict.)

When the parents were successful on their first goal, they moved on to the issue of an afterschool program. Initially rebuffed by a "no resource response" from the principal, they turned to the idea of a parent-run Homework Club after school. The aim was academic enrichment, and the principal consented to the use of school facilities. The Philadelphia Education Fund provided assistance in composing what turned out to be a successful funding proposal. Some teachers took part by lending their classroom materials and by referring students who needed help, and soon a "small group of teachers and parents were working together in new ways."[12] Parents gained skill and confidence working with the students, and teachers saw the parents in a new light. Though coming from a background of exclusion and marginality,

> parents learned how to research an issue of concern; they were trained in classroom management, instruction, and curriculum; they learned to write funding proposals; they gained the confidence to interview public officials; they led public meetings; and they created a political campaign to focus attention on their children's needs. The AOP organizing process provided parents the opportunity to learn the skills of civic participation.[13]

Again, several things are noteworthy. The externally supported community organizer was the catalyst, not the school staff. Yet, school staff, starting with the counselor, did provide essential and, over time, growing cooperation. The principal went along, a condition that is far from automatic.[14] Moreover, even though the effort started with its focus on safety around the school, it did move on to take up academic achievement and contributed to a change in the school-wide climate for learning. In addition, the participation by parents contributed to a greater understanding of the school situation and what was needed, as was the case in Pico Pico. "Wider participation expanded the scope of concerns considered."[15] And the gain in civic skills by parents stands as a significant accomplishment in its own right.

The particular details of the two cases should not obscure an extremely important lesson. In both cases the parents were active contributors to the education task. In the manner of the Houston PTO mothers, they were an integral part of the provision of the service. They played a role in what Joel Handler calls "service engagement," and thus were not passive recipients of "service delivery."[16] Nor were they adversaries of the school system. Rather, they became insiders able to help shape the mission of the schools, informing the task with their "local knowledge," contributing energy and resources to the task, all-in-all playing a part that educators could see as a valuable contribution. Educators had little reason to feel that their professional role was threatened. In their parent and neighborhood role, the parents did not assume control but they maintained a position of influence that affected their children's schooling. Hence, the kind of antagonism that sometimes characterizes school-community relations in low-income neighborhoods had no fertile ground in which to grow. Positive relations between school and community cannot be guaranteed, but, as these two cases show, lower-SES neighborhoods can be contributors to synergy.

The shortcoming of the two cases is a familiar one. It is the issue of limited scale. Both examples accomplish turn around at the neighborhood level, but not on a citywide scale. Both secured extra resources, obtained on a special-case basis, but despite positive results these resources did not expand to a wider basis. Those disinclined to approve of social intervention might say that money is not the answer and cite examples accordingly. The weakness of that simplistic response is that it ignores cases, like these two, in which additional resources have made a difference. Seen in this light, a lesson of the two mini cases is that although infusion of money is not a guarantee that intervention will be effective, it is often a necessary factor.

BREAKING THE ECOLOGY OF DISADVANTAGE

As chapter 2 made clear, several factors may come together, making families from lower-SES backgrounds constitute an ecology of disadvantage. Some factors grow from the meager resources found in lower-income households. Some, such as weak credentials of teachers, reflect the low priority given to educating lower-SES children. Individual factors accumulate in such a way that they shape attitudes and expectations among lower-SES children and also within the larger society about those children. Reformers often talk about "the culture of a school" without acknowledging that the climate inside a school may be greatly influenced by conditions of marginality that it shares with the surrounding community. If, out of this shared marginality, an atmosphere of despair and hopelessness takes hold, a few scattered initiatives will not turn the situation around.[17] Hence, a comprehensive approach is needed to set in motion a different ecology.

With an ecology of disadvantage as its target, the civic-capacity approach must move well beyond the usual menu of school reforms to call for a much wider range of involvements. And these involvements should not be controlled by educators, but be part of a broad effort to advance the development of children and youth and also to revitalize neighborhoods. Such a broad effort provides a potentially significant role for political leaders—the governors, mayors, and legislators who can redirect agencies to engage in collaboration and support that normal interagency turf protection impedes and that the historical separation of school districts makes more difficult (see chapter 9).

Moreover, top-level coalitions are insufficient. In their book, *Powerful Reforms with Shallow Roots*, Larry Cuban and Michael Usdan make the case that "securing teachers' endorsement and parents' support for changes are essential."[18] The prevalent notion that teacher and parental support can come later if those at the top have a clear vision, a good plan, and the courage to brush aside obstacles and marginalize those invested in the status quo is greatly weakened by the rise and fall of the Bersin superintendency in San Diego.

Under Superintendent Alan Bersin, San Diego was regarded by many as a model of comprehensive accountability with a management-oriented regime. Despite some evidence that test scores, at least at the lower grades, were beginning to respond under his plan, the aggressive "Do it fast, do it deep, take no prisoners" implementation style that Bersin adopted helped set the stage for his ouster. It remains an open question whether San Diego will jettison all of Bersin's initiatives or simply weed out those considered most objectionable and soften the mode of implementation. It is likewise unclear whether the initial gains will be sustainable. What does seem clear is that a one-dimensional, top-down management regime is problematic unless it is linked to a broader effort to engage the community in a supportive role.[19] Moreover, reformers who admire the Bersin model should be wary about implying that authoritarian leadership is an apt prescription for education systems serving lower-SES populations. Instead, effort should be directed into enhancing the capacity of lower-SES communities to act collectively on behalf of educational and other community improvements.

For those accustomed to thinking in highly individualistic terms, the civic-capacity approach may be jarring. It makes the assumption that individual academic capacities and an inclination to advance those capacities grow within settings heavily influenced by social class. And, the approach likewise assumes that those in the lower-social classes advance their capacities by mobilized efforts to replicate what middle-class children and youth enjoy, not just from their households, but from the entire class ecology in which they grow up. A civic-capacity approach, then, runs strongly counter to the conventional precepts that stem from "hyper-individualism." Yet it is also mindful of contributions that, with the right mix of supports, can come from lower-class communities, as illustrated in the mini cases of Pio Pico and the Watkins elementary schools.

BUILDING CIVIC CAPACITY FROM THE BOTTOM UP

Once it is granted that civic capacity is an essential contributor to educational performance, the next question becomes one of how to strengthen this capacity, particularly in lower-SES communities where resources are scarce and the inclination to act collectively is weak. In the 1960s, conservatives argued that resources intended for the poor were misdirected by being channeled through social-service agencies without really reaching the target population. Though perhaps overstated, the point stands as a proper caution. As private providers of various services increasingly populate the current school-reform terrain, we run the risk of again channeling money and effort in such a way that it reaches the poor only indirectly. The channels are different, but the pattern could be the same. Little effort goes into direct engagement of the lower-SES population, especially as a collective force. Why?

One reason is that, absent some extraordinary event, those in the bottom ranks of society are themselves not often assertive about claiming an active role. They face multiple problems. They have too few resources for the challenges they face, especially when poverty is concentrated and collective-resource capacities are especially meager. Compared to the upper reaches of the system of stratification, they are weakly organized for broadscale collective action. They have little history as an effective political force and have often had to absorb the social cost of change, whether from public policies such as urban renewal or from technological change such as a declining place for low-skilled labor. While the neighborhoods themselves might remain in place, the residents are often highly mobile; and their frequent exits weaken social networks and can generally attenuate the power and potential for political voice.[20]

Political and civic disengagement rests on far more than a scarcity of material resources. It stems partly from a weak sense of efficacy and, perhaps even more debilitating, a sense of being held in low regard by society. That these perceptions are grounded in reality makes them all the more resistant to change. Thus, past experiences of marginality are not easy to turn around, especially when the past is populated with a mix of unfulfilled promises and shallow policy efforts at problem solving. Such experiences give rise to a sense of being devalued,[21] a self-image that cannot be reversed by offering a new pedagogy, encouraging parent involvement, building a new school, recruiting mentors, bringing in business advisors for management issues, or making vouchers and other transfer options available. All of these are "silver bullets" that in the past have failed to do much to reverse the cumulative consequences of low social class.

Let us be clear, however, that in arguing that barriers to engagement include the psychological element of feeling devalued we are not positing a version of the culture of poverty. Our two mini cases of Pio Pico and Watkins Elementary make it clear that lower-SES parents care greatly about the opportunities available to their children. They can be mobilized to contribute to neighborhood improvement and academic advancement. The forces that differentiate them from the Houston PTO mothers are situational and have nothing to do with a subculture of a distinct and different set of values. Commonality rather than differentiation characterizes motivation. Verba, Schlozman, and Brady found that civic voluntarism is tied to resources, skills, and networks,[22] and we argue that these same situational factors impinge on the ability of a population to develop civic capacity in support of improved education. Moreover, situational factors are alterable by intervention. For one thing, intervention can supply additional resources where they are scarce. Consider the example of providing a community organizer in the case of Watkins Elementary. Intervention can also open up opportunities to develop skills in working collectively at problem-solving. As the example of the Pio Pico principal shows, people in key positions can generate momentum by going beyond the conventional management roles of administrators, and engaging and encouraging members of the community. Moreover, intervention can give durable form to a network, by fostering organizations and establishing set tasks around which people can gather and interact. The homework club at Watkins Elementary is a case in point.

The motives to improve education and neighborhood life are already in place across class and racial lines. These motives need only effective channels of action. For education, the challenge is understanding how to orchestrate a large number of related moves and sustain them over time so that there is a clear and

continuing message that lower-income students and their families are not devalued by society. Moreover, as the two mini cases suggest, some form of problem-
solving organization at the neighborhood level (with supporting ties to allies
beyond) seems to be an essential part of the overall effort. People in lower-SES
communities need to be active contributors. That they occupy a contributing
role and know that their contributions are highly regarded are the ultimate answers to the question, "How can communities turn around the feelings of some
residents that they are devalued?"

A civic-capacity approach means enlisting the active support of a wide array
of players, and in the process forging appropriate partnerships and alliances. The
main challenge, we believe, lies in working with those in society's lower strata
and achieving a proper balance between providing strategic assistance and al-
lowing room for a contributing role to take shape. Without the engagement of
the poor and near poor, educating those in society's lower strata will remain an
exercise in triage, that is, the application of scarce resources to a small number
of individuals who hold special promise for academic achievement. When this
happens, large numbers are written off and left to a fate of little promise.[23]

It takes positive synergy between community and school to get beyond triage,
and that positive synergy can come only if the lower-SES population is engaged.
Civic engagement, thus, cannot be limited to a few exceptional individuals. If it
is to be effective in problem-solving, civic engagement needs a broad base, and
for urban education that means wide engagement of the less advantaged.

Building civic capacity, then, is not about the isolated actions of individuals. It exists only when people see their interdependence and act because of it.
It involves thinking in collective terms and seeking to bring about some result
through collective effort. That is what is so well-developed among the Houston
PTO mothers and so often undeveloped among lower-SES populations. The key,
therefore, is to bring about circumstances in which people see that they share
concerns and have a common reason to act together.

But act to do what? Citizens are neither mere spectators nor passive consumers. Furthermore, their role is not that of an interest group that emerges peri-
odically to pressure educators and other public officials and then retreats with
members falling back into their private lives.

The full reality of civic engagement is not separate from ordinary life, but an-
chored in it. In the two mini cases of Pio Pico and Watkins Elementary, as well
as in the case of the Houston PTO mothers, people act together because they recognize that having an impact requires a series of combined efforts. Each household wants safe and effective schools for its children, but the path to that end

involves both collective action by citizens and cooperation between citizens and public agencies, along with occasional strategic supports from the nonprofit sector and civic-minded businesses.

Education illustrates an important lesson. Public policy is ultimately about blending governmental and nongovernmental efforts. Much of that blending occurs without much conscious intention. But it is nonetheless an inescapable reality. Again consider the PTO mothers in the Houston district of school board member Donald McAdams. Those well-off parents see themselves as acting largely to improve education for their children, but that activity draws them into addressing a wider set of needs. McAdams reminds us that these parents are far from selfless:

> Yes, they sometimes got into neighborhood wars over a principal change, the location of a new school, attendance boundaries, or pet projects that would benefit their neighborhood at the expense of another. Most of them saw school reform in terms of their child, their school, their neighborhood, this year. They could make life complicated and sometimes painful for their [school board representative]. But without them, it was difficult to build an effective public school. And without them I could not have been an effective voice for reform on the board of education, for they were my political power base.[24]

Consider the implications of these remarks. Many of the Houston parents saw themselves as acting as private citizens, meeting mainly family responsibilities, with perhaps some vague consciousness of having a community responsibility. But even if they had a narrow understanding of the obligations they were meeting, they developed skills and experienced a public setting. They developed or honed a capacity that could be applied to other issues in other circumstances. And above all, they understood that, by acting collectively, they possessed an enhanced capacity to meet their obligations (even if initially conceived narrowly).

Kristina Smock provides a useful analysis of approaches to organizing and activating community efforts. She observes that the civic model of citizens coming together around a common concern can develop a common identity around a shared fate. As one participant put it, "You're a different person if you know your neighbors than if you're kind of living in your own world, or isolated." Another explained, echoing Robert Putnam's theme of social interdependence,[25] "for a neighborhood to function, there has to be the give and take of it. And there has to be the looking out for [people] beyond your immediate household. And if that is freely given by you, hopefully it gets returned to you, if it ever comes up."[26]

Smock does not attribute this to an inner sense of duty, but to experience that comes out of personal concerns—in this particular case concern about neighborhood safety. Civic action need not spring from altruism.

Normative ties can, however, play a part. Smock cites another instance in which a network of organizations and institutions took shape around a common vision of a revitalized neighborhood. One participant explained: "They've been able to put this coalition of people together—agencies with different agendas and different politics and different ideas—and bring them all together to agree on [a plan]."[27] Another participant explained: "When you work at your job on a daily basis, you basically just see what's around you. You go out and handle certain specific tasks. But working with [the coalition], you're able to hear the concerns of other organizations. . . . So it kind of like lets you see the whole picture."[28]

The common theme running through these examples is that problem-solving activities can draw people into a broader understanding of the challenges they face. They develop this understanding, not out of an abstract sense of duty, but out of working on concrete issues. A sense of duty is more a result than the cause of this process. Civic engagement is, therefore a matter of acting in a collective context around a shared aim. Awareness of interdependence, as contrasted with an altruistic sense of duty, serves as the main motivating force. For the less advantaged, full awareness of interdependence may, as it did in Pio Pico and Watkins Elementary, depend on the school's or some other societal agency's creating a condition that invites collective action.

As suggested by Smock, awareness of interdependence may open up a wider sense of responsibility, and, if so, it typically comes not from exhortations about civic duty but through experiences of acting collectively. Part of the policy puzzle of reforming schools, then, is a question of how to create conditions favorable for engaging in collective actions.

Contrast the Houston PTO situation with that of lower-SES parents. It is not that the latter have bad "habits of the heart," nor a faulty set of values. It is that they lack positive experiences of acting collectively, have few resources for doing so, and live in a setting populated by others who also lack those experiences and resources. To the nonaffluent, the neighborhood is often a source of danger for their children and not a promising base for acting collectively.[29] In short, without some intervention there is a weak capacity for engaging in action that will blend constructively and synergistically with the neighborhood school and other neighborhood institutions. Moreover, in most lower-SES communities, if a capacity for acting collectively is developed beyond the reach of family ties, it is likely through the church rather than through public institutions. Yet, as Pio

Pico and Watkins Elementary show, public institutions, and especially schools, can serve as centers of activity around which civic capacity can be built in communities populated by the lower ranks of the system of social stratification. In other words, situational factors are important, but they can be altered to facilitate the building of civic capacity with a substantial base of citizen activism.

BRIDGING THE EXPERT-CITIZEN CHASM

One challenge to civic involvement is the often intimidating role of professionals in the field. For a variety of reasons, lower-SES parents are particularly inclined to leave education to the professionals.[30] In such situations, it is very tempting for educators to use expertise as a defensive posture and keep parents at a distance. One challenge in expanding civic capacity, then, is to break down the barrier between citizen and expert. For upper-SES populations, a high degree of formal education, combined with socialization into an assertive stance with organizations, can penetrate the barrier. By contrast, lower-SES people, on their own, typically lack the wherewithal to break through the barrier.

Note that what we are talking about is simply having full opportunity to interact with public institutions and the individuals who head and staff them. What the powerful mediating force of community organizing can do is break down the barriers. Organization means that instead of isolated individuals facing an institution staffed by professionals, citizens can act collectively and draw on the accumulated experience and expertise of the group. In this way, the power bases are not so imbalanced. Still, when a community organization faces recalcitrance, it may find that confrontation alone is not productive. Mark Warren, for example, talks about a recent trend toward combining "confrontational tactics with strategic efforts at collaboration and institutional development."[31]

So, in addition to organized neighborhoods, reform forces may find that they need receptive professionals. The move from confrontation to collaboration is tricky at best. But, because engagement cannot be confined to an oppositional stance, there is good reason to cultivate what Lisbeth Schorr calls the "new professionalism"; that is, professionals appreciative of and open to what the lay public can contribute in the forms of knowledge and effort. While posing tough questions is part of the process, as far as possible, engagement needs to be framed ultimately in positive terms.[32]

Because engagement currently has a distinct class skew, it needs to be addressed in a couple of ways. One is to provide lower-SES people with the experiences of acting collectively on the problems they face. Organizing takes the first step by moving from isolated individuals to group mobilization. The second step is to put community-school interaction on a foundation of mutual and complementary contribution. This means reframing the citizen-government relationship, appreciating but not exaggerating the role of the expert, and above all not underestimating the value of citizen contribution.

ELITE SUPPORT

The current widespread support for school reform is evidence of the general opinion that we should put young people on a path that leads to the mainstream economy and society. Building alliances around this aim is itself a form of civic engagement, and we believe it is something best done around particular initiatives addressing concrete problems. North Carolina's Smart Start and Kentucky's Prichard Committee are case examples. NCLB has put the matter high on the nation's agenda, and now the question is how to pursue these aims. We have argued that there is good reason to take a comprehensive approach and push civic engagement on that basis.

Not only is the support of business and other civic elites important, it also matters how these entities voice their support. As a detached expression of business sentiment, the support can sound like little more than a call for applying business methods to the management of schools. If that is the case, complex issues surrounding social and economic disadvantage remain unaddressed. Elite support may overlook a couple of realities. One is the fact that weak management is a symptom and not a basic cause. Another is that poor management could be rooted in the political weakness of lower-SES communities, which causes deficient citizen oversight, and not in willful disregard for sound practice. We should be wary, too, of the notion that business has an unambiguous and powerful incentive to reform schools; in central-city school-reform efforts, the corporate involvement has sometimes proven to be thin and easily distracted.[33] Business and civic elites are, however, not predestined to engage in a hollow dialogue. Smart Start, a partnership to support early childhood education in North Carolina, and the Prichard Committee, a statewide education-reform-support organization in Kentucky, provide examples of support for broad and sophisticated programs.

Business executives are accustomed to worrying about the soundness of investments, and there is no reason to expect them to worry less about social investment in the future generation. Private investments are typically surrounded by multiple checks. Support for social investment may depend on similar checks because it would be unrealistic to expect business executives to operate totally outside their accustomed patterns of action.

The Prichard Committee was funded by business from the beginning, but its role was one of advocacy, not operations. Smart Start is more instructive as an example of a complex form of operation. It involves both a state-level partnership and, with state backing, county-level partnerships, both of which also operate as nonprofits. Government funding from multiple levels and multiple-agency channels provides core support, and those funds, in turn, help attract significant private support. The state partnership is a nonprofit that works in collaboration with the state government's Division of Child Development. The nonprofit status gives the state and local partnerships civic prestige and standing that they would lack as strictly governmental entities, but the partnerships would not be the active enterprises they are without strong core support from the public sector.

The initiative gained further legitimacy from an independent performance audit, as well as from winning various awards. The initiative also combines local design with oversight and guidance from the state level. As a form of social investment drawing on both public and private resources, the initiative needs to be in good standing in the state's civic circles. Thus there are formal means to provide and protect that standing and give reassurance to business and other civic leaders that Smart Start is not "just another government program." Instilling business confidence requires more than articulating a rationale for business support; it calls for arrangements that hold promise money will be well spent.

CONCLUSION

In the approach we advocate, civic engagement is not action directed toward an abstract or a generic public-policy process, and not action aimed at pressuring public officials into accountability. It is about a class-skewed need to enhance citizen capacity and raise citizen awareness of the importance of their contributions. These include awareness of their contribution to educating the young, promoting public safety, and enhancing the quality of local life. Government can contribute to this awareness, but it cannot alone construct it or sustain it. Citizens have an essential contribution to make, and they need a fully developed awareness of their role as contributors to community problem-solving. This kind of awareness grows easily in upper-SES populations, as exemplified in the Houston case. In lower-SES populations this kind of awareness comes only with explicit planning and a concerted effort to carry out the plans.

Human nature is not the barrier to civic engagement, as some cynics might argue. Nor is a distinct lower-class subculture the barrier. Rather, engagement rides heavily on circumstances, and the challenge is to create favorable conditions. Citizens are most easily attracted to efforts that are close to home. That is why education (including early childhood and youth development) is an area that holds promise for enhanced citizen engagement. For upper-SES people, the gateways to engagement are open and at least somewhat inviting. For lower-SES people, the gateways are quite different, and past experiences make engagement considerably less inviting. This is the reason that efforts to organize lower-SES populations toward civic participation are valuable.

The more affluent middle class is quick to invoke the rhetoric of individual re-sponsibility, but that class is highly experienced and skilled at working in groups and in finding ways to weave themselves actively into the work of schools and other public institutions. Without comparable opportunity for public engage-ment, those in the lower reaches of the system of social stratification are largely on the outside looking in—and that all too easily becomes a self-perpetuating cycle. Building civic capacity to its fullest means countering that cycle among the lower strata, but such a countering effort also calls for elites to see that they also are part of a fabric of interdependence. They are potentially useful players in providing resources and legitimating actions for the empowerment of the lower strata. How elite relationships can be reconfigured is another phase of capacity building, and for now its analysis is left to a later occasion.

WHAT MAYORS CAN DO TO HELP BUILD SMART EDUCATION SYSTEMS

Michael K. Grady and Audrey Hutchinson

L arge and persistent differences in student success are challenging educators, community leaders, and civic officials to pursue bolder solutions to
low school performance, especially in our largest cities. The call for bold-
ness is the reason that the contributors to this volume embrace a broad definition of education, one that extends well beyond what we think of traditionally as
education—the delivery of academic content in school buildings for six hours a
day, five days a week. Rather, we argue for a "smart education system" that en-
gages the full storehouse of a city's educational resources to create a pathway of
successful youth development—academic, social, physical, emotional. Authors
of other essays in this volume have described this smart education system as a
"system of systems" or a "web of opportunities."

Based on their access to sources of civic power and to the bully pulpit, mayors play a unique role in a smart education system. The historical insulation of
districts from city politics has until recently isolated districts, leaving education
up to the schools. The renewed interest in mayoral involvement in education is
an implicit recognition of the need to bring civic resources to bear in support of
children and schools.

This chapter examines what mayors specifically are doing and what more
they can do to advance the principles of a smart system. We begin this chapter with a brief review of recent scholarship on the escalating involvement of
mayors in public schools at various levels. We examine the reasons that may-

ors choose to engage the education sector—even though doing so often means significant political risk—and outline the major forms of contemporary mayoral involvement. In the second section, we summarize a set of case studies in mayoral involvement from five cities in various stages of pursuing the principles of smart education systems. Finally, we propose four new areas where we believe mayors could make a difference in achieving the goals of a smart education system—a system in which the community and civic capacity is engaged and mobilized, where there is a clear commitment to equity in learning opportunities based on student need, and which produces higher levels of achievement for all students and accelerated learning for groups of students who have the farthest to climb.

THE CONTEXT OF CONTEMPORARY INVOLVEMENT OF MAYORS IN PUBLIC EDUCATION

While imperfect as a policy framework, No Child Left Behind has succeeded in shining a bright light on the wide disparities in achievement between different populations of students. Citizens and leaders alike cry out for a public accounting for these differences. This has prompted mayors of some cities to step into the breach. In the cases of New York City, Boston, and Cleveland, among others, mayors have asked for and been granted dramatic new authority over school-system management. These cases have generated most of the headlines; however, in other cities mayors with less formal power over schools have pursued more subtle strategies to mobilize the public to pressure for school improvement.[1] These mayors have focused on creating coalitions of organizations that can contribute to rich pathways toward educational and developmental success.

The recent resurgence of mayoral involvement in schools is seen as a watershed event in American-education history.[2] One outcome of the administrative progressive era of the early twentieth century was the creation of a firewall to insulate schools from the destructive effects of ward politics that ruled in large cities.[3] The intent of the reformers was to separate the pure business of educating the young from the politics of governing. This, the reformers reasoned, could be accomplished in part by putting professionally trained educational leaders, rather than political leaders, in charge of the day-to-day affairs of system management. So it's ironic, indeed, that mayors have reentered the fray of public education for some of the same reasons they were sent packing by progressive reformers a century ago.[4] What were then viewed as risks are now seen as assets—mobilizing mayors' political networks, blending municipal and educational resources, and cajoling individuals and groups to invest in the schools.

When questioned by skeptics about their motives for intervening in the schools, mayors respond by pointing out the cost of doing nothing.

Mayors have been driven to act because the public has grown impatient with the pace of school reform.[5] And they act by recruiting "break-the-mold" leaders such as Joel Klein in New York and Paul Vallas, first in Chicago and later in Philadelphia. Mayors act with a blend of political calculation, institutional mission, and an eye on legacy. They argue that the challenges of massive, costly, and complex education bureaucracies have outstripped the capacity of the system to manage them. The city government simply must step in to protect the futures of its young people and the economic and civic vitality of the city.

In a recent collection of articles on mayoral involvement, scholars report that current engagement of mayors in education is limited by local statute and system context. At one end of the spectrum sits the "total control" cohort, which includes Chicago, New York, Boston, and Cleveland, where mayors have substantial authority over both budget and system leadership. At the other end of the continuum are the low-to-medium involvement cities where mayors must use "back channels" to have an impact on quality of education issues. In the middle are mayors who operate in "partial control" or "partnership" models, where their authority over resources and power is more limited.[6]

On balance, mayoral involvement has had a positive effect on creating the conditions and capacities for smart systems—broader public support, reduction in institutional isolation, sharper focus on accountability, and improved organizational capacities.[7]

Yet others assert that mayors have yet to dent what they call the "instructional core" of education—namely, teaching and learning.[8] These authors argue that, to date, most of the successes of mayors have been at the periphery of education—more efficient business functions, enhanced technology, and stronger coalitions or partnerships. The research makes clear that mayors could do more to improve the instructional core of teaching and learning to create smart systems.

How can mayors target their resources and authority to strengthen the cornerstones of a smart education system? In the next section, we examine how four mayors have advanced the three principles of smart systems.

WHAT FOUR MAYORS ARE DOING TO BUILD SMART EDUCATION SYSTEMS IN THEIR CITIES

Mayors can do quite a bit to enhance educational opportunities and quality: build partnerships, tap municipal assets, cultivate local community capacity to lead school improvement, create new civic capacity for sustaining progress, to name a few examples. Often with an eye on the prize of improving teaching and learning, the mayors of Denver, Akron, Long Beach, and Nashville have employed practical, high-yield strategies, along with municipal resources of their offices, to rally their communities in support of education. And they accomplished this with only limited authority over the school system's budget or leadership.

As the following examples show, mayors' roles vary widely, depending on local circumstances. Laws, political culture, and community support for schools differ among cities, and the precise approach one mayor takes may not work for another. Nevertheless, these stories offer important lessons in public engagement for municipal leaders. They suggest effective approaches for mayors, identify minefields to avoid, and offer reflections on the challenges of sustaining engagement for teacher excellence and student learning.[9]

Forging a Vision and Civic Commitment in Denver to Improve Latino Academic Achievement

After a coalition of Latino community organizations and activists met with Mayor John Hickenlooper in 2003 to express their concerns about education, they proposed that he convene a summit on Latino academic achievement. Hickenlooper was receptive; the issue had already been raised by the Reverend Lucía Guzmán, executive director of the city's Agency for Human Rights and Community Relations, and María Guajardo Lucero, executive director of the Mayor's Office for Education and Children. Latinos are the largest and fastest-growing segment of the city's student population and are among those with the greatest needs; student-achievement data suggest that achievement gaps between white and Latino students are substantial and growing.

Engage the Community in a Broad-Based Summit

Guajardo Lucero sought input on the summit from a broad range of individuals and organizations. To her surprise, many more people wanted to participate in the event than she had expected. "Once people got wind of it, there was great interest," she said. The planning group was strategic about extending invitations and assigning roles for the summit. "It makes everyone's work harder to have so many people involved," says Hickenlooper. "But you end up with a final product that's far superior to whatever a city agency could come up with by itself."

In 2004, Hickenlooper convened the Mayor's Summit on Latino Academic Achievement. Some 300 business leaders, elected officials, community activists, and educators attended the daylong event, addressing issues like teachers' roles, parent engagement, the role of language, preschool, and access to higher education. By all accounts, the meeting was a success.

Keep to Clear Goals

"A lot of what the mayor's office can do is keep communicating different aspects of the challenge," Hickenlooper says, particularly "creating a sense of urgency" and "educating citizens and business that they can make a difference on something that's of great importance to them—their business's future, the city's future."

The conference focused on these goals. The Colorado Children's Campaign presented stark data on demographics and educational outcomes. Former mayor Federico Peña spoke to the business community: "We are losing the global war to produce the smartest and most creative workforce in this century. We must act now, and we must especially focus on Latino students." Kati Haycock, director of The Education Trust, provided local and national examples of schools and districts where Latino children achieved at high levels.

Keep the Momentum Going

Hickenlooper pledged to hold a follow-up meeting one hundred days after the summit to consider the next steps. The second meeting drew an overflow crowd—more than two hundred people—and led to new partnerships and pledges for action. Hickenlooper and his staff have kept the issue of Latino achievement high on the agenda in the Denver public schools. The mayor visits schools weekly and asks principals what they are doing to support Latino achievement.

These events did not magically create a citywide coalition for educational improvement. But they provided a rare opportunity for various sectors to meet and consider the issues, and brought new players, such as Latino activists, to the table. The business community and higher-education institutions have indicated that they are ready to undertake more comprehensive efforts to improve education in Denver. Linda Alvarado, president of a local construction company, says, "There are more than 50 percent Latinos in the Denver public schools. This is our workforce."

Mayor Hickenlooper played a vital role in uniting a set of disparate community and civic interests to focus on the issue of Latino achievement. The initial outcome was a coalition of leaders empowered to advocate for new resources and learning opportunities for this vulnerable population of students. The mayor's personal oversight of progress will bring a strong dimension of accountability to the effort and focus it on equity in results.

Collaboration on a "Seamless" Education System
within the Long Beach City Limits

Former mayor Beverly O'Neill has a photo in her office that depicts the mayor, the superintendent, the presidents of Long Beach City College and California State University at Long Beach, and a class of elementary pupils, all raising their hands, during a school visit by former U.S. secretary of education Richard Riley. The photo, O'Neill says, illustrates what city leaders have been trying to achieve over the past decade: a system in which all levels of education and the city government work together to make it possible to get a top-notch education from kindergarten through a master's degree, all within the Long Beach city limits.

Create a Partnership around a Common Mission

In the early 1990s, Long Beach schools were feeling the effects of an economic downturn and increasing violence. Former mayor Ernie Kell formed a task force to address education, economic development, and public safety and asked local businessman George Murchison to bring together the leaders of the educational institutions. In 1994, they launched a formal partnership to create a "seamless education system."

Much of the work of the partnership has focused on ensuring a smooth transition for students between high school, community college, and the university. "There are no secret formulas here," says Robert Maxson, former president of Cal State-Long Beach. "Public school English teachers, English professors from the community college, and English professors from the university get in a room. They look at the content and make sure it is seamless."

In response to criticisms by district staff that the Cal State teacher-education program was not preparing teachers adequately for city schools, the partnership retooled the program after seeking the input of school teachers, The resulting program is so strong, Maxson notes, that it comes with a warranty: if a teacher, supervisor, or principal believes that a Cal State graduate is not adequately prepared, the university will provide additional instruction or send a supervisor to work directly with the teacher on site.

Although the city government does not support the partnership financially, O'Neill has championed it and kept it on the front burner. "Every time [the mayor] gives a speech about the accomplishments of the city, she mentions the program. That gives it credibility and visibility," says Maxson, adding that the commitment of the leaders of the educational institutions also keeps the partnership thriving.

Strengthen Community Support

The partnership also reached out to the community. In the "Principal for a Day" program, community residents spend a day shadowing a school principal, which helps wipe away negative impressions, according to Judy Seal, the partnership's director. The partnership kept its ear to the ground in other ways as well; in response to parental concerns, it launched a nationally recognized school-uniform program.

Stronger support for education institutions is another favorable result of cooperation and engagement within the city. In 1999, its voters approved a $295 million bond issue for the Long Beach schools, with more than 70 percent support. "The city is proud of its schools," says O'Neill. "They know that you can go from kindergarten to a master's degree in the same city, and they are all outstanding institutions."

Data also show that student achievement, high school graduation rates, and success in college have improved. Long Beach was named the 2003–04 winner of the Broad Prize for Urban Education, which is given to a district that has made exemplary progress in raising achievement and closing achievement gaps.

Some worried that the partnership would wane after Mayor O'Neill left office in 2006. But others maintained that the partnership has become so entrenched in the community that it will remain, no matter who is mayor. According to Seal, "*Seamless* is a way of thinking and looking at education."

Mayor O'Neill and her higher education counterparts have put into place a cross-sector education collaborative that features many of the properties of a smart system of education. Creating a K–16 path of supports and opportunities clarifies for youth and parents what the future holds for students who persist. Moreover, the implementation and evaluation of the seamless partnership is informed by data and experience. Now that Mayor O'Neill has left office, the challenge will be to preserve the partnerships and energy that power this pathway to success.

Expanding Supports and Opportunities for Student Success: Building Community Learning Centers in Akron

Mayor Don Plusquellic of Akron saw an unparalleled opportunity when the state of Ohio created a capital fund for rebuilding schools. If Akron could raise matching funds, it would qualify for $800 million over fifteen years—but, to raise the money, voters would have to approve a tax increase.

On their first try, in 2002, Plusquellic and his supporters failed to convince voters to pass a countywide sales-tax referendum. Laraine Duncan, deputy mayor for intergovernmental relations, recalls, "Sadly, school districts outside Akron didn't see the benefit to their bottom lines, and county residents rejected the idea that they should participate in helping the Akron Public Schools."

Champion School Funding Campaigns

According to former deputy superintendent Donna Loomis, "Don cared so deeply about this issue that he was not going to leave a stone unturned to find a way to raise matching funds." He sought legal advice and found that Ohio laws allow cities to use income tax revenue to construct or improve "community learning centers" (CLCs). His staff developed a new measure, Issue 10, which would be voted on by Akron residents but would be levied on any individual who worked in Akron and would not be assessed against income from pensions, Social Security, or investment. The mayor and community leaders campaigned hard and, in 2003, voters approved the measure.

Duncan says that a key to the successful campaign was highlighting the fact that the community learning centers would be open to the public at all times, including summer months. The creation of the centers opened the door for new partnerships with nonprofits, says Loomis, such as the one that led to the recent groundbreaking for facilities to be shared by the Helen Arnold Community Learning Center and the Akron Urban League.

Another critical selling point during the campaign for Issue 10 was the impact that an $800 million infusion of construction funds—the largest capital expenditure program in the city's history—would have on Akron's economy. Businesses, unions, and residents of Wards 3 and 4, the locus of African American community life, all strongly supported the measure.

Create Partnerships to Rebuild Schools

To implement the plan to transform Akron's entire system of fifty-seven schools, the city and school district entered into a formal partnership governed by a joint-use agreement. Having already worked together on the Issue 10 campaign helped strengthen the relationship. "One of the stories from Issue 10 is how the school district and the city worked together on that campaign," says Loomis. "We realized that it's not the city's money or the school system's—it's the community's money." Superintendent Sylvester Small agrees. "What will make or break the partnership is the quality of relationships between our organizations—and that starts at the top with the mayor and me."

The partnership made a commitment that community residents would have a strong, active say in the design of the centers. After an initial phase of deciding how communities should participate, how extensive that role should be, and how it could be sustained, the partnership arrived at a process that recognizes constraints by assessing needs and assets with community leaders, developing a set of programming options, and holding open forums to gain community consensus about what option to use. One challenge the city and schools face, Duncan warns, is that enrollment projections—on which state funding is based— show declines. "Our Issue 10 campaign message promised that we'd all have all new schools," she says. But "some people are not going to have a school in their neighborhood."

Superintendent Small says he will consider the centers a success if they are in use from morning to night and the community, including residents who are not parents of students, takes pride and ownership of the buildings. The mayor agrees. "Only about 20 percent of the residents have school-aged children. . . . I am hopeful that, by opening the doors to the public and inviting them in, there will be a sense that we must all take responsibility for educating our children."

The community aspect of smart education systems is a prominent feature of the Akron strategy. Following passage of Issue 10, partnerships formed at several levels to plan and deploy resources to rebuild schools in Akron and enable high-quality teaching and learning. The city-schools partnership crafted the strategic plan to direct resource deployment and implementation of the CLCs. Likewise, school-community partnerships at the CLC level make key programming decisions about how to use available resources. In Akron, the challenge will be to preserve these various coalitions as the sledding gets tougher in the face of increasing pressure on resources, community concerns about the management of the CLCs, leadership transitions, and other factors that are predictable in a system where the city government, the schools, and community groups boldly share power and accountability for results.

Restoring Public Confidence in the Nashville Schools

Mayor Bill Purcell of Nashville recognizes that a predicate for mobilizing the community is public confidence that the schools are worth supporting. That confidence wasn't widely felt in Nashville when Purcell was elected mayor in 1999. Embracing education as the chief public-policy priority of his administration, he sees that the well-being of a city depends on developing future human capital—and the better than 80 percent of Nashvillians who voted for his reelection in 2003 seems to agree.

Cultivating strong bonds among individuals, organizations, and civic leadership has been Nashville's leading strategy to build stronger families and communities. And Purcell prefers not a takeover model but a shared-leadership model—one in which educators handle day-to-day management of the schools, and the mayor uses the unique leverage points of public opinion, municipal services, and funding authority to advance education goals.

Celebrating Schools: First Day and First Week

Nashville's public schools had been beleaguered by physical facilities in disrepair, stagnant test scores, chaotic learning environments, high teacher turnover, and loss of students to private schools and more affluent nearby districts. The poor reputation of the public schools discouraged new arrivals to the area from buying homes in Nashville. Purcell realized that he had to tackle existing problems before the public would support a budget increase for education.

Purcell convened a coalition of leaders from business, higher education, and community-based organizations, people who shared his belief in developing the talent of young people. In 1999, the coalition joined the mayor in sponsoring the First Day Festival, which has become an annual citywide back-to-school celebration on the Sunday before the first day of school. The festival included music, storytelling, puppet and magic shows, roving mascots, concerts aimed at teenagers, and back-to-school giveaways from many corporate sponsors. Parents were also encouraged to accompany their children to school on the first day, as Purcell did with his daughter.

By 2005, the event was attracting more than 20,000 people. It has united organizations and citizens who normally have little contact with one another. V.H. "Sonnye" Dixon, pastor of Hobson United Methodist Church and recent past president of the Nashville Chapter of the NAACP, says: "First Day is one time when we take down the walls that separate us and celebrate together."

Schools sponsor First Week activities to bring parents, neighbors, and community providers into the schools. One such event is a "Boo Hoo Breakfast" at Dan Mills Elementary for parents of new kindergartners. At Inglewood Elementary, a school counselor says, "The public libraries, Boys and Girls Clubs, and social service organizations all use this prime opportunity to sign up kids and parents for extended learning activities."

Building the Community's Confidence in Its Schools

Nashville has a rich heritage of business partnerships with the public schools, such as those arranged by the PENCIL Foundation, a local group that links businesses, organizations, and faith communities with public schools. Purcell introduced the Mayor's Honor Roll, listing local employers with release policies for employees to visit their children's schools, and he set an example by gaining approval for release time for city employees.

Public confidence in the Nashville schools was bolstered by First Day activities, an independent performance audit, and new Director of Schools Pedro Garcia's strong commitment to improving student performance. Believing that the public would now be willing to support increased annual funding for schools, Purcell requested, and the city council approved, an increase from $397 million in 2000 to $503 million in 2003, along with $165 million in capital funds.

Four years of steady achievement gains, increases in school funding, and greater community and business engagement created favorable conditions for school success. With great pride, school leaders reported in 2005 that Nashville schools showed significant, across-the-board achievement gains at all grade levels on the Tennessee Comprehensive Assessment Program.

Bill Purcell has decided not to run for a third term. But school board president Pam Garrett is not worried about the movement's survival. To quote her: "Anyone trying to alter any major aspect of this new commitment would face heavy resistance from the community and civic leadership."

When he ventured into the deep waters of public education, Bill Purcell understood that before he could call on community and civic leaders to invest in the schools he needed to do something about the alarmingly low public confidence in the schools. He had to make the case that the schools were indeed worth the investment of the public's time and resources. He worked to restore that confidence by regularly visiting the schools, ordering an external audit of system management, creating a community/civic coalition of support, and persuading the city council to "ante up" significant financial resources. In return, the mayor challenged the schools to produce better outcomes for all students and accelerate improved results for those farthest behind.

The Challenge of Sustainability

One common thread connects the challenges faced by these five preceding very different approaches to mayoral involvement: their long-term sustainability in the face of leadership change and shifting political winds. Engaging the public is not a one-time event. All the cities highlighted in this chapter, along with many other cities, face the continued challenge of maintaining and strengthening support for public education over time.

Denver's mayor recognized this challenge early on. He knew that a meeting like the Latino Summit could fire people up for a short time, but he also knew that the momentum could wane if the city did not follow up on the plans. The follow-up meeting he held one hundred days after the summit laid out action plans for all constituent groups. The good will generated at the two meetings will help ensure that the work continues.

Maintaining support is particularly challenging in a time of financial constraint. In Akron, lower enrollment projections from the state could force the city and schools to scale back their plans for rebuilding schools as community learning centers, since funding is based on student enrollment. Leaders are hopeful that residents will continue to back the plan even if fewer schools are rebuilt.

Inevitable changes in leadership also make sustaining engagement a challenge. In Long Beach, Mayor O'Neill stepped down in 2006 after twelve years as the leading champion of the city's seamless education partnership. But officials note that the partnership was not an issue in the election campaign; all the leading candidates supported it. The partnership is now the way the city government and its education institutions do business. Nashville's Mayor Purcell has decided not to seek a third term; in 2007 a new mayor will be elected. The school board president is not worried, though. She believes that business leaders and the community would block an attempt to dismantle traditions that have built up around the first-day-of-school festivities.

Perhaps the best outcome for public engagement exists when a community is so engaged in its schools that it cannot envision any other way of doing things. When this is the case, education—and the city—can only benefit. The four cities highlighted in this chapter have shown some of the paths toward that goal.

THE NEXT FRONTIER FOR MAYORAL ENGAGEMENT IN EDUCATION

As noted in the preceding pages, the greatest impact most mayors have had on the schools has been on system infrastructure: management practices, facilities, information technology, fiscal capacity, and the like. What is less common—but essential—is the direct intervention by mayors to improve the quality of teaching and learning. In the preceding section we showed how some mayors are beginning to make a difference in the core issues of teaching and learning. We close by noting four areas of contemporary education reform especially important for mayoral involvement. In a large city it is the mayor who has the resources and political reach to sustain a city's journey on the path to a smart system.

Equity-Based Teacher Assignment System. Municipal leaders can influence the debate about how educational resources are allocated to schools. Typically, school budgets are determined on a per-pupil, need-neutral basis. But mayors can encourage the assignment of teachers and deployment of instructional resources in ways that are sensitive to the aggregate needs of the student body. Student-based budgeting in Oakland and an incentive-pay system in Denver are two of the bolder efforts to encourage the districts' most talented and experienced teachers to work in schools serving high concentrations of vulnerable students. Mayor Hickenlooper of Denver actively supported a tax increase to fund the incentive pay system in that city. Other mayors will have to take similar risks to implement bold, yet needed, reforms, including engaging in teacher contract negotiation, something city leaders have been loathe to do until now.

Teacher Incentive Programs. A companion strategy to student-based budgets involves the use of civic and municipal resources to create incentives for attracting educators to schools in high-need communities. A number of city leaders have been actively involved in the design and implementation of these types of strategies in recent years. The administration of New York mayor Michael Bloomberg launched a program that offers housing subsidies of almost $15,000 to mathematics, science, and special education teachers who agree to work in low-performing schools. San Jose sponsors the Teacher Homebuyer Program to compensate for the high cost of home ownership in the Silicon Valley. And higher education has gotten into the business of teacher incentives as well. For example, Yale Urban Teaching Corps Fellows receive full funding for a master's degree course of study, plus a stipend of $18,000. In return, graduates commit to teach in a New Haven public middle or high school for a minimum of three years.

Information Technology and Data Systems. Often city, government, or corporate partners can lend valuable technical expertise to a district committed to building high-quality data systems to support instruction and school management. State-of-the-art information technology generates high-quality data that enable better decisionmaking at both school- and system-management levels. Similarly, collaboration between education and other city agencies has the potential to assemble a wider range of indicators of students' well-being than those traditionally used by school systems. And cities like Boston, Charlotte-Mecklenburg, and Philadelphia are developing sophisticated student-information systems that are being used by teachers, principals, and system leaders alike.

Civic Capacity to Turn Around Failing Schools. The consequence of No Child Left Behind with the strongest political charge is a school's designation as low performing. When a school fails to show progress over a period of time, the district and state are required to intervene. Traditionally, these interventions entail school or staff restructuring, but are mostly restricted by the limited resources the system or state can afford to invest. Rare indeed are efforts to mobilize civic capacity and community-based resources as part of a comprehensive strategy to improve low-performing schools. This pattern of behavior ignores the storehouse of talent and educational resources—libraries, museums, other cultural institutions, city agencies, community-based providers, colleges and universities—that are resident in local communities. In some cities, though, municipal leaders are showing the way to mobilize needed resources. For example, at the urging of Mayor David Cicilline of Providence, Rhode Island, local organizations have formed a consortium to support Hope High School's effort to implement a corrective action plan ordered by the state commissioner of education. These partners have stepped forward to commit significant resources, including personnel to support the efforts of Hope's teachers and students.

PART IV

GETTING SMARTER:
TWO CASE STUDIES

CREATING A SMART DISTRICT
IN HAMILTON COUNTY

Jesse B. Register

The merger of the Hamilton County Department of Education and the Chattanooga Public Schools occurred on July 1, 1997. Although this is not a story about the merger, it is important to describe briefly the events and circumstances surrounding the merger as background leading to the creation of a smart district in the newly formed system. Chattanooga Public Schools was an urban district that served approximately twenty-one thousand students, the majority of whom were minority and from low-income families. The Hamilton County District was a suburban and rural district of approximately twenty-two thousand students from primarily blue-collar and middle-class families. Ninety-five percent of the students in the county system were white, with about 20 percent attending private schools.

The pending merger created animosity in both systems and in the community. In a general election in November 1994, the residents of Chattanooga had voted to dissolve the city school system. By state law they could do so, and the county would then have the responsibility for operating the schools. Residents of the county who did not live in the city of Chattanooga didn't get to vote, and the majority didn't want to merge with the city school system. Residents in the suburbs thought the county system was better.

The decision was controversial even in the city, and court action forced a second referendum in November of 1996. The attempt to overcome the outcome of the first election was led by members of the African American community. The recall failed, and plans for the merger moved forward.

At the same time, the structure of government was changing for school districts in Tennessee, a reality that added another adjustment for the public schools in Hamilton County. The method of selecting superintendents was being standardized in the state so that elected boards of education would appoint superintendents. Prior to this change in state law, the Hamilton County Commission appointed its board of education and the superintendent. Therefore, the first superintendent of the merged system was also the first superintendent appointed by an elected county board of education.

The Board of Education made a decision to hire the superintendent for the new system early. After I was selected for the position, I began preliminary work in October 1996. This included visiting schools, meeting people, becoming a part of the community, and beginning a planning process to unify the two districts. In January, I replaced the retiring Hamilton County Superintendent and continued the planning process for the remainder of the school year. It was an advantage to have from October to the middle of January without the requirements of office.

The two districts had a combined total of eighty schools in an area covering almost six hundred square miles: the differences in communities and schools across the county were striking.

This chapter outlines some of the major actions that educators and community leaders undertook to erase inequities and build a smart district focused on results, equity, and community (see chapter 3). The district is now poised to create stronger partnerships with community agencies and organizations and build a smart education system that will serve all of the children of Chattanooga and Hamilton County effectively.

STRIKING INEQUITIES

As an illustration of the contrast between the county system and the city system at the time of the merger, consider Bachman Elementary School in the county and Hardy Elementary School in the city. Bachman was a small K–2 school in the Signal Mountain community that had an excellent reputation, as did the upper elementary school, Thrasher, to which Bachman fed students. In terms of student achievement, Bachman and Thrasher were perennially among the top-performing elementary schools in the state. The population of each was almost entirely middle- to upper-class in socioeconomic status, and parent participation and support was excellent. One fundraiser a year, a donation to the Mountain Education Fund, generated well in excess of $100 per pupil per year for all the schools in the community.

Teachers from across the district bid on teaching vacancies as they occurred, but there was very little turnover in these two schools. When an opening did occur in one of them, many good applicants lined up. The stability of the faculties and quality of the teachers were excellent. Although the building was old, the atmosphere in it was warm, cheerful, and inviting. A new elementary school that would serve grades K–5 was scheduled to replace Bachman.

Hardy was an upper elementary school (grades 3–5) located in a densely populated part of Chattanooga. The student population of the school was 100 percent African American, and 99 percent were eligible for free lunches.

The facility at Hardy was old and in a state of disrepair, and the atmosphere was dismal; there was really nothing attractive in the building. The adults who worked there were lethargic and negative.

At the beginning of the first year of the merger, a teacher at Hardy was accused of striking a child with some instrument in front of the other children in the room. An investigation revealed that the incident wasn't the first occurrence of this kind for the teacher; she ruled by intimidation, and the physical punishment had the impact of setting the classroom tone for the year. Unfortunately this incident was reflective of the culture of the school, one in which the children were often the victims. After charges for dismissal were brought against the teacher, she received considerable support from some colleagues and from members of the community. The dismissal was upheld by the board, but in a heated public meeting. Two years later, Hardy was identified as possibly the lowest-performing elementary school in the state.

It became apparent that a culture enabling poor teachers to remain in place existed in both systems, although in different ways. In the county system, the process was jokingly referred to as "swap day." When mediocre teachers had outlived their welcome in one school community, they were transferred to a school in another community, and the time clock started again, leaving a number of teachers that had been transferred around the district for many years.

In the city, teachers who couldn't survive in a particular school or who received too many complaints from the community, ended up in inner-city schools. Hardy was of the schools that had become a safe haven for less-than-satisfactory teachers. Over the years, as these teachers grew in number and years of experience, they came to control the culture in these schools.

A Lack of Good Data on Student Achievement

Standardized data from both systems was surprisingly hard to get, and what was available provided only summary information. Disaggregated data for groups of children or by school were unavailable. It was impossible to tell how Title I schools were performing, how minority children were performing, how special needs children were performing, how economically disadvantaged children were performing, and how ESL children were performing.

Maybe the lack of data reflected attempts to hide the facts from the general public. More likely, there was not enough staff focused on gathering and analyzing the data. Furthermore, the state education agency couldn't supply the disaggregated data either.

The situation changed in 1999, when the state's commissioner of education began placing greater emphasis on student achievement data across the state as pressure for accountability grew politically, and achievement data by school was published. Using that state data, a private watchdog group prepared a report that listed the lowest one hundred schools in the state based on student achievement. Of the twenty lowest performing schools in the state, Hamilton County had nine. It was not a surprise that those schools were the nine high-poverty, inner-city schools that had previously gone without much public attention.

A General Lack of Confidence

Many minority constituents in the city were afraid that their children would be lost in the larger crowd of a merged system, or even worse, neglected or discriminated against by those in power. Even so, as reported earlier, the second general election in the city approved the dissolution of the city system with support from most elected officials in the city.

One motivation for the leadership's support of the merger was financial, in that the city of Chattanooga would no longer be legally bound to put city revenues into a unified district. Instead, the financial responsibility would fall to the county government. The second reason was a lack of confidence on the part of much of the leadership and general public that the city school system could be successful against the challenges it faced.

Much of the leadership that supported the merger also believed that the former county school system did not have the capacity to improve the schools. Even though the district was considered successful in many ways, it was not perceived as an innovative district, and the leadership had virtually no experience with a disadvantaged and minority population.

When the unification was certain, there was sentiment that a better school system could emerge, but there was also much skepticism. A common feeling was that the new superintendent wouldn't last two years because of anticipated disruption and political sabotage. Previous mergers in the state had resulted in numerous lawsuits over salary and benefits issues, and similar actions were expected in Hamilton County.

Trust had to be earned from many different segments of the community. Smart decisions had to be made, and the new district had to show signs of effectiveness before it could expect to get more community support. Despite anticipated difficulties, creating a new smart system was a matter of survival for a viable public school system in Hamilton County.

A Decade of Change

In 2007, almost ten years later, Hamilton County is a changed place. The striking inequities of teacher quality have all but disappeared. The achievement gap is disappearing for minority and disadvantaged children, and trends in student achievement are very positive over the past four years. The district is on the cutting edge of high school reform in the country.

An organization now exists that is unlike either of the two previous school systems. The governance structure, size, organizational culture, vision and goals, policies and operational procedures, demographics of the workforce and student population, the district's prominence in the country, and the perception of public education have all changed.

Change is not easy, nor does it guarantee the development of a more effective or smart system. The remainder of this chapter will identify key lessons learned from the effort of the Hamilton County school system to evolve into an effective and successful organization that is, in many respects, a good model for other districts across the country.

LESSON 1:
DEVELOPING ORGANIZATIONAL CULTURE IS
AN ESSENTIAL PREREQUISITE FOR SYSTEMIC CHANGE.

In some ways the merger of two systems can be viewed as the ultimate opportunity to create a new vision, establish a new organizational culture, and modify the focus of the district. After all, in a merger, the organizational structure undergoes fundamental change, and the existing institutional culture, so resistant to change in established organizations, can be dissolved.

In reality, though, it is not so easy to change a school culture because of its institutionalization and resistance to change. Most people in the schools and even in the central administration from the previous systems remain through a merger. The attitudes and beliefs of those people and the institutional values of those schools tend not to change even during the merger of districts.

In Hamilton County, attention to attitudes and beliefs that formed the organizational culture in the city and county systems was unavoidable because the cultures of the two districts were so different. Left alone, those differences would lead to a dysfunctional new school system.

Two dysfunctional beliefs that had to be confronted were:

- Many teachers and principals believed that a school that serves a concentrated percentage of minority and disadvantaged children could not produce high achievement.
- Many teachers and principals had become complacent or smug because average test scores were high but masked achievement gaps, and the school failed to meet the potential of all students.

Schools or systems that merge, or otherwise change by force, are not the only ones in which obstructive attitudes exist. In all districts, the culture of an organization and the beliefs and attitudes of the people in it will either support or inhibit the creation of effective schools and systems. Carefully examining the attitudes, beliefs, and actions of teachers and administrators that cumulatively affect, if not establish, the organizational culture of an educational system is a critical first step in creating good schools and districts.

In Hamilton County it was very important to examine differing points of view on the following issues:

- The attitudes and beliefs of teachers and leaders toward the education of all children
- Inequities among schools and actions to take to address those inequities
- A common vision and focus for the district
- Common goals within schools and across the district
- A sense of ownership and responsibility for helping students improve achievement
- A sense of teamwork and support for the weakest schools in the district
- A sense of collective efficacy

The leader of the district is the only person who can successfully initiate a meaningful examination of the organizational culture if the culture is to change. In Hamilton County, with the merger of the two districts and with the arrival of a new superintendent, timing was right to examine the culture of the organization.

Topics like the seven preceding attitudes and beliefs could not be effectively addressed briefly, so the combined district began to tackle them soon after the merger by conducting twice-yearly administrative retreats. The summer retreat was for all administrators in the district, and the winter retreat was for principals and line administrators only.

These retreats were an opportunity to present ideas, lead discussions, and conduct activities that focused on attitudes and beliefs of the district leaders. Outside experts contributed by adding their perspectives. For example, Larry Lezotte, a leader in effective-schools research, and Michael Fullan, an internationally renowned expert on educational leadership and change, led some sessions at the retreats. The intention was to create a change in individual and group attitudes about the goals of public education and the ways in which leaders approach the work.

As the leader of the district, I shared my beliefs about public education, the children we serve, equity and issues of double standards, the power of effective groups, attitudes leaders should bring to their work in the district or schools, and other topics related to creating a positive organizational culture.

Influencing the attitudes and beliefs of the leaders in the district was a critical step in creating a new organizational culture. Changing attitudes takes time, so persistence is important. I no longer felt apologetic for repeating the ideas about basic beliefs and goals for the district. With time and perseverance, the "unmentionables" became topics that could be discussed in Hamilton County, and attitudes and beliefs did, in fact, change.

Now, ten years after the merger, it is possible to characterize the prevailing attitudes in the district as the following:

- The district and school focus is on instruction.
- Every child has a right to a good teacher every year.
- Principals must know what effective instruction looks like and be good instructional leaders.
- The twin goals of the district are equity and quality.
- The central office exists to support the work in classrooms and schools.
- The district is only as strong as its weakest link (school).

Creating the Vision

Once these new beliefs became part of the culture of the district, it was possible to develop a vision statement for the district. Doing so had two purposes. First, it would establish common focus so that our common efforts were directed toward the same goals. Second, the process of crafting a vision statement would help solidify the senior staff's attitudes and beliefs. By participating in the process. team members had to reveal any fundamental differences of opinion about the work of the system. Indeed, the process takes time. After three years, different points of view among members of the executive staff still needed to be addressed.

After much discussion and thought, the leadership crafted a vision statement that accurately reflected a common set of new attitudes and beliefs about public education and the education of all children:

> Hamilton County Schools is a diverse school system committed to creating, fostering, and supporting an environment that offers opportunities for success for all.

This articulation of a common vision reflecting the new culture could not have been adopted earlier. The time invested in rethinking the attitudes and beliefs of the district staff was well worth it.

Just as important as crafting the statement was planning for its adoption by the school board and the community. After the senior staff drafted the statement, they presented it to the board, which then held a retreat to wrestle with the words and intentions of the vision.

As it did with the executive staff, the discussion of the vision statement clarified the attitudes and beliefs of the various members of the board. These discussions were critical to developing and maintaining a common focus and direction for the system, because board members representing very different districts had to embrace a common direction.

To their credit, the nine elected board members were able to agree to the basic principles contained in the vision. Their view was for the common good of public education in the entire district, and not on narrow, personal interests that could be divisive and harmful to the creation of a smart district. Although the board was never unanimous on basic beliefs, seven or eight of the nine members were always in agreement. In the end, the board officially adopted the vision. Not one word was changed!

Developing a Strategic Plan

The Hamilton County vision statement proved to have powerful meaning in the district. It was not just a set of words that simply graced school walls and websites. Instead, it became the basis for the district's operations.

After extensive discussion at a board retreat, the board and superintendent decided to develop an accountability plan for the district, with goals and strategies for improving student achievement. The components of the plan were identified and agreed upon, and as superintendent I was asked to start developing components of the plan with the district staff.

The board indicated from the outset that the plan should

- include goals and benchmarks for improved student achievement;
- hold the district and individual schools accountable for results;
- provide performance incentives.

The process of developing this plan was strengthened by the fact that the school board and the administrative leadership in the district worked cooperatively during the next year to complete the plan. For several months, the district staff analyzed student achievement data and considered the balance of pressure and support when holding high-performing as well as low-performing schools accountable. Performance incentives were debated with an eye toward their acceptability to teachers and the union. Finally, the staff deliberated about the kind of support system needed for teachers and schools to meet the expectations of the accountability plan.

Extensive deliberation occurred during this planning process and regular communication with the board took place. Feedback from the board was essential during the months of work that went into the development of the plan. On occasion, outside consultants were used to lead board discussions, but most often the board and superintendent discussed the plan development in work sessions. Facilitators included John Norris, an independent consultant and specialist in group dynamics and race relations, and Norm Fruchter, director of the Community Involvement Program, now at the Annenberg Institute for School Reform. The board was patient while data and strategies were researched and discussed, and the best strategies were selected for the strategic plan. Senior administrative staff took most of the 2000 school year to develop the plan.

Dialogue with the teachers union was important and deliberate. The union actively participated in developing the system of rewards that was incorporated in the final product, and this system was included in the negotiated contract the next year. Collaboration with the union continued to be very important as work in the district proceeded.

A five-year plan was developed and approved. It was concise enough to communicate effectively, and it became a public relations document for board members and administrators to use in promoting the district in the community. The strategic plan, very consistent with the vision of the district, was received well and helped move the focus of the community away from the merger and toward school improvement and student achievement.

At the core of the improvement strategy were two basic principles that became the focus of district reform for the next five years. First, every child must have access to a teacher or teachers of high quality every year. Second, a support system necessary for teachers to be successful must be provided at every school. Priority schools would receive increased support necessary for them to become successful, and they would be subject to corrective action if success was not attained in a reasonable period of time.

A balance was struck between accountability and support, and between school and district responsibility. Low-performing schools would be held accountable for improving the academic achievement of their students; however, the district and ultimately the community was also accountable for the resources and support system needed to attain the desired results.

The balance between district and school responsibility also created a sense of partnership toward common purpose. As the strategic plan was presented to the school board for adoption, and then to district leadership, school staffs, and the community, this dual responsibility was carefully articulated. As a result, the plan did not generate animosity between school and district staff. Instead, the plan promoted a focus on good instruction and the elimination of double standards regarding teacher quality.

The plan was well conceived and very much on track by the time the federal No Child Left Behind Act was enacted.

LESSON 2:
REDESIGNING ORGANIZATIONAL
STRUCTURE AND PRACTICES ENABLES RESULTS.

Attending to attitudes and beliefs, articulating a vision for the district, and then developing a strategic plan to accomplish that vision are important first steps in reform, but too often meritorious plans are never implemented in school systems. The leadership of a smart district must be prepared to aggressively restructure the district office if that is necessary to obtain the desired results.

In the first year of the merger, two significant weaknesses in the school system emerged. These became the focus of the two major reform initiatives of the district. The central office was restructured over the next three years to address these weaknesses.

The first reform initiative focused on low-performing schools in the district. The striking inequity, the double standards, and the resulting wide achievement gap between poor and minority students, on the one hand, and more affluent white students on the other, were the targets of this effort. The consequent work involved the reconstitution of thirteen schools, including nine elementary schools that were among the lowest-performing schools in the state. Most of the principals of these schools were replaced, and teachers had to reapply for their jobs; a third of the teachers did not return to their original schools. And the district implemented leadership development and support programs for these schools.

The second initiative focused on reinventing high schools. Concerns from the business community, as well as parents, about the rigor and relevance of instruction and learning in high schools were loud and justified. In response, the district, which became one of seven sites participating in a national initiative sponsored by Carnegie Corporation of New York to redesign high schools, raised graduation requirements across the board, and broke down large high schools into small learning communities.

The capacity of the district to successfully tackle the reconstitution of elementary schools and the reinventing of high schools was dependent upon changing the organizational structure of the central office. Equally important was making sure that the right people were in key positions to see that the reform initiatives were successful. Central office reorganization took place in steps over several years as adjustments were made to address the urban reform and high school redesign needed to accomplish of the vision of the district and and the implementation of the strategic plan.

District restructuring came on the heels of the merger and the organizational changes necessitated by that merger. These changes—coupled with budget cuts that made it impossible to add staff—posed a significant threat to the staff of the district's central office. Positions less critical to the new vision or accomplishing the strategic plan of the district were eliminated. Some staff left the district; others sought different positions in the district; some were transferred to other positions in the district office or in schools; and some stayed and have become outstanding leaders of reform.

At the same time, the district created two new units that were vital to the strategic plan and vision. First, the district formed a division of data and accountability and appointed as director a former principal with a doctorate specializing in statistics and mathematics. Since the creation of the department, the director has become one of the most sought after people in the district office. Principals and others actively seek his assistance as they analyze their data and plan improvement strategies.

Second, the district formed a division of urban education, headed by an assistant superintendent. In addition to the line authority to select and replace principals, the assistant superintendent was empowered with flexible resources to provide the support system necessary to turn around the low-performing schools. Later, because of the success of the division of urban education, the entire central office was similarly structured.

In order to focus squarely on instruction, two associate superintendent positions were established. Reporting directly to the superintendent, they were the associate superintendent for secondary education and the associate superintendent for elementary education; each had line authority to appoint principals. Department heads and directors of programs with resources were appropriately assigned to these two associate superintendents, as was the curriculum and instructional staff.

The division of curriculum and instruction and the division of school operations were both eliminated and those resources were assigned to the two associate superintendents. Most importantly, the fact that the school system's focus was on quality instruction in every school was reinforced by placing elementary and secondary education at the top of the organization chart. The stated purpose of the work of all departments was to support and improve instruction in the district.

This idea was further reinforced by the decision to decentralize instructional leadership by reassigning most of the instructional staff at the district office to individual schools. The idea was to place instructional expertise and support as close to the classroom as possible.

All district-level curriculum and subject-area specialist positions that were not directly responsible for administering programs or budgets were eliminated. The resources from those positions were then used to staff new school-based instructional-specialist positions in the schools. These specialists, called consulting teachers, were assigned to schools to support new teachers and to plan and coordinate professional development for their schools.

LESSON 3:
PARTNERSHIPS PROVIDE
RESOURCES AND SUPPORT FOR IMPROVEMENT.

The Hamilton County School System has had tremendous support from local and national partners in the major reform initiatives undertaken in the district.

The strength and the success of these partnerships have been a recurring theme since merger. With limited resources, skepticism in the community, and the history of the two districts, the creation of a smart district would have been very unlikely without the active support and participation of partners in the reform initiatives of the district.

Resources were one part of the value added by the partnerships. The Public Education Foundation of Chattanooga (PEF) and the Benwood Foundation of Chattanooga joined to contribute $7.5 million to the urban initiative with the express purpose of eliminating low achievement in schools designated as low-performing in Hamilton County.

But their support was not open-ended. Following the release of the list of low-performing schools in the state, the chairman of the Benwood Foundation board of directors and its new executive director invited the superintendent to a meeting and issued him a challenge. It was to devise a plan to get all schools off the low-performing list. Resources were guaranteed if the Benwood Foundation board considered the plan to be a good one.

Other than the original supportive relationship with the PEF, the Benwood initiative was the first public affirmation of substance that supported reform from outside the district. The strength of the partnership grew as the PEF and the Benwood Foundation joined in the urban-reform initiative with the district. That partnership has continued for more than five years.

PEF has also provided invaluable support for efforts to strengthen teacher quality. With PEF support and outside grants, the PEF and the district conducted very extensive and valuable research on the quality of teachers in the district overall and specifically in the low-performing schools. Student data that measured academic growth was available from the state value-added system, and was used to conduct research on quality teachers on a voluntary basis.

To determine what was needed to build good faculties in all schools, the Hamilton County Education Association, the teachers union, became a willing and valuable partner, and along with the PEF and the district worked cooperatively to interview and survey good teachers in the low-performing schools and from across the district. This research formed the data base for making strategic decisions about recruitment and retention of good teachers.

The Mayor of Chattanooga also joined the partnership when he took office. After meeting with district and community leaders, listening to their concerns, and studying the challenges of the district, he established the Community Education Alliance, a group of the city's business and civic leaders, to contribute its expertise even though the city was not legally responsible for funding the public schools.

Out of the alliance came a proposal to provide salary bonuses to high-performing teachers who would agree to teach in the low-performing schools for four years. Even though it was only one part of a comprehensive plan to support the low-performing schools, the effort was significant because it drew public attention to the issue and new partners to the table. The teachers union, the school system, local foundations, and the Mayor's initiative all agreed on new strategies and incentives to recruit groups of high-performing teachers to the low-performing schools.

In order to engage teachers in the low-performing schools in the reform effort, the executive director of the Benwood Foundation, the president of the PEF, and the superintendent held faculty meetings in all of the targeted schools. We were greeted with much skepticism. Some people obviously didn't want us to be there. They were either satisfied with their current positions and did not want to transfer or threatened by the pending intervention. Others did not believe that the proposed support was a reality, nor did they believe that the intervention would be supportive and effective. The PEF president was actually sought out after one of the meetings and told not to waste the money!

However, the partnerships created visible community support for the work to be done in the low-performing schools. That support included receptions at the Mayor's house and a range of incentives for teachers. After seeing support from inside and outside the district and new faculties assembled after reconstitution, new attitudes started to develop. New and effective school-based leadership teams, visible recognition and support from the district and community partners, and a system of incentives suddenly made the schools more attractive to prospective teachers.

Another local foundation, the Weldon F. Osborne Foundation, saw the progress and potential for making a real difference in the quality of the urban schools, and asked to join the effort. A grant was given to the University of Tennessee at Chattanooga to develop a master's degree program with special emphasis on urban education. Teachers who agreed to teach in the urban schools were given full scholarships for the program.

One of the most important partnerships was with the teachers union. As in most urban districts, a significant roadblock to employing large numbers of good teachers in the schools existed in the hiring process of the district that was a part of the negotiated teacher contract. The process was very cumbersome. Every position in the district had to be individually posted, and teachers in the district had to be given time to apply for each posted position. As positions were filled through transfers, new vacancies would occur and the time-consuming process would begin anew for each vacancy.

The inner-city schools were the most negatively affected by the transfer process because of the revolving doors that existed for many of the better teachers in those schools. As vacancies occurred in the district, the best teachers in the urban schools would apply for transfer and then leave. The devastating result was that the inner-city schools were left with the most vacancies at the end of the hiring season. For the urban schools, it was a vicious cycle of always hiring teachers last after the best ones had already gone elsewhere.

In 1998 and 1999, a crucial change was planned in the negotiations process and that paved the way for changing the transfer policy. In 1999, the district and the union agreed to abandon traditional bargaining and accept collaborative, or interest-based bargaining. District and union leadership received training together, and the collaborative bargaining model was implemented.

The transfer policy in the district was one of the "sacred" cows of the union and district, and changing that policy would have been impossible in an adversarial bargaining relationship. Instead, the negotiating team and the union leadership understood the problems and worked with the superintendent to develop a new transfer policy.

The change enabled the system as a whole to fill vacancies weeks earlier. In 2001, under the old system, the urban schools had thirty classroom teaching vacancies on the first day of school. In 2002, with the new system in place, there were only *two* classroom teaching vacancies in the district on the first day of class!

Additional strategies that take advantage of the effective partnerships have been adopted. Teacher recruitment fairs, new teacher orientation programs and other mentoring strategies have been undertaken jointly by the union, the district, and some foundation partners.

LESSON 4:
BROAD OWNERSHIP HELPS ENSURE SUCCESS.

While the low-performing-schools initiative was targeted on a small number of schools with the greatest need, the high school initiative involved all of the district's high schools. And as cities across the country are finding, changing an enduring institution like the American high school is a difficult task under any circumstances. To succeed, all stakeholders have to take ownership of the initiative.

To achieve that end, a leadership team was formed. It included the superintendent, the president of the PEF (the fiscal agent for the Carnegie grant), and key district and PEF leaders. All high school principals were engaged in the planning process at the outset, and then the decision was made to involve all high school teachers, as well as parents, students, and community members, Leadership teams from each of the high schools were established, and a very inclusive planning process was begun.

Each school was given the autonomy to conduct its own planning process and was supported by having access to data. Surveys of faculty, parents, and students were developed for the schools so that each could begin building a data base from which to develop a plan for reform that was tailor-made for it and its student body.

Every high school teacher in the district had ample opportunity, in fact received encouragement, to participate in developing plans for the reform. In order to engage many in the process, retreats were held at the outset and continued on an annual basis. Leadership teams that included administrators, teachers, students, and parents gathered at the retreats. There was time to interact with teams from other schools, and appropriate training and development sessions were available based on expressed needs of the groups.

Guiding principles for high school reform evolved through the planning process, and all schools were expected to address those guiding principles. Within those parameters, however, each school planning team was allowed much flexibility in determining the shape of reform for that school.

Each school had to submit an annual plan and budget that was approved by the district and PEF leadership team. Funds were allotted directly from the PEF to the schools on an annual basis to afford maximum flexibility and ease in using the funds. Decision making and appropriate accountability were balanced.

A good example of the success of the flexible use of funds can be seen in an unusual but smart decision of the leadership team at one particular high school. The faculty there was stable and, for the most part, satisfied that its approach to high school curriculum and instruction was the right one. Not many teachers in this school wanted to change, even though the student-achievement data and changing student demographics strongly indicated a need for change.

In order to broaden the perspective of these teachers, the leadership team in the school brought the entire faculty to New York City to visit a number of high schools that not only served a diverse student population but also had adopted some innovative changes in instruction and curriculum. The visit opened the entire faculty's eyes to new and different thoughts, attitudes, and approaches. They came away energized and eager to implement changes in their school.

As a result of the initial approach to reform, a very high degree of ownership in the reform effort has been realized. Teachers, parents, students, and administrators across the district support reform measures that are very extensive.

Rather than bemoaning another initiative or program, school faculties and administrators are very protective of the reforms that have been planned and are being implemented. Even though some principals were reluctant to consider change at the outset, they are now, individually and as a group, strong supporters of the reform.

LESSON 5:
LEADERSHIP DEVELOPMENT INCREASES
THE CAPACITY OF A DISTRICT TO MANAGE CHANGE.

Most change that will be sustained comes from the people within a district. Therefore, quality investment in all professionals through leadership development and professional development will significantly enhance the capacity of a district to implement change. Furthermore, districts must not assume that this is a responsibility that will be met by colleges or other institutions.

The demographic makeup of the leadership team in the Hamilton County Schools at the time of merger was alarming. More than half of all administrators were eligible to retire within five years. Seventy-five percent of high school principals were eligible to do the same, and the demographic make up of assistant principals as a group was no better.

There was very little focus on leadership development and limited professional development activities for district leaders. Therefore, a priority was placed on building both the present and future leadership capacity in the district. The goal was to reach existing administrators, to create a pipeline for the development of new administrators, and to increase the number of teachers who had leadership development opportunities provided by the district.

Since the time that leadership development was established as a priority, an outstanding and comprehensive leadership program for the district has been devised with the help of the PEF and a grant from the Annenberg Foundation. The program has been sustained through the decade.

One focus of the leadership program has been to build the instructional leadership capacity of principals. Over the years, many outside experts have been brought in for the principals and administrators. More recently, inside expertise in the district has been used to continue to build the instructional leadership skills of the district administrators, principals, assistant principals, consulting teachers, coaches, and other teachers.

Several years ago, a Leadership Fellows Program was established for classroom teachers with leadership potential. After five years, the ranks of entry-level administrators, as well as recently appointed principals, are filled with Leadership Fellows. The school-based consulting-teacher ranks are also heavily populated with leadership fellows.

Many other staff development opportunities exist for all administrators in the district. These include regular opportunities to participate in Critical Friends Groups, book clubs, workshops and special presentations from consultants, and countless more.

Leadership development for high school reform and for urban education has been coordinated with the overall leadership program of the district. For example, high school principals meet one day a month to work on the high school reform initiative. Ideas and best practices are shared, current research is presented, and outside presenters are used when appropriate. High school principals no longer work as competitors or in isolation from their colleagues. They learn much from each other and take what they learn back to their respective schools.

District operations have changed as a result of the leadership program. Principal meetings are often held in schools, with the mornings planned by the associate superintendents. The focus is always on instruction. Whole-group meetings are restricted to an hour after lunch, and they too are structured to focus on the key issues facing the district.

CONCLUSIONS AND LESSONS LEARNED

The nine-year period since the unification of the Hamilton County Schools has seen much change in the district. Sustained improvement in student achievement is indicative of progress made in the district as a whole. Much progress has been made toward reducing the achievement gap, eliminating striking inequities for inner-city schools, and developing a vision for systemic high school reform.

The proportion of children reading at grade level in the nine inner-city schools that were subject to restructuring has risen in five years from 18 percent to 74 percent. The goal is 100 percent, but the progress toward the goal is strong and sustained. Other standardized measures of student achievement in the inner-city schools have comparable results.

The lower standard for the quality of teachers in urban schools has been completely eradicated. These school faculties are now inviting their suburban neighbors to participate in the staff development opportunities that they are creating. Teachers are proud to be a part of these schools.

High schools are showing good standardized-test results, and other key benchmarks that indicate success are positive. For example, the ninth-to-tenth-grade promotion rate has improved significantly. The ninth-grade roadblock is being eliminated.

In attaining these results, Hamilton County has learned some important lessons about how reform can be sustained and broadened. These lessons are described below.

Smart districts must develop an effective communications plan and invest in infrastructure to implement the plan.

In 2005, the Annenberg Institute for School Reform conducted a Central Office Review for Results and Equity (CORRE) for the district as a part of an education summit initiated by the Hamilton County Mayor (see chapter 3). By far the most significant need identified was for an effective communications plan for the district.

Much of the district's success in reform was better known in national education circles than in the local community. The district failed to make a sufficient investment in communications to tell its story locally, and budget cuts and criticisms over the central office's size hampered efforts to build communications capacity.

Change undertaken in the district was aggressive, and the opponents of change were vocal and skilled critics. Although the focus and direction of the district never strayed amid the critics' attacks, the local image of the district was not nearly as good as it should have been.

More attention over the years to public relations could have garnered much better local support. During 1999 and 2000, a private grant supported the use of a private communications firm that very effectively managed a communications plan for the district; it was so successful at generating support that the county commission approved a tax increase for the district during that period. Unfortunately, the grant lasted only two years, and the district could not continue the communications funding at the same level as the grant had.

Funds have presently been restored to the district budget to support a communications director and department, and a new director of communications is now on board.

Smart districts must maintain a focus on instruction while existing in a political environment.

There are many factors that contributed to an intense and antagonistic political climate for the Hamilton County School System during its first ten years of existence. In addition to a change in governance structure that shifted power from one elected body to another, many hard decisions were made that created political controversy. These included adopting a new pupil assignment plan and establishing attendance zones; removing personnel decisions from political influence; and changing fiscal policies and philosophy to direct additional resources toward schools with the greatest need. Although the board of education remained steadfast and focused, the political controversy grew.

In August 2004, the county mayor recommended a tax increase for schools and for general county government, and in an unusual move the county commission rejected his recommendation. Some vocal commissioners called for the resignation of the superintendent.

In an effort to unify the community, the county mayor organized and conducted an Education Summit in the 2004–05 school year that included the CORRE led by the Annenberg Institute.

Despite the opposition in the county commission, it was obvious that public support was growing stronger for the school system and the direction in which it was headed. The support was bolstered by the positive results in student achievement. Faced with such support, the commission changed its position the following year and approved a tax increase to support the construction of five new schools and an increase in the operating budget sufficient to give good increases in salary and benefits to teachers.

With the additional financial and political support secured, I submitted my resignation to the Board of Education in October 2005, with an effective date of June 30, 2006. The strategy was to give the school board ample time to conduct a search and employ a new superintendent prior to the next local elections, which would take place in the summer of 2006.

A new superintendent was appointed and took office on July 1, 2006, and in the August election, the control on the county commission continued to shift. The political climate presently appears to be very positive, and many see a solid majority of six out of nine commissioners being supportive of the schools.

Major reform efforts of the district remain intact, and I, the former superintendent, serve in a consulting capacity to the new superintendent for his first year. Through the political turmoil, there was a concerted effort to keep the focus of the district and community on improving the quality of education in the public school system. The importance and effectiveness of keeping that focus and vision is apparent. Now the district is poised to continue its improvement and to enlist more support from the community to strengthen instruction and learning for all students in Hamilton County.

"WE ARE EACH OTHER'S BUSINESS": THE PLACE OF PARTNERSHIP IN SMART EDUCATION SYSTEMS

Dennie Palmer Wolf and Jennifer Bransom

PAUL ROBESON

That time we all heard it, cool and clear, cutting across the hot grip of the day.
That major Voice. That adult Voice. forgoing Rolling River,
forgoing tearful tale of bale and barge
and other symptoms of an old despond.
Warming in music—words devout and large, that we are each other's harvest:
we are each other's business:
we are each other's magnitude and bond.

—Gwendolyn Brooks

C ities have the greatest resources and the greatest number of people who never experience those resources. Nowhere have we been able to harness the libraries, parks, museums, and other public spaces to create cities that are engines of opportunity. Few, if any, major education reform strategies (even those that appear outward-looking, such as mayoral control or the creation of a diverse portfolio of schools) explicitly seek to transform their city, or even a portion of it, into the kind of "engine of opportunity" that it could be. The funding, programs, strategic planning, and staff of these cultural resources are totally separate—even in fierce competition—in most cities. Children, families, and the future lives of cities are all the poorer for not being "one another's business."

173

The central thesis of this volume is that building smart education systems could be a major strategy for creating cities that develop and distribute opportunities (see chapters 8, 9, and 12). The core premise of this chapter is that building "smart" systems demands three ways of becoming "each other's business." And cities and their partners are only beginning to practice these: (1) in-depth cross-sector collaboration, (2) collecting and using evidence about whether programs make a difference, and (3) shared systems of opportunity. As a way of exploring these new forms of civic work, the chapter presents a case study of the evolution of the Dallas Arts Learning Initiative (DALI), a citywide effort to ensure that all children learn *in* and *through* the arts. Underlying this discussion are two convictions: (1) that the arts (and cultural activity more broadly) offer fertile ground for learning how to provide educational opportunity more equitably, and (2) that many of the lessons learned in the cultural sector can be transferred to other sectors such as health care and nutrition, postsecondary education planning, and the reintegration of students who have been in the juvenile justice system.

BECOMING "EACH OTHER'S HARVEST": THE ROLE OF ARTS AND CULTURE IN BUILDING AND RENEWING COMMUNITIES

In writing about the work of many cultural organizations, particularly those serving local communities, Adams and Goldfarb point out that as diverse as this work is, the individuals and organizations involved are often united by a set of underlying principles.[1] These include the beliefs that creativity is a common, not a rare, phenomenon and that all children, not a few, deserve the experience of being an author or an artist; that all cultures are fundamentally equal—equivalently but distinctively wise, skilled, and complex; that diversity is a social asset, part of a multiclass, multirace commonwealth; and that creating new meanings or teaching someone else to do the same is fundamentally a political act, insofar as it expands capacity and allows for challenge and difference. It was no mistake that the New Market Theater was closed down for its performances of *Othello* in the last days of apartheid South Africa.

Even in the pragmatic and technical United States, there is a long tradition of community activists using the arts and culture to redistribute intellectual and social capital and to challenge the status quo. At Hull House, Jane Addams convinced immigrant parents to continue practicing their traditional arts as a way of demonstrating to their children that their mothers and fathers were anything but the "wogs" and "polocks" the nativists sneeringly called them. During the

Depression, the Works Progress Administration of the New Deal created parks, murals, and documentary photography that testified to "everyman's" right to imagine and strive. Dorothea Lange's "Migrant Mother," a product of the WPA, continues to remind viewers that despite exhaustion, dirt, and poverty, every mother has hopes—just as they do—for the future of her children. The civil rights movement used the shared covenant of spirituals to insist that there was a larger human community to which all people belonged and where every person was entitled to the same guarantees and dignities.

In many cities and towns, community choirs and theaters, pick-up bands and open-mike spoken-word performances are among the rare venues where people cross class, race, and gender lines and where the assumption that talent is correlated with first language, address, or skin color is in abeyance.[2] This tradition is not just a nice bit of history; it is potentially a resource to be reckoned with. It is no accident that the most racially and ethnically integrated honors and Advanced Placement courses in many city high schools are classes in music, media, or visual arts.[3] Nearly a third of the New Century High Schools that have been created in New York City have a cultural organization as their core partner, partly because these organizations can be rallied and partly because of the belief that the demands inherent in striving in a field like writing, music, or film can be among the most powerful and motivating experiences an adolescent can have.

These examples pose a double challenge. First, do U.S. cities and towns have the vision, determination, and political will to organize their multiple but fragmented resources (e.g., schools, libraries, museums, afterschool programs, work experiences) into a connected education system accessible to all students? And second, how will the institutions and educators involved work together to ensure that the children and youth they work with all experience opportunities to invent, create, question, and lead?

BECOMING "EACH OTHER'S BUSINESS": CROSS-SECTOR GENIUS AND COHERENCE

Dallas isn't called "Big D" for nothing; its current Chamber of Commerce tag line is "Live Large, Think Big." Like many cities of its size and economic base, Dallas is full of culture: theaters; a symphony; dance; a major art museum; a $275 million performing-arts center that will open in 2009 with new facilities for opera, theatre, music, and dance; a new Latino arts and cultural center; and one of the most boldly designed outdoor sculpture gardens in the nation. But if, in the mid-1990s, someone tallied the extent to which young people had access to those resources, numbers would fall into two starkly different columns: one for the "haves" and one for the "have-nots." Budget cuts had pared away arts and music programs in the schools, and the mounting pressures for accountability for raising reading and mathematics scores more than filled the academic schedule, particularly in the lower-scoring schools serving the city's poorest children.

In 1997, a concerned Long Range Planning Committee of the Dallas Cultural Affairs Commission hired Big Thought, a local nonprofit organization that had coordinated arts education programs, to gather data on the availability and accessibility of educational outreach programming offered by the city's arts and cultural institutions. After reviewing reports from the Office of Cultural Affairs, the Dallas Independent School District (Dallas ISD), and many organizations from the cultural community, the commission quickly concluded that the task was more of a challenge than they had anticipated: there was no coordinated system for collecting such data, and no one agency was overseeing the quality and distribution of the city's cultural education services.

In concrete terms, this meant that within the same district, some public schools were arts rich, while others were starved. While a favored quarter of the district schools received multiple performances, residencies, master classes, and field trips, an estimated 75 percent received none. In essence, the majority of students could finish high school without ever having attended a school-sponsored cultural field trip or live professional performance. With 82 percent of Dallas ISD students coming from low-income families, the likelihood that the vast majority of Dallas schoolchildren would ever experience a professional arts program outside their school building was very small. Believing in the potential benefits of these programs to all children, not only those attending the most advantaged and well-organized schools, the Dallas Cultural Affairs Commission advocated the creation of a citywide partnership to address this disparity.

Cultural as Well as Artistic Learning

A year later, the City of Dallas, Dallas ISD, and arts and cultural organizations formed a new citywide consortium, Dallas ArtsPartners, designed to guarantee the equitable and high-quality delivery of educational services from sixty diverse cultural institutions to participating public elementary schools. Despite its name, the consortium included much more than arts education programs; historic sites, science museums, the arboretum, and other institutions were also represented. The concept was to foster cultural learning and build an infrastructure that shared the full range of enrichment with families and children throughout the city. To accomplish this work, businesses and local foundations made major financial contributions, and offered in-kind services that ranged from public relations to the use of conference and meeting spaces.

The programs offered by Dallas ArtsPartners came in many forms: school-day performances, field trip performances, artist residencies, master classes, workshops, and guided tours. These experiences all incorporated firsthand experiences with creative professionals (dancers, instrumentalists, scientists, historians, journalists, archaeologists, and so on). The program was aimed at strengthening instruction in the classroom through two kinds of support: the knowledge and teaching skills of community professionals, and the help of ArtsPartners Integration specialists, who worked closely with educators to help them design curricula that used the arts and culture to enrich subject-matter learning.

Going Beyond the School Day

Even at this early stage, it was clear to the partnership that in-school work was vital, but far from sufficient, and that this work with children had to be amplified by work with their families. As 21st Century Community Learning Centers, a federally sponsored afterschool program, spread across the city, ArtsPartners became one of the district-designated providers for the arts and cultural strand of programming. This designation provided a chance to think through the problem of how afterschool sessions could enrich and amplify in-school curricula without becoming just a homework center or the site for extended remediation. Thus, at one elementary school, the afterschool staff worked hand in hand with the day-school staff to provide reading clinics that would support children's reading development in ways that were both demanding and motivating. Throughout the year, in these sessions, children read the books that the Dallas Children's Theater was using in its current season's shows. All children received copies of the books to read and discuss at home. On Saturdays, families went to performances with their children and then came together to talk about how the director and actors had transformed a text into a performance. This was a partnership based on the complementary "genius" of schools and afterschool programs with a common goal for urban students: reading at high levels.

Similarly, ArtsPartners used a program called "Summer in the City" to introduce families to the concept of the city as a larger campus for learning. For ten consecutive days, yellow school buses picked up third through sixth graders and at least one adult from each family at ten elementary schools throughout the city. (In the early years of this program, teachers and artists noticed that family members would follow in cars so that all their children could attend. Soon the program expanded to acknowledge this interest.) What was beginning to emerge was the early blueprint of a connected network of programs, accessible to whole families, not just the children in designated schools. There was a growing sense that the blueprint could become a citywide curriculum for participation in the city's cultural life, if certain conditions were met: (1) each sector or service contributed what it did best; (2) the plan harnessed, rather than ignored, the energy and interest of families—the adults and children living together; and (3) the sectors gave sustained attention to creating a coherent system, as acknowledged by the stakeholders: providers, teachers, families, and children.

In 2001, after three years of operation, the district, the city, and ArtsPartners felt the need for evidence of the return on its investment of approximately $2.4 million annually, half to purchase services and half to staff and implement the programs. As a first step, the Dallas ISD Department of Research, Evaluation, and Information Systems produced an initial report comparing Texas state accountability data for schools that participated in ArtsPartners programs and schools that did not.[4] Preliminary findings from these data showed that those who participated in ArtsPartners programs outperformed a matched set of elementary schools on standardized measures of academic performance. This data propelled the city, district, and ArtsPartners to decide that the program was strong enough to increase its scope. Thus, by school year 2002–03, the program had become universal, offering arts learning to each of Dallas's 101,000 public elementary school students, and aligned professional development to 6,000 general-classroom teachers and arts and cultural educators from approximately sixty cultural organizations.

BECOMING ONE ANOTHER'S "BUSINESS": EVIDENCE OF MAKING A DIFFERENCE

The city, the district, and ArtsPartners demonstrated that they had constructed a productive, stable, and large-scale partnership that guaranteed universal access to a network of cultural experiences usually beyond the means of most poor and working-poor families in Dallas. But orderly distribution and equitable provision of resources are only the technical side of equalizing opportunity to learn. These guarantee an *intended* curriculum, but what matters more is the *enacted* curriculum (see chapter 4). Having a ticket and a bus ride to a performance of Dallas Black Dance Theater guarantees a student only the opportunity to attend the performance, not the chance for classroom discussions or writing, or the opportunity to return for another performance.

Similarly, the enacted curriculum is not the *learned* curriculum. Unless a student can connect to, understand, extend, and transfer what she learned from the dance, the experience is only "an afternoon out" (see chapters 2 and 4). To go from the efficient provision of arts and cultural learning programs to significant effects on student learning requires a radically different type of partnership.

In 2001, ArtsPartners, working with the district and national research partners, undertook a longitudinal study aimed at understanding and improving the work carried on by ArtsPartners. Designing and conducting the study involved "becoming one another's business" at an entirely new level by joining two distinct working cultures, each with its own traditions of evidence. The first of these cultures was that of artistic and cultural partners—Dallas Children's Theater and authors from the Writers' Garret—a world in which a work or performance speaks for itself and individual creators can establish their own criteria for quality. The second realm was that of school-district accountability, which had become closely focused on quantitative evidence of increasing student performance as measured by the common instruments and metrics of large-scale state tests. As the process of designing this study unfolded, markedly different forms of partnership work emerged, including building shared capacity and mutual respect, defining shared and valued common outcomes, examining results, and developing a deeper understanding of successes and needed improvements.

Building Shared Capacity

The study was designed to build the capacity of local partners to think together about the quality of the ArtsPartners programs as a means to enrich students' in-school learning.[5] Rather than use a team wholly composed of outside researchers, the Dallas project selected and trained a mixed group that included graduate students in education and psychology, current and retired classroom teachers, and community youth workers, as well as staff members from ArtsPartners and some of the participating providers.

The participants represented the different races and cultural backgrounds of the children of Dallas ISD. As a result, when interviewing students or scoring samples of student work, they brought critical funds of cultural knowledge to the table. For instance, when scorers had difficulty making sense of the written work of younger bilingual students, Spanish speakers could urge the scorers to read the work aloud—with the emphasis and rhythm of spoken language—in order to find the sense in it. The mix of races and ethnicities guaranteed a variety of perspectives in the making of all major decisions. At the same time, the mix of partners from key sectors ensured that the discussions and ques-

tions raised in the study found their way into the district's teacher-training programs as well as to the education departments of arts and cultural organizations across the city.

Finally, it was important to develop trust and mutual respect within the collaboration.[6] Cultural educators—the writers, performers, scientists, and others—who would be coming into classrooms insisted that they did not want to be
only "footstools" for subject matter learning; they wanted to teach the big ideas
and deep skills of their fields; for example, they taught astronomy, not songs
about the planets. At the same time, classroom teachers did not want their mandated instruction to be portrayed as flat and dull compared to learning infused
with arts and culture. Instead, the point was to develop a design that acknowledged what good classroom instruction accomplished and how it could be en-
riched if teachers had artists, historians, or scientists by their side.

Establishing Shared and Valued Outcomes

Designing the study also entailed identifying outcomes that both public school
educators and cultural organizations valued highly.[7] This discussion was not
easy because the two sectors had long served the same children—but essen-
tially worked in parallel, not integrated ways. A common challenge was student
literacy. Even on the relatively low expectations Texas Assessment of Academic
Skills (TAAS) test, only 68.7 percent of third graders met minimum standards
(the level below proficient) in reading in 2001. Thus, the district was struggling
to help students move from the basic to the proficient level of achievement in
literacy. For children to attain this goal, they would need help with inferential
and critical reading as well as with the structure of argumentative and informa-
tive essays.

The discussions helped district educators see arts and culture in a new light:
music scores, paintings, and even exhibitions at the planetarium were complex
texts that demanded sophisticated interpretation. Also, cultural providers could
think of themselves as partners in the classroom providing children with multiple symbol systems through which to capture and share their ideas and experiences. The decision to focus mutually on literacy began what was to be a long-
running discussion about the importance of providing students—particularly
those acquiring academic English and those with learning disabilities—with
the opportunity to assume the role of authors with the responsibility of creating and editing original works, no matter what their current reading and writing levels were. This took the form of students creating personal works, even
though these works might contain errors. Seeing examples of the resulting stu-

dent work and video clips from their interviews changed how teams of researchers, and the teachers with whom they worked, viewed the participating students. Increasingly, they saw that even struggling learners have the capacity to imagine, invent, and investigate.

With considerable work, a model emerged. It called for a classroom lesson and a partnership lesson that focused on similar content and also student performances. For example, in a classroom lesson, sixth-grade students read a selection of stories and biographies on the theme of courage and persistence. Then, using multiple texts, they investigated the life of Jesse Owens, and finally wrote a short profile about him. Subsequently, the same group of sixth graders engaged in a partnership lesson in which they read accounts of the experiences of children in the Holocaust, and then they visited the Dallas Holocaust Museum and recorded exhibitions that most caught their attention and the questions they had. They used their notes to craft thoughtful interview questions for the curator of the museum. Finally, each child received an identity card based on the history of a child during the Holocaust; for example, one child might have lived in the Warsaw Ghetto; another might have escaped to Italy. The children then wrote about what they had learned, incorporating details from what they had seen, read, and heard. Researchers observed student behaviors, collected and scored student work, and interviewed students about their learning processes in both the classroom and the partnership lessons.

Examining Results

Each year the results from the previous year were reported and discussed at a meeting hosted by ArtsPartners, which included members of the central office, school board, participating classroom teachers, principals, arts and cultural providers, and researchers. The meeting was less a presentation and more a forum for asking questions. For example, in the first year, a board member was concerned that the data was not disaggregated to show results for English-language learners. His challenge led to a discussion of how well the overarching category captured the myriad of migration patterns, literacy histories, and legal statuses of the students whom it labels.

In the second year, disappointing student results showed that classroom units involving sciences and social sciences were less successful in improving students' approaches to learning or literacy than earlier units that had integrated the arts into classroom teaching. In thinking about why these units had not succeeded, all the partners realized that they had assumed that the same approaches would work across the different disciplines. Teachers also acknowledged their need for more professional development in the sciences. These results, though sobering, were the impetus for much more careful matches between cultural and academic outcomes. The results also showed that much more work was needed for the model to be equally effective across domains.

Developing a Deeper Understanding of Effects

In much of the current work on equitable distribution of educational resources, there is a profound confusion between provision and learning. For instance, if a middle school has up-to-date computers and software, time in the schedule for labs, and an instructor assigned, then the schools "have" the technology students need. But, in actuality, if the "wetware" is missing—the computer instructors, the older students with computer savvy, the thoughtful vice principal who creates time for students who do not have Internet access at home—all students may not benefit from the school's hardware and software.[8]

The qualitative data from the longitudinal interviews suggested that the Dallas program could have done much more to produce learning. Across the different schools, virtually all the children participated actively in the residencies and trips. But for some children these events were simply briefly delightful, while for others the experience ignited a string of activities and effects. As evidence accumulated across schools and the years of the study, Big Thought researchers and staff worked with teachers and students to develop a deeper understanding of the difference between an enjoyable event and an experience with lasting effects.

The longitudinal study followed a population of high-poverty black and Latino children across multiple years. Twice a year the children took trips to venues throughout the city or worked intensively with a cultural specialist. A smaller core of students was interviewed each semester about their work, and asked to talk about what they had experienced working with the cultural partner. Interviewers specifically addressed children as learners—individuals with minds, imaginations, and plans. They asked about the origins of their ideas, the choices they made in creating a work, and how they improved a work along the way. As a result of this process of talking about learning, students shared explanations of how they think, how their imaginations work, and what ideas they were mulling over. Significantly, it is the subset of children who were regularly interviewed that showed the most dramatic gains in their learning. Apparently, the experience of being seen as "a mind at work" leaves as deep an imprint as doing the work itself.

Another challenge the project confronted was how to help students extend their experience once they returned home. A student who meets a watercolorist and then goes home to a drawer full of paper and markers, and a grandfather who will make her a "gallery" on the kitchen wall, is in a different residency than the child who does not have the place, the supplies, or the human support to continue the work once the field trip or artist's visit is over. This was a sobering and important lesson for providers. In response, artists began to teach explicitly for transfer and continuity. They improvised journalists' notebooks for children to take home and keep; they designed backpacks containing the supplies that would make an instant studio or lab at home and allowed students to check them out. Furthermore, interviewers discovered that perhaps the most powerful form of transfer occurred when students went home and taught siblings or neighbors what they learned, so artists incorporated the ability to reteach into their teaching. Many Big Thought providers and curriculum writers had to learn, rather than assume, what it takes for something to be a lesson, not just an event.

Many of the students were keenly aware that they were learning and seeing things that were special. They talked often and freely about going back to their neighborhoods and homes and sharing with their siblings and neighbors what they had learned from the drummer, the actress, or the trip to the planetarium. Across the years of the study this finding has coalesced into two linked realizations: First, educators typically box students into the role of receiver, rarely thinking about how an eight-year-old might become a classroom helper the following year, and then a mentor, and eventually an assistant teacher. Second, and more broadly, students rarely have the opportunity to serve as the brokers and carriers of important cultural messages about learning.

Rethinking Who Learns

The results of the longitudinal study also highlighted the need for a broader view of stakeholders. Since its founding, Big Thought has concentrated on creating a supply of arts and cultural learning that could be distributed through the public schools. But talking with students made it clear that the supply is far from enough. On a regular basis, children talked about how their family members and guardians helped them build an initial interest into a talent or pastime by seeking out free classes, buying birthday presents of markers or books, or searching libraries and book stores to locate an author who had done a residency at the school. As a consequence, Big Thought has redefined its constituency to include families. In child-care settings throughout the city, artists now work with families and their preschool children to create both a generation of students who expect the arts as a part of their school experience and a generation of adults who will select schools and afterschool programs based, in part, on the availability of high-quality arts and cultural learning.

BECOMING ONE ANOTHER'S "MAGNITUDE": BUILDING PATHS AND COMMUNITY DEMAND

The longitudinal study yielded a number of hoped-for large-scale findings, including concurrent improvement in students' learning behaviors, improvements in student writing, and even some gains in standardized reading scores that lasted into middle school. But the study itself also yielded other dividends. Its rigor, and Big Thought's sizable investment in organizational learning and cross-sector capacity building, convinced both local and national funders to take notice of what was going on in Dallas.

Building Paths

Simply sampling a smorgasbord of opportunities is not the same as discovering a talent or passion and pursuing it over time. In the first case, a child is always a beginner, a novice, or a first-time visitor. In the second case—often pursued by middle class families—students have the chance to develop substantial skills, to climb the rungs within an organization, to go on excursions and trips, to form relationships with a corps of youth workers and teachers, and possibly to become a part of youth leadership.[9] Thus, since its inception, Big Thought has been making other investments in building a system of arts and cultural learning across the city, a system that could create paths for children and families to develop their interests and skills.

For example, Big Thought added an early-learning preface to their elementary school work. This included the North Texas Wolf Trap Early Learning Through the Arts, where artist-educators teach early childhood caregivers in preschools, in Head Start centers, and in child-care facilities to use the arts as a means of engaging two- to five-year-olds in early reading readiness learning. In-school programming was supplemented by Library Live, free monthly arts programs in all twenty-four Dallas public libraries designed to motivate children to read, promote intercultural appreciation, and offer families fun learning opportunities. The series also aims to establish libraries as community centers, safe places for families to gather throughout the year for education and inspiration.

There were also additional programs for older students, particularly those with the greatest needs. For instance, Creative Solutions, a program that mentors teens on probation to build skills and encourage creative thinking, working in teams, problem-solving, and giving back to the community. The program has two components: An intensive eight-week summer session and a series of residencies conducted on weekends during the school year.

Building Community Support and Demand

Building on its recognition of the force and energy of families, Big Thought's Family Initiative, which is funded by the Ford Foundation, has organized a community infrastructure and implements activities to achieve three goals:

- Increase diversity in the access and use of the city's cultural resources by families
- Promote the support and involvement of parents—including other family members, such as grandparents and other caregivers in a household—in arts education to improve academic achievement in Dallas ISD
- Organize trained coalitions of families to advocate for and sustain the institutionalized funding of arts and cultural learning opportunities

As the work moves into its next phase, a major goal is to create a distribution system for arts and cultural learning different from the downtown hub that characterizes many urban areas. Over the next six years, Dallas ArtsPartners and its partners Dallas ISD and the City of Dallas—including representation from the Dallas Public Libraries, the Office of Cultural Affairs, and the departments of Public Information, Strategic Customer Service, Parks and Recreation, and the Dallas Police—plan to establish thirty neighborhood centers that will host additional learning opportunities for participants of all ages. A major goal is to build support and demand for arts and cultural learning throughout the population of families living in the city. Such support is essential to withstand shifts in political and economic fortunes and sustain arts and cultural learning over the long haul.

BECOMING ONE ANOTHER'S "BOND": BUILDING EXCELLENCE AND EQUITY AT SCALE

In 2005, The Wallace Foundation selected Dallas and New York City as the two sites in which to invest so that they could create a *system* of high-quality arts learning. This system is envisioned as a network of opportunities that will encompass in-school instruction, afterschool programs, and a network of neighborhood centers spread throughout the city. The system also hopes to provide continuing paths for arts and cultural learning that families and children, from early childhood through adolescence, can pursue. Building this new initiative, DALI, is an opportunity to take "being one another's business" to a new level.

The work is just beginning. But in the spirit of planning backwards, the partners (Dallas ISD, Big Thought, The Wallace Foundation, and cultural providers) have fleshed out a bold vision of the "system of systems" they want to create. In addition, this consortium has begun to develop the research tools for tracking the opportunities that exist, who uses those opportunities, and who benefits from their engagement with these forms of enhanced and extended learning. While this model is tuned to arts and cultural learning, it also provides a compelling framework for measuring and improving a smart education system at scale in virtually any domain: health and nutrition, postsecondary opportunities, and so on.

At the heart of this model is a commitment to move from the provision of services to the production of learning. It outlines four major dimensions of systems building: scope, excellence, shift of ownership, and sustainability.[10]

1. *Scope (Supply and Demand).* This dimension refers to the evidence that what is offered (the supply) expands to met the demand of children and families throughout the city and that over time the supply grows to match what children and families are seeking. For example:

- Does the number of opportunities to engage in arts and cultural learning grow over time? Both in school and out of school?
- Are those expanded opportunities equitably distributed across neighborhoods?
- Do poor and minority families have the information and supports they need to take advantage of what is available?

2. *Excellence and Path.* This dimension refers to the quality of the arts learning and the degree to which individuals seek to stay engaged across time and venues. For example, in arts instruction:

- Does the arts instruction model urge students to think and perform as artists?
- Does the arts instruction set high levels of expectation?
- To what extent do young people stay engaged as they change schools and neighborhoods?
- Are coherent, unbroken pathways to arts learning established over time so that children can pursue the arts in and out of school?

3. *Shift of Ownership (Increasing Equity and Engagement).* This dimension refers to the evidence that the arts and cultural education is reaching new groups of individuals (students and adults) and providing equitable and sustained ac-

cess to those individuals, independent of their wealth, location in the city, or other distinguishing characteristics. In addition, it identifies shifts in ownership—who becomes involved as a provider, a site, or a funder—of the program. For example:

- Are neighborhood and school arts and cultural gaps closing over time?
- Are teachers, parents, and students taking ownership for DALI programming?
- Over time, are families better informed about and better able to find opportunities matched to the different talents and artistic/cultural interests of their children?

4. *Sustainability and Coherence.* This dimension considers the extent to which the different subsystems are linked and supported independently and codependently, one to another through institutionalized infrastructure. Thus, this dimension refers to the way in which bodies like the City of Dallas, Dallas ISD, local foundations, major Dallas cultural institutions, the media, and funders operate as genuine partners. For instance:

- Is arts programming a regular, sustained presence in schools, in afterschool programs, and in neighborhood centers throughout the city?
- Do media, schools, and cultural organizations collaborate on creating more channels of information about new opportunities that reach a wider range of audiences?
- How are the school district, the city of Dallas, and community foundations cooperating to ensure long-range funding for DALI?
- Is arts education programming a growing budget line-item for Dallas ISD? For the city of Dallas in its many divisions?

CONCLUSION:
WHAT IT TAKES TO BECOME ONE ANOTHER'S
"HARVEST, BUSINESS, MAGNITUDE, AND BOND"

This chapter has highlighted the effort to create a smart education system in one sector (arts and cultural learning) in one city (Dallas). This effort has drawn partners into new ways of working together: (1) in-depth, cross-sector collaboration, (2) data-informed accountability, (3) building systems (both networks and paths) of opportunities, and (4) building community support and demand. This work has encompassed almost a decade. It has involved unfamiliar choices and considerable negotiation. And the work is projected for another decade—a long span in an urban community. But, if replicated, it is work that could turn urban neighborhoods, maybe even whole cities, into engines of opportunity.

The early school reformer, Horace Mann, convinced the American people that public financing of a system of universal education was a sound idea. One of his arguments was that it would serve as "the flywheel of equality." One hundred and seventy years later, it is growing clear that schools alone can't drive equality of opportunity; families and their children need entire communities to act as engines of opportunity. If this were the case, three things would be true. First, families who are poor, who have cut short their own education, or who are mobile for economic reasons could, in the span of a generation, "learn the ropes" so that their sons and daughters would prosper intellectually, socially, and culturally in schools and the wider community. Second, students who depend on public institutions for formal, sequential learning would follow paths from childhood to adulthood that allow them to develop their talents and aspirations.[11] Finally, we would have as major "dashboard" indicators for a city's viability: (1) the number of years it takes for a working-poor family to begin to thrive economically, culturally, and educationally; (2) the proportion of its children who attain their aspirations; and (3) the number of a city's government agencies, institutions, and leaders who work together over time to make this possible.

PART V

A VISION FOR THE FUTURE

FROM SMART DISTRICTS
TO SMART EDUCATION SYSTEMS:
A BROADER AGENDA FOR
EDUCATIONAL DEVELOPMENT

Warren Simmons

The heightened attention devoted to district reform in recent years is a welcome development. It represents a recognition that the reform movement's attempts to ignore or bypass districts would fail to yield results in an equitable way, and that the state-based or school-by-school approach would be unlikely to engage communities in a way to sustain reforms over time.

The district efforts have begun to yield promising results. Analyses of district reforms in Boston, Charlotte-Mecklenberg, Houston, San Diego, Philadelphia, and Christina, Delaware, reveal significant gains in students' literacy and mathematics achievement, as measured by state and local standardized tests.[1] In some instances, these gains have been corroborated by the results of National Assessment of Education Progress (NAEP), an independent assessment sponsored by the U.S. Education Department. NAEP's Trial Urban District Assessments compared reading and mathematics performance in ten urban districts (Atlanta, Boston, Charlotte, Chicago, Cleveland, the District of Columbia, Houston, Los Angeles, New York City, San Diego) with results obtained in the nation at large from 2002 to 2003. These comparisons showed that the average performance of students in Atlanta, Los Angeles, and New York City improved on NAEP's fourth-grade reading assessment during that period. Moreover, the average NAEP mathematics scores of students in Charlotte exceeded the averages obtained by students nationally in grades 4 and 8.[2]

When combined, the results of national, state, and local assessments reveal that changes in district governance and operations are beginning to generate improvements in student outcomes. But these data raise concerns as well as hope. Most of the reported gains have been confined to the elementary and middle grades. Unfortunately, achievement gains in high school have not kept pace with the progress made in earlier grades.[3] In addition, despite the gains made by many African American and Latino students, a significant number of these students continue to fail to meet NAEP or state criteria for proficiency. In other words, while they are making real progress, their performance is not commensurate with their state's definition for being at or above standard.

This evidence indicates that the efforts to redesign and strengthen districts, while important, are not sufficient. Educators and community members must intensify or expand their efforts so that the vast majority of students, particularly African Americans, Latinos, and students from low-income families, move beyond basic skills to attain levels of performance needed to participate meaningfully in our democracy, in the global economy, and in their communities. This chapter examines some of the shortcomings of existing efforts and describes some of the additional supports students and schools need to achieve the more ambitious and essential aims. I lay out a vision for a "smart education system" that provides needed supports for children and families, and conclude with some steps that districts and communities can take to begin to build such systems.

DISTRICT REFORM:
PROMISING RESULTS, DIFFERENT PATHS

In general, districts have pursued three paths toward reform: managed instruction, professional learning communities (or communities of practice), and portfolios of schools. These approaches are not discrete; rather, they often co-exist, by design or default. However, district leaders often choose to put into the foreground one of these paths as their primary approach, even as they implement other strategies at the same time.

Managed Instruction. Inspired by the work of Community District 2 in New York City,[4] many districts (e.g., Los Angeles Unified, Charlotte-Mecklenberg, Providence, and Norfolk) have developed districtwide curriculum and instruction programs to produce marked gains in students' mathematics and literacy achievement. Generally speaking, districts stressing this strategy

- set high standards in literacy and mathematics;
- mandate a core curriculum for both subject areas;
- provide districtwide professional development aligned with the district's standards and curricula;
- create a cadre of principals, central office staff, and teacher leaders who provide content-based coaching and instructional support in schools on an ongoing basis.

This approach relies heavily on centralized guidance and support for teaching and learning, but in many instances the alignment and coherence is also achieved through a mix of centralized guidance (e.g., mandatory core curricula, professional development, and school accountability regimes) augmented by the initiative of teachers and principals working in professional learning communities that are supported by local and national reform support organizations.

Communities of Practice/Professional Learning Communities. Districts emphasizing this strategy may also employ mandatory curricula or offer a recommended set of curricular options that reflect district and/or state academic standards. However, as McLaughlin and Talbert note, districts pursuing the community-of-practice strategy accent the importance of building school-based learning communities where teachers and administrators collaborate to

- develop a shared vision, language, and standards of practice;
- share and analyze evidence regarding the impact of practice on student engagement and achievement;
- enhance teachers' professional judgment and ability to use data to advance practice and student learning;
- cultivate a school culture that promotes learning and continuous improvement for adults and students.[5]

Boston Public Schools (BPS) is a leading example of a district that blends a managed-instruction strategy with a community-of-practice approach. The district ensures instructional focus by employing a common curriculum in language arts and mathematics that is aligned with the district's standards. Further focus and coherence is achieved through the use of literacy and mathematics coaches, who conduct professional development in schools using a Collaborative Coaching and Learning Model. In addition to centralized guidance, Boston has also established Instructional Leadership Teams in every school to amplify local expertise and to build cultures supporting collaboration and continuous improvement in every school. To support the work of these school-based professional learning communities the district has introduced MyBPS, a web-based system that provides student data by classroom and school.[6]

The efficacy of a community-of-practice approach toward district reform is beginning to be reflected in the progress made by a network of schools and districts in Northern California supported by Springboard Schools (formerly known as the Bay Area School Reform Collaborative).[7] Oak Grove and Alameda Unified School Districts in the Bay Area, along with Long Beach Unified School District, have made strides in creating district supports and a culture that advances teacher collaboration and evidence-based judgment.

Portfolios of Schools. A third approach to district reform is reflected in the work of school districts in Philadelphia, Chicago, and New York City. While these districts incorporate elements of managed instruction and communities of practice, they tend to put into the foreground the importance of designing a system that can support a portfolio of schools. Such a system includes a range of schools, including those operated by nonprofit and for-profit organizations, as well as those operated by the district, in order to provide options for students and families and a range of approaches to match varied student needs.

This approach emphasizes the importance of innovation and choice as levers for improvement. The School District of Philadelphia has the most explicit and comprehensive portfolio model to date (see chapter 5). There, and elsewhere, external providers are largely involved in supporting the growing number of small high schools and schools requiring intervention because of chronic underperformance. In the latter case, the multiple provider and portfolio approach appears to be less a product of explicit district redesign than an additional lever for school support and intervention.

As the newest of the three approaches to district reform, there is little data available on the portfolio approach. Specifically, there is little research on the cultural and structural changes districts must make to balance greater autonomy with accountability for schools operated by external organizations. More importantly, there is little data on the effectiveness of the approach itself. In a preliminary assessment of Philadelphia's portfolio model, Research For Action reported that "test score data thus far show some improvements in math and reading, with overall levels remaining comparatively low and with no provider or intervention strategy standing out as being much more effective than others."[8]

SMART DISTRICTS: THE CHALLENGES AHEAD

Despite their promise, these efforts at district reform face two significant limitations. The challenge ahead will be to address these limitations and move forward to accomplish the ambitious aims of reformers.

The first challenge is sustainability. With an average tenure of two and three-quarters years for most urban superintendents,[9] districts are constantly buffeted by shifting reform winds. And old reforms do not necessarily go away when a new leader comes in with a new strategy; districts possess the vestiges of multiple reforms that operate amidst the principal strategy pursued by current system leadership.

Moreover as Hubbard, Stein, and Mehan observed, reform is political and cultural as much as it is technical.[10] Philadelphia's struggles under David Hornbeck's leadership in the late 1990s, and more recently, Alan Bersin's departure from San Diego, are reminders that a shift in district leadership and reform strategy can occur despite substantial gains in student achievement. Reforms that fail to build political support and promote favorable attitudes, beliefs, and norms are as susceptible to failure as those that are technically unsound.

The belated recognition of the political and cultural dimensions of reform is reflected in the renewed emphasis on community engagement as an essential element of district reform (see chapters 6 and 8). At the same time, districts face the technical struggle of balancing their approaches to reform in order to build the capacity needed to sustain reform and achieve results at scale—meaning raise achievement and narrow performance gaps in the vast majority of schools, not just a few.

A second challenge is to understand the qualitative changes in knowledge and skill required for students to move beyond basic levels of performance to attain proficiency. Unfortunately, our national preoccupation with standardized test scores fosters the misconception that learning can be reduced to knowledge and skills that can be taught and learned additively. For instance, on the 2003 NAEP reading assessment, the average scores of African American and Latino fourth graders in Boston were twenty-three and twenty-four points, respectively, lower than the average obtained by their white counterparts. Without additional information about the qualitative meaning of these numerical gaps, it would be easy to assume that they could be closed by having African American and Latino students work harder and longer.

In fact, though, attaining higher levels of performance requires qualitatively different skills. To attain proficiency in reading, and beyond, students must possess the ability to comprehend what they have read, analyze its connections with their own experiences, and make broad inferences that go beyond the text. Simply getting better at the basic skill of decoding is not enough.

The mismatch between the skills and knowledge requirements of the global economy and democratic society and the limited conceptions of learning assessed by standardized tests reflects the dangers inherent in using tests rather than the standards themselves as the major driver of school reform.[11] The premium placed on creativity, collaboration, interdisciplinary work, communication, cultural literacy, and technology should also undermine the credibility of reforms grounded in discipline-based work practiced largely using print materials in classrooms and at home. Basic skills alone cannot catapult all students, especially those on the unfavorable side of the achievement gap, to the educational achievement levels required for success in today's world.

CAN SCHOOLS MAKE THE DIFFERENCE ALONE?

Despite heartening evidence that a growing number of schools serving African American, Latino, and low-income students can beat the odds and produce dramatic improvements in academic performance,[12] a lack of resources and stability within many large urban school districts and the poor communities they serve prevent success from spreading across schools and over time. Hurricane Katrina revealed painfully that the economic, social, and cultural levies that isolated and impoverished generations of New Orleans' poor and African American residents were active accomplices to the educational failure produced by the public school system's mismanagement and turmoil.[13] But these economic, social, and cultural levees are not unique to New Orleans; they exist in many of this country's major urban cities. And, as with New Orleans before the hurricane, in these cities poverty is often hidden; downtown revitalization and neighborhood gentrification efforts have eliminated the towers of public housing complexes that once made poverty highly visible in places like Chicago, Baltimore, and Newark. While cities have progressed in decreasing the concentration of poverty through mixed-income developments and rent subsidies, it is not at all clear that these strategies have countered the effects of inadequate health care and nutrition, high levels of transience, low rates of parental education, and cultural isolation that continue to distress low-income families.

The deleterious effects of poverty on children and families have led an increasing number of voices to revisit the 1966 Coleman Report, which attributed the largest portions of variance in school achievement to variations in family characteristics rather than school quality. In reflecting on the controversy stoked by Coleman's findings, Gordon and Bridglall attributed much of the negative response to the national political context of the 1960s.[14] Coleman's report posed a major threat to fledgling federal and state efforts to enforce the U.S. Supreme Court's *Brown v. Board of Education* decision to end segregation and address the inadequate distribution of resources in the nation's schools. Critics of Coleman's study were concerned that it would lend credence to explanations that placed the burden of failure on the characteristics of poor families and their children, rather than on the flaws present in their schools. Gordon and Bridglall acknowledge that while the Coleman Report's critics succeeded in maintaining the nation's commitment to integration and quality schooling, they did so by fostering what the authors call the "over-identification of education with schooling," thereby obscuring the importance of family and community that amplify effective school-based curriculum and instruction.[15]

Family and Community Capital. Gordon and Bridglall identified seven types of family and community capital or resources that form essential supports for learning: financial, cultural, health, personal, human, social, and polity. The financial and health disparities between poor and middle-income families have been well catalogued by Rothstein[16] and others. And the achievement gap revealed by tests results, graduation rates, and advance course enrollments speaks to shortfalls in academic knowledge and skills among the poor that Gordon and Bridglall reference as human capital. But the broader social, cultural, personal and political costs of poverty often receive less attention. Cultural capital has probably received the most consistent research attention over time, although the political culture wars fought in local and state boards of education, as well as in the federal education department, have forced this topic underground. Nonetheless, decades of research have documented the harmful effects of the mismatch between the cultural knowledge and learning styles emphasized in schools and those prevalent among racial and ethnic minorities, and among women as compared to men.[17]

One of the most significant aspects of family and community capital is the availability of social networks that provide access to information and opportunities. The impact of poverty on a family's ability to create effective social networks is not widely understood because these networks are often hidden assets employed by more privileged families. For instance, being known and valued by educators in selective schools often helps privileged parents navigate the admissions processes from daycare to college; but the advantages do not exist for parents in poverty. The presence or absence of this kind of capital also mediates opportunities in housing and employment. A cumulative paucity of financial, social, cultural, health, and human capital also heightens a loss of polity and personal capital, a sense of belonging to and being invested in a larger community (polity capital) along with a sense of personal agency and efficacy (personal capital).

SUPPLEMENTARY EDUCATION

Gordon and Bridglall note that middle-class and affluent families often have the resources needed to build the various forms of capital that enhance and extend school-based learning. The music lessons, sports leagues, national and international travel, concerts and museum visits, and internships that dominate the weekend and afterschool experience of more advantaged children and youth serve to build the networks, values, dispositions, and knowledge that reinforce and accelerate school-based learning. By contrast, many of the supplemental resources available to low-income children in afterschool programs—often in the form of remedial basic skills instruction—tend to *decelerate* learning further by failing to make connections between academic content and the more meaningful, complex, and rewarding challenges found outside school. The dulling effects of basic skills instruction is echoed in the voices of struggling students who lament the fact that their school assignments are not sufficiently challenging.[18]

Instead of compounding academic failure by combining low-quality instruction during the regular school day with narrowly conceived remedial instruction after school, Gordon and Bridglall argue that communities should provide supplemental education for poor children that would entail "services related to health and nutrition, guidance, tutorials, mentoring, summer enrichment, travel, exposure to institutions of high culture, and [experience with] the social networks through which opportunities for upward mobility are mediated."[19] The strength and urgency of their argument is underscored by studies revealing that the national economic revival that occurred during the 1980s and 1990s was accompanied by a gradual decline in the availability and quality of supplemental supports for poor adolescents and preschool-age children.[20] The paucity of supports for learning leaves poor children and youth with the daunting task of meeting the skill requirements for the creative economy while being equipped with low-quality schools and minimal access to community resources for learning.

School-Based Supplementary Services

Unfortunately, the No Child Left Behind Act (NCLB), one of the most powerful levers for education reform in schools serving poor and minority students, exacerbates the inadequacy of supplemental resources for low-income children. Under the law, students in persistently low-performing schools are eligible to receive "supplemental educational services"; however, the statute restricts the definition of these services to tutoring and other forms of remedial academic instruction.

This shortcoming is offset somewhat by Title IV of the same act, the 21st Century Community Learning Center Program (CLC). First authorized in 1994, this federal program provides funds to states and districts to create afterschool programs that offer services that come closer to what Gordon and Bridglall envisioned. Although NCLB strengthened CLC's emphasis on academic instruction, CLC programs are also encouraged to foster academic enrichment through activities emphasizing the visual and performing arts, recreation, technology, and character education. The program now operates in over 6,800 elementary schools spread across 1,600 districts.

A recent evaluation of CLC programs, however, found that the program produced disappointing results. In comparing the performance of 1,258 students who were randomly assigned to CLC programs with the outcomes produced by 1,050 students in a control group, James-Burdumy et al. found that CLC participation had no significant impact on homework completion and standardized test performance in reading or mathematics.[21] Even more distressing, students in CLC programs experienced more behavior problems during the regular school day (suspensions and other disciplinary actions) as compared to students in the control group. The researchers speculated that the disappointing academic results were due to poor alignment between the regular school and afterschool educational activities. They also suggested that the expected rate of improvement in test score performance might exceed what is possible, given the quality of support and sporadic participation of students in CLC programs. While these explanations are plausible, the rise in negative behavior found among CLC participants in comparison to the control group raises serious questions about the program's impact on broader youth development outcomes, such as self-discipline, collaboration, and respect for peers and adults.

Unfortunately, CLC's impact on academic outcomes is mirrored in the evaluation results of other afterschool programs such as the Beacons Schools Initiative in New York City and the afterschool Program sponsored by The After School Corporation.[22] Though these evaluations indicate that the programs yielded more positive results for youth engagement, they generally show weak gains in academic achievement, as measured by grades and standardized tests. Reflecting on these disappointing evaluation findings, Kane suggested the need for afterschool programs to strengthen enrollment and participation by requiring

parental commitment as a prerequisite for enrollment, and by identifying leading indicators to academic test score improvement (e.g., increased attendance
and homework completion, improved grades) that may show improvement prior
to yielding results on standardized tests.[23]

While these changes may be warranted, enacting them would do more to
make afterschool more like school, and reduce the ability of these programs to
offer the kinds of enrichment experiences that enable middle-class and more affluent students to acquire the various forms of capital that support higher levels of achievement and development. Moreover, one has to question the efficacy
of a strategy that relies on urban schools that are often already beleaguered by
poor performance, lower teacher quality, high staff turnover, and inferior facilities and materials to serve as hubs for extended services.[24] The student, parent,
and community alienation that is often engendered by years of failure present a
formidable barrier to establishing the foundation of trust between the school and
the community needed to create strong linkages between learning assets in and
outside school. Supplemental educational supports that rely solely on schools
as a primary source for learning and development, then, overlook the fact that
many schools lack sufficient resources and that stronger resources may be available in other organizations such as churches, temples, and mosques, community development organizations, reform support organizations, businesses, and
cultural institutions.

THE DEVELOPMENT MODEL

Rather than extend services in schools that may be weak to begin with, many
districts are experimenting with what Warren refers to as the "Development
Model"—encouraging community organizations to create or operate schools as
a way of blending the staff, programs, and services these organizations often
already operate in community settings with academic programs provided during regular school hours.[25] The El Puente Academy for Peace and Justice in New
York City is a notable example of this trend. El Puente, a community-development organization located in North Brooklyn, established the academy in 1993.
It capitalizes on the larger organization's programs in art and culture, community health, and environmental improvement to provide meaningful tasks, as
well as adult and peer mentors, and to promote students' contributions to their
school, families, and community.

In contrast to the school-as-hub service model, the development approach
broadens and builds connections among a variety of assets that communities

possess to support student learning. These include funds of knowledge that are often not tapped in school, but remain highly useful and meaningful.[26] For instance, parents and relatives who are highly skilled workers, as well as immigrants who were once professionals in their former countries, can contribute their skills and knowledge to help develop students' skills and interests. Moreover, unlike the school service model, the development approach focuses on strengthening students along with their families and communities. This approach expands the availability of resources needed to build the various forms of capital for students to move beyond basic skills, and reduces the extent to which academic advancement alienates students from their families and communities.

Intersections between the Development Approach and District Reform

El Puente Academy was the product of a larger school reform effort sponsored by what was then known as the New York City Board of Education, in partnership with a local reform support organization, New Visions for Public Schools. Since 1993, New Visions and the district (now called the New York City Department of Education) have supported the development of well over one hundred new schools operated in partnership with arts and cultural institutions, community development groups, health centers, and higher education institutions.

Over time, as the number of schools operated by partnerships between the Department, New Visions, and local groups expanded, their presence compelled the district to enact reforms that would make this approach to supporting schools the rule rather than an exception or limited experiment. The growth of schools operated by external groups under district contracts, charters, or other forms of agreement has forced school boards, central offices, and unions representing teachers, support staff, and administrators to refashion policies and practices to encourage flexibility, innovation, and collaboration while maintaining accountability for performance and attention to core-curriculum guidance. The emergence of smart districts that govern and manage portfolios of schools has created opportunities for the expansion of school-community partnerships, along with increased pressure for the kinds of district reinvention needed to ensure attention to equity and excellence in outcomes and practice. The interdependence between school-community partnerships and district reform is evident in the development of the New Century Schools in New York City, in the schools operated by nonprofit and for-profit providers in Philadelphia, and in the school networks being established by the Oakland Unified School District.

The Emergence of Local Education Support Networks

As the number of partnerships involving schools and external organizations ex-pands, districts and communities must ensure that their growth does not deplete the availability of quality partners for the next generation of interested schools and communities. The push to attach partners to individual schools, however, can quickly strip communities of available assets and deny scarce resources to others. In addition, assignment of organizations to individual schools under-mines the ability of both parties (schools and partners) to share knowledge, tools, and strategies across schools and community organizations. The attach-ment of partners to individual schools also fosters a needless quest for "unique-ness," with each school and partner seeking to make its approach or theme distinct from that of others. This rush to distinctiveness often elevates innova-tion over quality, as though poor parents and students value variety over effec-tiveness. (Oddly enough, many of the same districts that promote educational choice and innovation for poor students and families embrace the rigorous uni-formity of Advanced Placement courses and college-prep curricula when cater-ing to the needs of middle-class and more affluent parents.) The point here is that innovation without quality represents no choice at all. Furthermore, dis-tricts using partnerships must strike a balance between innovation and quality and should rethink approaches that limit scarce community resources to indi-vidual schools.

From Smart Schools to Local Education Support Networks

As districts consider how to generate more leverage from the development strat-egy, several are collaborating with colleges and universities, reform support groups, and community-development organizations to establish partnerships that support networks of schools rather than individual ones. These neighbor-hood-based networks of schools and partner organizations are known as Lo-cal Education Support Networks (LESNs). The shift of emphasis from school-based partnerships to LESNs allows multiple schools and partners to pool their resources (e.g., knowledge, tools, funds, facilities). Moreover, LESNs typically treat a local neighborhood or community as a hub for learning, thus increasing opportunities to engage families, cultural institutions, businesses, faith institu-tions, and community development organizations in the design and implemen-tation of learning activities.

LESNs typically strive to pursue an integrated approach to academic, cogni-tive, social, and cultural development, and treat the development of strong fam-ilies and communities as an essential component of school reform. Two examples of LESNs illustrate different ways school network-community organization partnerships have pursued this approach,

The Harlem Children's Zone. The Harlem Children's Zone (HCZ) is a nonprofit community-based organization that furnishes a range of services, including day care and preschool programs, parenting classes, violence prevention initiatives, tutoring, cultural activities, and health care services, to more than 8,600 economically disadvantaged children in Central Harlem. During the bulk of its 30-year history, HCZ (formerly the Rheedlen Centers) was limited to providing its school-based supports at the end of the regular school day, thus reducing opportunities to enrich both the schools' curricula and HCZ-provided, community-based education supports through collaboration. The barriers that prevented this collaboration were removed, however, when HCZ was awarded a charter to operate a school. The charter agreement has allowed HCZ to establish the Promise Academy, a school that will eventually serve up to 1,300 students from preschool through grade 12.

Adding a K–12 school to its portfolio of services enabled HCZ to develop a more comprehensive network of supports for child and youth development— one that removes artificial boundaries between learning in school and in community settings. The presence of a K–12 school also allows HCZ to build a pathway of supports for learning and development from birth through adolescence, thus reducing the arduous tasks that parents and students often face as they seek to create a "through-line" for learning in the visual and performing arts, science and mathematics, or law and social justice as students move from elementary to middle and high school. Developing educational pathways out of a patchwork of school programs, while difficult for parents with means, is almost impossible for families with limited resources with respect to time, transportation, finances, knowledge, and social networks.

St. Hope Academy/Public Schools. Led by Kevin Johnson, a former professional basketball player, St. Hope Academy was established in 1989 in Oak Park, a neighborhood composed largely of poor and working class families in Sacramento, California. The academy was designed to serve 250 students in grades 3 through 12 by offering integrated academic and youth-development programs in health, language arts, drama, mathematics, music, and character development, among other areas. The academy also augmented students' school-based learning activities with adult mentors and neighborhood-development activities that reinforced ties among academic achievement, career development, and community revitalization in and beyond Oak Park. As part of Sacramento Unified School District's high school transformation effort, St. Hope was granted a charter to transform Sacramento City High—a large, comprehensive, and underperforming high school—into five separate small schools. The original academy has now been incorporated into an independent charter school district serving close to 2,000 students. The charter district includes an early childhood development program, an elementary school, a middle school operated in conjunction with the Knowledge Is Power Program (KIPP), and five small high schools specializing in the arts, health sciences, law and public services, mathematics, engineering and science, and business and education.

True to its broader focus on community development, the St. Hope Public School District continues to connect its educational programs to larger economic- and community-development efforts in Oak Park, which include opening a range of new small businesses like a book store, theatre, and coffee shop. Like the Harlem Children's Zone, the St. Hope Public School District recognizes that strong families and communities provide vital assets to support students' educational growth.

SMART EDUCATION SYSTEMS: A NEW OLD IDEA

District transformations such as the ones in Philadelphia, Oakland, New York City, and Chicago that result in school systems with permeable, rather than closed, boundaries have enhanced opportunities to strengthen and align school- and community-based learning activities by incorporating the assets of communities in ways that integrate in- and out-of-school learning opportunities on a systematic basis. At the same time, LESNs in New York, Sacramento, and other communities are able to draw on the resources of schools, community organizations, higher education, and cultural and faith institutions to construct meaningful learning activities that incorporate academic, cognitive, social, and cultural components of learning. And they have done so without sacrificing high standards and attention to basic skills, something that schools would find difficult to do alone under the pressure to improve standardized test results.

The next step in the transformation of these systems to support high levels of learning for all students is to connect the neighborhood web of educational supports that LESNs provide with the citywide partnerships that have the capacity to engage a broader range of partners. We call this bigger system a "smart education system."

The concept of a web of resources that a smart education system entails is not a new idea. The Annie E. Casey Foundation's New Futures Initiative, launched in 1987, was one of the first comprehensive multi-city efforts to improve education outcomes in high-poverty communities. It fostered public polices and practices that would integrate services across multiple systems (e.g., health, education, employment, child welfare, social services, juvenile justice) to support improved education and related outcomes for students.[27] New Futures pursued this strategy by promoting the development of new local governance structures called collaboratives to act as interim mechanisms connecting fragmented delivery systems. Toward this end, collaboratives composed of elected officials, business leaders, public agency officials, parents, and community representatives were formed in each of the seven New Futures communities to develop localized approaches to system integration and alignment.

In reflecting on the lessons learned from New Futures, the foundation and its partners noted that, "in many low-income communities, service-system and institutional-change initiatives like New Futures may, by themselves, prove insufficient to transform educational, social, and health outcomes. The emerging lesson is that in some environments, system reform efforts must be augmented by social capital and economic-development initiatives that target the whole community."[28] While the failure to build social and economic capital in poor neighborhoods prevented New Futures from reaching its full potential, it is noteworthy to point out that, at the time, local education systems faced minimal pressures for systemic change. New Futures was launched well before the standards movement raised expectations for learning and created national and state assessments that unmasked the full dimensions of the achievement gap and pressured districts to change under threat of state takeover of schools and entire school districts.

Moreover, state and mayoral oversight of school districts have allowed the collaboratives, which were voluntary structures under New Futures, to become formal governance mechanisms. In cities like Boston, Chicago, and New York, where mayors have direct control over the schools, the school superintendent is a member of the mayor's cabinet.[29] Increased mayoral control of education, then, has enhanced the ability of municipal governments to form strategic alliances among the school district, other city agencies, cultural institutions, and businesses using the authority and bully pulpit of mayors. These alliances create policies and conditions that foster the development of a smart education system.

What Is a Smart Education System?

In order to understand what we mean by "smart education system," it is helpful to unpack each word in that phrase.

Smart. While the word "smart" has a particular educational connotation, the word has also acquired a specialized meaning in the world of technology. In contrast to conventional technologies, which do one thing over and over again, smart technologies are nimble and are able to learn and adapt to new situations. They are thus more efficient and provide the services that are needed.

For example, conventional dishwashers use the same amount of water for each wash, no matter how many dishes are in the rack. Smart dishwashers, by contrast, are able to "know" how many dishes are in the rack and adjust the amount of water they supply. Further, they "learn" the habits of the user and make adjustments for someone who tends to wash more dishes or another who washes less each time.

In similar fashion, a smart education system is nimble, adaptive, and efficient. It provides differential supports to different young people and families, depending on their needs. It is able to attract new partners to augment its capacity when needed. And it collects and uses data and makes adjustments depending on what is working and what needs to be changed.

Education. Clearly the inequities in access to resources and services are vast. "Educational" does not mean "academic," however. The range of services provided in a smart education system is rather broad—everything from afterschool activities to cultural enrichment to internships in local businesses, and much in between. In addition, the services also help remove some barriers to learning that many young people face. For example, many young people who are in foster care endure frequent disruptions to their schooling because they frequently move from house to house—and school to school. A smart education system would engage the foster care system to minimize such disruptions and ensure that young people in foster care can continue to learn in an uninterrupted way. But what really distinguishes a smart education system is its focus on educational services. The goal is to ensure that all young people are supported in and out of school in their learning and other areas of development (e.g., health, social skills, cultural competence, character development, motivation, and self-discipline) that support academic achievement.

System. The services and supports that a smart education system provides already exist in most cities, for the most part. But as New Futures recognized, they do not constitute a system. Young people and their families must negotiate their own way through the opportunities that are available, and if they make it through them at all, it is almost by accident rather than design.

A system, by contrast, is aligned to the needs of the community. School districts and their partners in city agencies and private organizations—with community members acting as full partners—locate services and supports where they are needed and in ways the community wants. They coordinate such services to avoid duplication and make it easier for children and families to take advantage of them. They disseminate information about available opportunities widely. And they provide transportation and other supports to make access easier.

In addition, the agencies and organizations that provide services pool their resources to ensure the availability of high-quality services that are customized to meet the needs of students, families, and communities. And they are accountable to the community—people know who is in charge and whom they can hold responsible for achieving excellence and equity.

What Does a Smart Education System Look Like?

The kind of smart education system we envision does not yet exist, citywide, in any city in the United States. However, the press for school district transformations that promote high standards and the decentralizing of decisionmaking and resource control (fiscal, human, material) to school networks and community partners provides an essential foundation for change. This practice must be accompanied by citywide governance structures that forge interfaces among city agencies with responsibility for children, youth, and families, as well as with cultural institutions and museums, businesses, and nonprofit organizations that provide services to support student learning. Moreover, linking neighborhood-based and citywide alliances ensures a more equitable exchange between elites and grassroots organizations than is possible through citywide collaboratives that are often dominated by the perspectives, politics, and values of elites.

A smart education system, then, is dependent upon community engagement that engenders the effective exchange of ideas and information between elites and grassroots community leaders and organizations. To provide one example, in a community, less-privileged members may have a definition of valued arts activities that differs from the one developed by more-advantaged members of the community. The result is a potential conflict: to some in a city, legitimate arts are defined as classical music and playing in orchestras, while to other less-advantaged, culturally diverse groups arts could involve hair-weaving, painting of fingernails, and a variety of activities that actually add value and are important in a community, but aren't valued by all members. An engaged community that provides equitable access to information and decision-making for grassroots and "grass-top" organizations provides both the demand for continued improvement and support for the sometimes difficult decisions that improvement entails.

By contrast, as the recent history of reforms shows all too clearly, a lack of engagement can scuttle technically sound improvement efforts based on political, social, or cultural conflicts, or as Carolyn Akers, the director of the Mobile Area Education Foundation in Alabama, is fond of saying, "Education reform isn't rocket science; it's political science."[30] In many cases, though, it's both: reform involves the technical challenge of building new structures as well as the political challenge of rearranging power relationships. Creating a smart education system is no different.

The technical challenges can be formidable. Many cities lack the capacity even to conduct an inventory of existing services. Budgeting and information systems vary widely among agencies and organizations and may be technically incompatible. And few cities have the experience of using new information to drive policy changes.

Technology can help alleviate some of the technical challenges. Denver, for example, has used global positioning systems and census data to match the availability of recreation facilities in high-poverty neighborhoods. And Boston and other cities have developed sophisticated student-information systems that could be used to create an extensive database of information on learning opportunities in and out of school. But the challenge, there and elsewhere, is to enable district and community leaders to understand how to use the information effectively.

The political challenges are perhaps more substantial. Many cities that have attempted to forge partnerships between districts, community groups, and other agencies have found that school districts tend to want to take the lead in such partnerships and are reluctant to cede resources or authority. In other cities, political leaders are eager to spread services evenly, rather than concentrate them in areas with the most need. And few organizations have a history of working together; bringing them together sometimes breeds suspicion about motives.

Building a Foundation for Smart Education Systems

Strong communities are as vital to the development of smart education systems as they are to successful schools. The relationships among people in successful schools corresponds with Sergiovanni's definition of "community" as people "bonded to a set of shared ideas and ideals" in a way that is "tight enough to transform them from a collection of I's into a collective We."[31] Another aspect of community that often characterizes examples of successful reform is what Kretzman and McKnight describe as an internal focus where "the primacy of local definition, investment, creativity, hope and control" is emphasized.[32] This significance of an "internal focus" is evident in the knowledge that school staff seem to have about the students and their families, in their understanding of the resources required to accomplish their work, and in their commitment to achieving their collective goals. Many successful urban schools, like El Puente and the St. Hope Academy, began by making important shifts in their thinking about external communities as revealed by their outreach strategies and collaborative stance with families and community-based organizations and groups. In partnership with community, these schools have also taken a critical step to move beyond the enumeration of deficits to the identification of assets that may already exist, both in school and in the community.

The LESNs outlined in this chapter apply these principles to create a network of learning opportunities grounded in the assets and experiences of schools and key partner organizations within a specified neighborhood or community united as much by shared values, experiences, and aspirations, as by physical boundaries set by geography or politics. Smart education systems, however, require the development of shared values, experiences, and aspirations across a diverse swath of communities that exist within most cities—the communities flush with energy and ambition based on new housing and business development, and those with equal hope and ambition but with fewer resources (political, social, fiscal) available to support their efforts. The cities that build wary, sometimes temporary, but often productive alliances between the multiple communities within their borders possess a common set of features that act as scaffolding for cross-cultural and cross-sector dialogue and action and that collectively represent the beginning of an infrastructure to support and sustain smart education systems.

These four features are:

Leadership Development. Cities comprise diverse communities with varying sources of leadership (e.g., neighborhood associations, unions, community development corporations, faith institutions, social clubs, civic organizations, governmental agencies, arts and cultural institutions). These varied sources pose a challenge for developing leaders with a core set of shared values, beliefs, and knowledge from communities with divergent experiences and cultures. Building a consensus and knowledge base, while respecting differences, requires skilled and concerted cross-sector leadership development that is often lacking at the local level. Advocates, community leaders, government officials, and school board members with major roles in education often come to this endeavor with little formal or shared knowledge about education practice and policy, and few vehicles to address this shortcoming. In comparison, state and national leadership is supported by a bevy of organizations such as the Council of Chief State School Officers, the Business Roundtable, the National Governors Association, and the Learning First Alliance, all of which strive to build cross-sector understanding and consensus about the current status of education and its implications for future policies and practices. There are few local equivalents of these organizations, yet these types of supports are sorely needed to provide a common foundation for shared understanding and collective action.

Local intermediary and reform-support organizations, such as the local education funds in Chattanooga and Portland, and the collaborative in El Paso, have included this role in their already crowded portfolio of work. In addition, local affiliates of the Industrial Areas Foundation assume this responsibility for parents and community groups. These organizations, however, often perform this function as a byproduct of their other work, rather than as an explicit responsibility, and they often do so with little direct funding from foundations. To develop the leadership needed to strengthen and expand cross-sector coalitions, local communities and their partners must invest in leadership development that will create and inform a network that includes local government leaders and their key staff, school board officials, union leaders, community-based organizations, faith institutions, and higher education representatives, among others.

Applied Research. As with education, the various systems that provide support for youth and community development offer diverse services that vary widely in quality. The quality varies within programs as well as between them; a low-performing school might include an exemplary arts program, for example. But the heterogeneous nature of these services contributes to varied perceptions of the nature of the "elephant." And often, these differing perceptions fuel conflicts about the nature and urgency of problems based on experiences that vary along lines of race, ethnicity, income, and neighborhood.

Applied research provides an essential base for building a shared understanding of a system and its differential impact on outcomes and experiences in specific settings. While guided by theory, organizations such as Research For Action in Philadelphia, Education Matters in Boston, the Consortium for Chicago School Research and the Annenberg Institute's own Community Involvement Program (formerly housed in New York University's Institute for Education and Social Policy) conduct research on problems posed by local constituents that include community-based organizations, school districts, local funders, and municipal leaders. In doing so, they pay specific attention to the enactment of policy and practice with an eye toward understanding how and why change achieves or fails to reach desired outcomes within or across communities. Research of this kind is more context sensitive and practice oriented than traditional scientific research and evaluation activities that often seek to minimize or control the very factors (e.g., teacher and student mobility, practitioner choice and motivation, prior levels of achievement, community resources) that affect the shape and progress of reform.

While these controls help isolate and determine the effects of a particular intervention, they also obscure and oversimplify the forces educators, students, parents, and advocates must confront when they apply a design under the varying conditions that exist across schools and communities. To build smart education systems that improve the quality and effectiveness of reform, local leaders and practitioners need more information and data that discern the course of implementation, not just its destination. These data often fuel constructive discussions in superintendent cabinet meetings, local business roundtable gatherings, editorial board briefings, teacher network meetings, parent and community forums, and labor-management negotiations—the very settings that the scientific-research community struggles to reach through national clearinghouses, regional laboratories and centers, and scholarly journals.

Local "Skunk Works" or Innovation Incubators. Contrary to the widespread perception that we know little about "what works" in education, school districts and other systems, in fact, confront a cornucopia of "best" practices, "effective" programs, and evidence-based designs. What they often lack is the knowledge and means to incubate and adapt "proven" practices at the scale needed to improve and connect learning activities across distinct communities. Although this challenge is complicated by basic research and evaluation studies that overlook implementation prerequisites, a growing number of university- and community-based nonprofit organizations are creating for school systems what Lockheed, the aircraft corporation, called "skunk works": a site for applied research and development.

Examples of organizations partnering with local school districts to support the design and implementation of new ideas include the Bay Area Coalition for Equitable Schools; New Visions for Public Schools and the Center for Arts Education, both in New York City; the Boston Plan for Excellence and Center for Collaborative Education, in Boston; and the Philadelphia Education Fund along with Foundation, Inc. Their work includes the development of small schools, arts curricula and programs, authentic forms of student, school, and district assessment, and the development of school networks operated by nonprofit and for-profit organizations. Local skunk works have also helped national and lo-cally developed designs make the mutual adaptations needed to foster improve-ment rather than chaos within larger systems of schools.[33] The critical role played by these organizations is often ignored by national research and evalua-tion studies focused more narrowly on outcomes and design fidelity, rather than adaptations required by varying contexts.

Alternative Governance Structures. Structural or policy barriers that require the intervention of independent governing bodies involving different sectors (e.g., education, housing, health, social services) stymie even the best design and implementation efforts. Educators in secondary schools, for example, are often frustrated by student attendance and behavior problems exacerbated by poli-cies and practices followed by the foster care and juvenile justice systems that operate beyond the reach of schools but whose presence is felt deeply by them just the same. Similarly, community groups operating recreation, education, and health programs chide districts for policies that limit their access to students and facilities while calling for families and neighborhoods to do more.

To achieve the kind of smart education system we envision, communities must restructure larger systems in education, health, recreation, and economic development that pose boundaries for cross-section planning and collaboration. While the creation of cross-agency collaboratives and neighborhood councils represents a step in the right direction, these arrangements are usually volun-tary and operate within the constraints of systems that fragment communities and families into isolated individuals with specific needs.[34] Mayoral cabinets for children and families established in Boston and New York lend authority to these arrangements, but often sacrifice community engagement for centralized collaboration.

Public Engagement Mechanisms and Strategies

When local governing bodies are slow to respond to felt needs, communities can pursue change through court actions, appeals to state and federal governments, and the building of local demands for change. All of these actions involve some form of public engagement to raise awareness, build constituency, and drive ac-tion. Data from public opinion surveys indicate that the American public, over-whelmingly, considers education a top national priority.[35] However, these same surveys show that the public believes that the nation's schools are not equipped to provide a high-quality education for all.

As a result, the volume has been turned up on the "quiet revolution": public engagement. Yet we have much to learn about the design and implementation of effective strategies to engage the public within and across communities in different regions of the country. To advance this work, communities need a broader understanding of how partnerships and leadership emerge and develop, given differences in context and purpose, as well as the kinds of tools and expertise that individuals and organizations need to heighten the quality and effectiveness of their engagement strategies in the context of an ever-changing community.

Vision and Action Artifacts

The leadership, research, and public engagement endeavors outlined previously often lead to the production of vision frameworks and action plans intended to guide ongoing or periodic reviews of progress and action by the community. The form these vision statements and frameworks take varies considerably, along with the manner in which they are distributed and used. Despite the paucity of information about promising practice in this area, communities continue to extrapolate the business sector's emphasis on the importance of mission statements and action frameworks for organizational development and restructuring. Given the importance placed on these tools, several questions warrant further study:

- What level of detail and sophistication is necessary for these frameworks to inform and engender action on the part of key target groups and systems?
- What corollary activities, tools, and products are needed to augment these frameworks so multiple groups can inform their development and use them to guide changes in policy and practice?
- How might different audiences modify these resources over time to address the need for continuous, evidence-based inquiry and adaptation to promote equity and excellence?
- What role can educators, community-based groups, intermediary organizations, higher education institutions, and others play in the development and modification of these resources over time?

CONCLUSION

While much work remains to define and develop the scaffolds needed to create smart education systems, the potential payoff is high. And there is a strong desire on the part of municipal leaders, community organizations, and philanthropic groups to work through the challenges. For years, cities and funders have tended to focus either on schools or on out-of-school learning opportunities, even while recognizing that each needs the other. But they have been reluctant to work together. The demands to close the achievement gap and the innovations and outcomes resulting from system transformation informed by community development could finally create optimal learning environments. These would be the kinds that partnerships, educators, and community leaders have long sought, ones needed in smart education systems to build creative communities that drive an economy and derive benefits from it.

NOTES

Introduction

1. Richard Rothstein, *Class and Schools* (Washington, DC: Economic Policy Institute, 2004).
2. Craig Jerald, *Dispelling the Myth Revisited: Preliminary Findings from a Nationwide Analysis of "High-Flying" Schools* (Washington, DC: Education Trust, 2001).
3. Rothstein, *Class and Schools*.
4. Center for the Study of Social Policy, *Building New Futures for At-Risk Youth: Findings from a Five-Year Multi-Site Evaluation* (Washington, DC: Center for the Study of Social Policy, 1995).
5. Annie E. Casey Foundation, *The Path of Most Resistance: Reflections on Lessons Learned from New Futures* (Baltimore: Annie E. Casey Foundation, 1995).
6. Constancia Warren, Michelle Feist, and Nancy Neverez, *A Place to Grow: Evaluation of the New York City Beacons, Summary Report* (New York: Academy for Educational Development, 2002).
7. Annenberg Institute for School Reform, *School Communities That Work for Results and Equity* (Providence, RI: Annenberg Institute for School Reform, 2002).

1. The Real Achievement Gap

Robert Rothman

1. Diane Ravitch, "As American as Public School, 1900–1950: Introduction," in *School: The Story of American Public Education*, ed. Sarah Mondale and Sarah B. Patton (Boston: Beacon Press, 2001).
2. Patricia A. Graham, "Assimilation, Adjustment, and Access: An Antiquarian View of American Education," in *Learning from the Past: What History Teaches Us about School Reform*, ed. Diane Ravitch and Maris A. Vinovskis (Baltimore: Johns Hopkins University Press, 1995).
3. U.S. Census Bureau, *Profile of the Foreign-Born Population of the United States* (Washington, DC: U.S. Government Printing Office, 2001).
4. Laura Lippman, Shelly Burns, and Edith McArthur, *Urban Schools: The Challenge of Location and Poverty* (Washington, DC: National Center for Education Statistics, 1996).
5. William O'Hare and Mark Mather, *The Growing Number of Kids in Severely Distressed Neighborhoods: Evidence from the 2000 Census* (Baltimore: Annie E. Casey Foundation, 2003).
6. Elaine Allensworth, *Ending Social Promotion: Dropout Rates in Chicago after Implementation of the Eighth-Grade Promotion Gate* (Chicago: Consortium on Chicago School Re-

search, 2004); Jenny Nagaoka and Melissa Roderick, *Ending Social Promotion: The Effects of Retention* (Chicago: Consortium on Chicago School Research, 2004).

7. Christopher B. Swanson, *Who Graduates? Who Doesn't? A Statistical Portrait of Public High School Graduation, Class of 2001* (Washington, DC: Urban Institute, 2004); Robert Balfanz and Nettie Letgers, "Locating the Dropout Crisis: Which High Schools Produce the Nation's Dropouts?" in *Dropouts in America*, ed. Gary Orfield (Cambridge, MA: Harvard Education Press, 2004).

8. National Center for Education Statistics, *The Condition of Education 2005* (NCES document no. 2005-094; Washington, DC: US Government Printing Office, 2005).

9. Council of the Great City Schools, *Beating the Odds: A City-by-City Analysis of Student Performance and Achievement Gaps on State Assessments* (Washington, DC: Council of the Great City Schools, 2006).

10. National Education Association, *Report of the Committee of Ten* (accessed from http://tmh.floonet.net/books/commoften/mainrpt.html)

11. Quoted in Jeffrey Mirel and David Angus, "High Standards for All? The Struggle for Equality in the American High School Curriculum," *American Educator* 18 (Summer 1994): 4–42.

12. See Jeffrey Mirel, "The Traditional High School," *Education Next* 6, no. 1 (Winter 2006); Jeffrey Mirel and David Angus, *The Failed Promise of the American High School, 1890–1995* (New York: Teachers College Press, 1999); Arthur Powell, Eleanor Farrar, and David K. Cohen, *The Shopping Mall High School: Winners and Losers in the Educational Marketplace* (Boston: Houghton Mifflin, 1984).

13. Mirel, "The Traditional High School."

14. John Bransford, Ann Brown, and Rodney Cocking, eds., *How People Learn* (Washington, DC: National Academy Press, 1999), p. 19.

15. Fred M. Newmann and Associates, *Authentic Achievement: Restructuring Schools for Intellectual Quality* (San Francisco: Jossey-Bass), pp. 27–28.

16. Warren Simmons and Lauren B. Resnick, "Assessment as the Catalyst of School Reform," *Educational Leadership* 50, no. 5 (February 1993): 11–15.

17. Marc Tucker and Judy B. Codding, *Standards for Our Schools* (San Francisco: Jossey-Bass, 1998), p. 58.

18. Lynn Olson, "Progressive-Era Concept Breaks Mold: NASDC Schools Explore 'Project Learning,'" *Education Week*, February 17, 1993, p. 1.

19. Robert Rothman, *Measuring Up: Standards, Assessment, and School Reform* (San Francisco: Jossey-Bass, 1995).

20. Rothman, *Measuring Up.*

21. Thernstrom made these comments at a 2004 forum sponsored by the Harvard Graduate School of Education. See http://forum.wgbh.org/wgbh/forum.php?lecture_id = 1441. Also see Abigail Thernstrom and Stephan Thernstrom, *No Excuses: Closing the Racial Gap in Learning* (New York: Simon and Schuster, 2003).

22. Diane S. Rentner and Others, *From the Capital to the Classroom: Year 4 of the No Child Left Behind Act* (Washington, DC: Center on Education Policy, 2006).

23. Rentner, *From the Capitol to the Classroom.*

24. Linda Darling-Hammond, "From Separate but Equal to No Child Left Behind: The Collision of New Standards and Old Inequalities" in *Many Children Left Behind*, ed. Deborah Meier and George Wood (Boston: Beacon Press, 2004), p. 18.

25. Edmund W. Gordon and Beatrice L. Bridglall, "The Challenge, Context, and Preconditions of Academic Development at High Levels" in *Supplementary Education: The Hidden Curriculum of High Academic Achievement,* ed. Edmund W. Gordon, Beatrice L. Bridglall, and Aundra S. Meroe (Lanham, MD: Rowman and Littlefield, 2005).

26. See William Schmidt and Others, *Why Schools Matter: A Cross-National Comparison of Curriculum and Learning* (San Francisco: Jossey-Bass, 2001); Andrew C. Porter, "The Effects of Upgrading Policies on High School Mathematics and Science" in *Brookings Papers on Education Policy 1998,* ed. Diane Ravitch (Washington, DC: Brookings Institution Press, 1998).

27. See Jeannie Oakes, *Multiplying Inequalities: The Effects of Race, Social Class, and Tracking on Opportunities to Learn Mathematics and Science* (Santa Monica, CA: Rand Corporation, 1990); Michael S. Knapp and Associates, *Teaching for Meaning in High-Poverty Classrooms* (New York: Teachers College Press, 1995).

28. Edmund W. Gordon, "The Idea of Supplementary Education," in *Supplementary Education: The Hidden Curriculum of High Academic Achievement,* ed. Edmund W. Gordon, Beatrice L. Bridglall, and Aundra S. Meroe (Lanham, MD: Rowman and Littlefield, 2005).

29. National Council on Education Standards and Testing, *Raising Standards for American Education* (Washington, DC: US Government Printing Office, 1992).

2. City Kids, City Families

Dennie Palmer Wolf and Heather A. Harding

1. See Jane Addams, *Twenty Years at Hull House* (Boston: Bedford/St. Martin's, 1999); Lewis Hine, "Record Group 102, Records of the Department of Commerce and Labor" (National Archives Information Locator, Children's Bureau, 2006); William Julius Wilson, *When Work Disappears: The World of the New Urban Poor* (New York: Alfred A. Knopf, 1996).

2. Heather A. Harding, "City Girl: A Portrait of a Successful White Urban Teacher," *Qualitative Inquiry* 11, no. 1 (2005): 52–80.

3. On-line dictionary for Microsoft Word.

4. Christopher Spencer and Helen Woolley, "Children and the City: A Summary of Recent Environmental Psychology Research," *Childcare, Health and Development* 26, no. 3 (2000): 181–198.

5. Martha Nussbaum and Amartya Sen, eds., *The Quality of Life* (New York: Oxford University Press, 1993); Amartya Sen, *Development as Freedom* (New York: Alfred Knopf, 1999); Amartya Sen, *Inequality Reexamined* (New York: Russell Sage Foundation, 1992); Alberto Minujin, Jan Vandemoortele, and Enrique Delamonica, "Economic Growth, Poverty, and Children," *Environment and Urbanization* 14, no. 2 (2002): 23–43.

6. Edmund W. Gordon and Beatrice Bridglall, "The Idea of Supplementary Education," *Pedagogical Inquiry and Praxis* no. 3 (March 2002): 1–4; Charles V. Willie, "The Real Crisis in Education: Failing to Link Equity and Excellence," *Voices in Urban Education* 10 (Winter 2006): 11–19.

7. Priscilla Little, "The Idea of Supplementary Education," Harvard Family Research Project, "Complementary Learning," *Evaluation Exchange* 11, no. 1 (Spring 2005): 7.

8. Jason Booza, Jackie Cutsinger, and George Galster, *Where Did They Go? The Decline of Middle-Income Neighborhoods in Metropolitan America* (Washington, DC: Brookings Institution Living Cities Census Series, 2006).

9. Gary Orfield and Chungmei Lee, *Why Segregation Matters: Poverty and Educational Inequality* (Cambridge, MA: Civil Rights Project at Harvard University, 2005).

10. United Nations Children's Fund, *The State of the World's Children, 2006: Excluded and Invisible* (New York: UNICEF, 2005).

11. Paul Jargowsky and Rebecca Yang, "The 'Underclass' Revisited: A Social Problem in Decline" (working paper, Brookings Institution, May, 2005).

12. Alan Berube, "Gaining but Losing Ground: Population Change in Large Cities and their Suburbs," in *Redefining Urban and Suburban America: Evidence from Census 2000,* ed. Bruce Katz and Robert E. Lang (Washington, DC: Brookings Institution Press, 2003).

13. See, for example, Douglas S. Massey and Nancy A. Denton, *American Apartheid: Segregation and the Making of the Underclass* (Cambridge, MA. Harvard University Press, 1993); Jonathan Kozol, *The Shame of the Nation* (New York: Crown, 2005).

14. Brookings Institution Metropolitan Policy Program and Population Reference Bureau, *Kids in the City: Indicators of Child Well-Being in Large Cities from the 2004 American Community Survey* (Washington, DC: Brookings Institution, August 2006).

15. Mark J. Stern, *Is All the World Philadelphia? A Multi-City Study of Arts and Cultural Organizations, Diversity, and Urban Revitalization* (working paper no. 9, University of Pennsylvania, Philadelphia, May 1999).

3. Smart Districts as the Entry Point

Marla Ucelli, Ellen Foley, and Jacob Mishook

1. See chapter 9; also see Warren Simmons, Ellen Foley, and Marla Ucelli, "Using Mayoral Involvement in District Reform to Support Instructional Change," *Harvard Educational Review* 76, no. 2 (2006): 189–200.

2. See Annenberg Institute for School Reform, *School Communities that Work for Results and Equity* (Providence, RI: Annenberg Institute for School Reform, 2002); Annenberg Institute for School Reform, *Reforming Relationships: School Districts, External Organizations, and Systemic Change* (Providence, RI: Annenberg Institute for School Reform, 2003); Mark Berends, Joan Chun, Gina Schuyler, Sue Stockly, and R .J. Briggs, *Challenges of Conflicting School Reforms: Effects of New American Schools in a High-Poverty District* (Santa Monica, CA: RAND, 2002); Susan J. Bodilly, *Lessons from New American Schools: Prospects for Bringing Designs to Multiple Schools* (Washington, DC: RAND, 1998); Patricia Burch and James Spillane, *Leading from the Middle: Mid-Level District Staff and Instructional Improvement* (Chicago: Cross City Campaign for Urban School Reform, 2004); Richard Elmore and Deanna Burney, *Investing in Teacher Learning: Staff Development and Instructional Improvement in Community School District #2, New York City* (New York: National Commission on Teaching and America's Future and Consortium for Policy Research in Education, 1997); Mary A. Ragland, Rose Asera, and Joseph F. Johnson Jr., *Urgency, Responsibility, Efficacy: Preliminary Findings of a Study of High-Performing Texas School Districts* (Austin: University of Texas, Charles A. Dana Center, 1999); Linda Skrla, James Joseph Scheurich, and Joseph F. Johnson Jr., *Equity-Driven Achievement-Focused School Districts* (Austin: University of Texas, Charles A. Dana Center, 2000); Jason Snipes, Fred Doolittle, and Corinne Herlihy, *Foundations for Success: Case Studies of How Urban School Systems Improve Student Achievement* (Washington, DC: Manpower Demonstration Research Corporation and Council of the Great City Schools, 2002); Wendy Togneri and Stephen E. Anderson, *Beyond*

Islands of Excellence: What Districts Can Do to Improve Instruction and Achievement in All Schools (Washington, DC: Learning First Alliance, 2003).

3. Barbara Neufeld, Dana Roper, and Carol Baldassari, *Year I of Collaborative Coaching and Learning in the Boston Public Schools: Accounts from the Schools* (Cambridge, MA: Education Matters, July 2003).

4. Claire Handley and Robert Kronley, *Challenging Myths: The Benwood Initiative and Education Reform in Hamilton County* (Chattanooga, TN: Kronley and Associates, 2006); Public Education Foundation, "Benwood Initiative: Rapid Reading Gains at Eight Urban Elementary Schools Prove that Excellent Teaching Means Every Child Will Learn" (accessed September 6, 2006, from http://www.pefchattanooga.org/www/docs/1/benwood/).

5. Interview for Boston case study, October 2005.

6. Interview for Boston case study, October 2005.

7. Interview for Boston case study, October 2005.

8. Burch and Spillane, *Leading from the Middle*, p. 4.

4. Teaching and Learning in Urban Districts

Deanna Burney and Kenneth Klau

1. National Research Council, *Testing, Teaching, and Learning: A Guide for States and School Districts* (Washington, DC: National Academy Press, 1999).

2. Annenberg Institute for School Reform, *Findings and Recommendations from the Central Office Review for Results & Equity conducted in partnership with the Annenberg Institute for School Reform and the Portland Schools Foundation* (Providence, RI: Annenberg Institute for School Reform, 2005).

3. Education Resource Strategies (ERS) and Annenberg Institute for School Reform, *Becoming a Capable and Accountable System: A Review of Professional Development and Curriculum in the Baltimore City Public School System* (Providence, RI: Annenberg Institute for School Reform, 2004).

4. ERS and Annenberg Institute, *Becoming a Capable and Accountable System*.

5. Maryland State Department of Education, *Maryland's Report Card: 2003 Performance Report* (accessed October 2, 2006, from http://msp2003.msde.state.md.us/lea.asp?K = 30AAAA).

6. David Tyack and Larry Cuban, *Tinkering toward Utopia: A Century of Public School Reform.* (Cambridge, MA: Harvard University Press, 1995).

7. Mary H. Metz, "How Social Class Differences Shape Teachers' Work," in *The Contexts of Teaching in Secondary Schools,* ed. Milbrey McLaughlin, Joan Talbert, and Nina Bascia (New York: Teachers College Press, 1990), pp. 40–107

8. Marc S. Tucker and Judy B. Codding, *Standards for Our Schools: How to Set Them, Measure Them, and Reach Them* (San Francisco: Jossey-Bass, 1998)

9. Annenberg Institute for School Reform, *Findings and Recommendations from the Central Office*.

10. Tyack and Cuban, *Tinkering Toward Utopia*.

11. Lauren B. Resnick, "From Aptitude to Effort: A New Foundation for Our Schools." *Daedalus* 124 (1995): 55–62.

12. Annenberg Institute for School Reform, *Findings and Recommendations from the Central Office*.

13. Linda B. Stebbins, Robert G. St. Pierre, Elizabeth C. Proper, Richard B. Anderson, and Thomas R. Cerva, *Education as Experimentation: A Planned Variation Model. Volume V: An Evaluation of Follow Through* (Cambridge, MA: Abt, 1977).

14. ERS and Annenberg Institute, *Becoming a Capable and Accountable System.*

15. ERS and Annenberg Institute, *Becoming a Capable and Accountable System.*

16. Annenberg Institute, *Findings and Recommendations.*

17. ERS and Annenberg Institute, *Becoming a Capable and Accountable System.*

18. Annenberg Institute, *Findings and Recommendations.*

19. ERS and Annenberg Institute, *Becoming a Capable and Accountable System.*

20. Annenberg Institute, *Findings and Recommendations.*

21. ERS and Annenberg Institute, *Becoming a Capable and Accountable System.*

22. Jere Brophy, "How Teachers Influence What Is Taught and Learned in Classrooms," *The Elementary School Journal* 83, no. 1 (1982): 1–13.

23. Based on Brophy, "How Teachers Influence What Is Taught," and Andrew C. Porter and John L. Smithson, *Defining, Developing, and Using Curriculum Indicators* (CPRE research report series no. RR-048; Philadelphia: University of Pennsylvania, Consortium for Policy Research in Education, 2001).

24. Brophy, "How Teachers Influence What Is Taught," p. 7.

25. ERS and Annenberg Institute, *Becoming a Capable and Accountable System.*

26. ERS and Annenberg Institute, *Becoming a Capable and Accountable System.*

27. Annenberg Institute, *Findings and Recommendations.*

28. Charles Abelmann and Richard Elmore, *When Accountability Knocks, Will Anyone Answer?* CPRE Research Report Series RR-42 (Philadelphia: Consortium for Policy Research in Education, 1999); Eric Wenger, *Communities of Practice: Learning, Meaning, and Identity* (Cambridge: Cambridge University Press, 1998), pp. 3–15, 72–102.

29. Clayton Cristensen, Howard H. Stevenson, and Jeremy Dam, "The Tools of Agreement" (Harvard Business School note 399-080; Cambridge, MA: Harvard Business School, 2001).

30. Abelmann and Elmore, "When Accountability Knocks."

31. Abelmann and Elmore, "When Accountability Knocks."

32. ERS and Annenberg Institute, *Becoming a Capable and Accountable System.*

33. Annenberg Institute, *Findings and Recommendations.*

34. Ronald A. Heifetz and Marty Linsky, *Leadership on the Line: Staying Alive through the Dangers of Leading* (Cambridge, MA: Harvard Business School Press, 2002).

5. The Diverse-Provider Model

Kenneth K. Wong and David Wishnick

1. Alex Molnar, Glen Wilson, and Daniel Allen, *Profiles of For-Profit Education Management Companies 2002–2003* (Tempe: Arizona State University Commercialism in Education Research Unit, 2003).

2. Paul T. Hill, Christine Campbell, and James Harvey, *It Takes a City* (Washington, DC: Brookings Institution Press, 2000).

3. Ann Marie Donahue, *Ethics in Politics and Government* (New York: H. W. Wilson, 1989), p. 221; also see Herbert J. Walberg and Joseph L. Bast, *Education and Capitalism* (Palo Alto, CA: Hoover Institution Press, 2004).

4. Kevin Bushweller, "Education Business," *Education Week*, December 3, 2003.

5. Center for Education Reform, *All about Charter Schools,* http://www.edreform.com/index. cfm?fuseAction = document&documentID = 1964 (accessed October 10, 2006).

6. Carrie Lips, "Edupreneurs: A Survey of For-Profit Education" (policy analysis no. 386, Cato Institute, November 20, 2000, p. 18).

7. Catherine Gewertz, "Philadelphia Cheers Better Test Scores," *Education Week,* September 1, 2004.

8. Katrina Bulkley and Patricia Wohlstetter, eds., *Taking Account of Charter Schools* (New York: Teachers College Press, 2004).

9. Kristen Loschert, John O'Neil, and Dave Winans, "Cash Cow," *NEA Today* 23, no. 1 (2004; accessed at www.nea.org.neatoday/0409/coverstory.html).

10. Donahue, *Ethics in Politics and Government,* p. 219.

11. Alex Hernandez and Matthew Mahoney, "Is the Private Sector Qualified to Reform Schools?" *Education Week,* September 18, 2002, pp. 34, 38.

12. Robert Maranto, "A Tale of Two Cities: School Privatization in Philadelphia and Chester," *American Journal of Education* 111, no. 2 (February 2005): 151–190.

13. Government Accountability Office, *Public Schools: Insufficient Research to Determine Effectiveness of Selected Private Education Companies* (report no. GAO-03-11; Washington, DC: Government Printing Office, 2002).

14. Government Accountability Office, *Public Schools: Comparison of Achievement Results for Students Attending Privately Managed and Traditional Schools in Six Cities* (report no. GAO-04-62; Washington, DC: Government Printing Office, 2003).

15. John Fitz and Brian Beers, "Education Management Organizations and the Privatization of Education in the US and the UK," *Comparative Education* 38, no. 2 (2002): 137–154.

16. "School diversity" can involve more than diverse service providers. It can (and, in Chicago, does) involve magnet schools, schools for gifted students, and targeted schools run by the central district, itself.

17. One other "smart" reform initiative is the Community Schools program.

18. Rosalind Rossi, "Sun-Times Insight: Exploring the Issues of the Day," *Chicago Sun-Times,* July 8, 2004, p. 16.

19. "Renaissance 2010 School Types" (accessed January 22, 2007, from http://www.ren2010. cps.k12.il.us/types.shtml).

20. For instance, Edison Schools, Inc., manages Chicago International Charter School Longwood Campus.

21. Information from http://www.ren2010.cps.k12.il.us/docs/Renaissance_2010_Cohort_II_ Schools.pdf and Ihejirika, Maudlyne, "Education Powers Up," *Chicago Sun-Times,* September 1, 2006.

22. "Left Behind: A Report of the Education Committee," paper prepared by the Civic Committee of the Commercial Club of Chicago (July, 2003).

23. Stephanie Banchero, "2010 School Reform Off to Wobbly Start," *Chicago Tribune,* April 10, 2005, p. 1.

24. Jeremy Mullman and Greg Hinz, "School Plan Falls Behind," *Crain's Chicago Business,* February 6, 2006, p. 1.

25. Lori Olszewski, "Way Cleared for Teachers to Walk Out," *Chicago Tribune,* October 30, 2003, p. 1.

26. Rosalind Rossi, "Big Coalition Unites Against Daley School Plan," *Chicago Sun-Times,* October 26, 2004, p. 22.

27. Rosalind Rossi, "Renaissance 2010 Draws 57 Applications in Second Round," *Chicago Sun-Times,* August 23, 2005, p. 24.

28. Rosalind Rossi, "Critics Say Schools Plan Too Vague on Closings," *Chicago Sun-Times,* September 14, 2004, p. 20.

29. Elizabeth Duffrin, "Slow Progress amid Strife," *Catalyst* 12, no. 6 (March 2006; accessed at www.catalyst-chicago.org/news/index.php?item = 19352cat = 23).

30. "Metro Briefs," *Chicago Sun-Times,* September 22, 2006.

31. Ihejirika, "Education Powers Up."

32. Stephanie Banchero, "Private Donors Shore Up Schools," *Chicago Tribune,* October 1, 2006. In a Letter to the Editor of *Crain's Chicago Business,* Arne Duncan and Donald Lubin, the chairman of the Renaissance Schools Fund, claim that $40 million had been pledged as of October, 2006. See Arne Duncan and Donald Lubin, "Letters to the Editor: Ren 2010 Plan on Track, School Leaders Counter," *Crain's Chicago Business,* February 13, 2006.

33. Mullman and Hinz, "School Plan Falls Behind."

34. Mullman and Hinz, "School Plan Falls Behind."

35. Susan Snyder and Connie Langland, "Ridge, Street Talk of Takeover," *Philadelphia Inquirer,* October 26, 2000.

36. Jolley Bruce Christman, Eva Gold, and Benjamin Herold, *Privatization "Philly Style": What Can Be Learned from Philadelphia's Diverse Provider Model of School Management?* (Philadelphia: Research for Action, June 2006), pp. 3–4.

37. Christman et al., "Privatization 'Philly Style,'" p. 4.

38. Christman et al., "Privatization 'Philly Style,'" p. 11.

39. Christman et al., "Privatization 'Philly Style,'" p. 14. See Jeffrey R. Henig, Thomas Holyoke, Natalie Lacerino-Paquet, and Michele Moser, "Privatization, Politics, and Urban Services: The Political Behavior of Charter Schools," *Journal of Urban Affairs* 25 (2003): 37–54, for the original paper cited by Christman et al.

6. The Role of Community Engagement

Richard Gray and Lamson Lam

1. Paul E. Barton, *Parsing the Achievement Gap* (Princeton, NJ: Educational Testing Service, 2003); Child Trends Data Bank, *Parent Involvement in Schools* (accessed October 5, 2006, from www.childtrendsdatabank.org/pdf/39_pdf.pdf); Kathleen Cotton, *Educating Urban Minority Youth: Research on Effective Practices* (Portland, OR: Northwest Regional Educational Laboratory, 2001); Joyce L. Epstein, *School, Family and Community Partnerships* (Oxford: Westview Press, 2001); Joyce L. Epstein and Susan L. Dauber, "School Programs and Teacher Practices of Parent Involvement in Inner City Elementary and Middle Schools," *Elementary School Journal* 91, no. 3 (1991): 289–305; Norm Fruchter, Anne Galletta, and J. Lynn White, *New Directions in Parent Involvement* (Washington, DC: Academy for Educational Development, 1992); Eva Gold, Elaine Simon, and Chris Brown, "A New Conception of Parent Engagement: Community Organizing for School Reform," in *The Sage Handbook of Educational Leadership,* ed. Fenwick W. English (Thousand Oaks, CA: Sage, 2005); Anne T. Henderson and Nancy Berla, *A New Generation of Evidence: The Family Is Critical to Student Achievement* (Washington, DC: Center for Law and Education, 1994); Anne T. Henderson and Nancy Berla, *A New Wave of Evidence: The Impact of School, Family and Commu-*

nity Connections on Student Achievement (Austin, TX: Southwest Educational Development Laboratory, 2002); Lamson Lam, "Test Success, Family Style," *Educational Leadership* 61, no. 8 (2004):44–47; U.S. Department of Education, *Mapping out the National Assessment of Title I: The Interim Report* (Washington, DC: U.S. Department of Education, 1996).

2. Norm Fruchter, Richard Gray, and Edwina Branch-Smith, *Mobilizing Community Engagement: A Framework for Success for All Students* (New York: Academy for Educational Development, 2006).

3. Fruchter et al., *Mobilizing Community Engagement.*

4. Anthony S. Bryk and Barbara Schneider, *Trust in Schools* (New York: Russell Sage Foundation, 2002).

5. Kevitha Mediratta and Norm Fruchter, *From Governance to Accountability: Building Relationships that Make Schools Work* (New York: Drum Major Institute for Public Policy, 2003).

6. For examples of the dynamic of PTAs versus community-based parent groups, see Eric Zachary and shoal olatoye, *Community Organizing for School Improvement in the South Bronx: A Case Study* (New York: Institute for Education and Social Policy, 2001); and Kevitha Mediratta and Jessica Karp, *Parent Power and Urban School Reform* (New York: New York University, Institute for Education and Social Policy, 2003).

7. Zachary and olatoye, *Community Organizing*; Colleen Larson and Carlos Ovando, *The Color of Bureaucracy* (Stamford, CT: Wadsworth/Thomas Learning, 2001).

8. Richard Gray and Laura Wheeldreyer, *Community Organizing for School Reform in Baltimore* (New York: New York University, Institute for Education and Social Policy, 2002).

9. Andrew Gitlin, "Bounding Teacher Decision-Making: The Threat of Intensification," *Journal of Education Policy* 15, no. 2 (2001): 227–257.

10. Lam, "Test Success, Family Style."

11. Examples of grassroots organizations include neighborhood-based housing and improvement associations, community development organizations, local service providers, community-based organizing groups, neighborhood-based religious institutions (churches, synagogues, mosques, and others), and community centers that provide and host a variety of adult and youth services.

12. Anne C. Kubisch, Patricia Auspos, Prudence Brown, Robert Chaskin, Karen Fulbright-Anderson, and Ralph Hamilton, *Voices from the Field II: Reflections on Comprehensive Community Change* (Washington, DC: Aspen Institute, 2002).

13. Zachary and olatoye, *Community Organizing*; Kavitha Mediratta, Norm Fruchter, and Anne Lewis, *Organizing for School Reform: How Communities Are Finding their Voice and Reclaiming their Public Schools* (New York: New York University, Institute for Education and Social Policy, 2002).

14. Under a reorganization of the New York City school system, the thirty-eight community school districts, including District 9, were subsumed into ten regions; District 9 became part of Region 10. However, New York City leaders allowed District 9 to remain an entity temporarily after the reorganization, because of the success of CC9. The collaborative has since been renamed CCB (Community Collaborative for the Bronx).

15. Natalie Bell, "Brooklyn Parent Group to DOE: Move Forward on Middle School Reforms," *New York Teacher* (accessed October 10, 2006, from http://www.uft.org/news/teacher/reforms/).

16. Harwood Group, *Will Any Kind of Talk Do? Moving from Personal Concerns to Public Life* (Bethesda, MD: Kettering Foundation and The Harwood Institute for Public Innovation, 1996).

17. Harwood Group, *Will Any Kind of Talk Do?*

18. These groups include Community Involvement Program of the Annenberg Institute for School Reform, the National Center for Schools and Communities at Fordham University, Bay Area Coalition for Equitable Schools, and the Institute for Democracy, Education, and Access at UCLA.

7. Leveraging Reform

Kavitha Mediratta, Amy Cohen, and Seema Shah

1. Gail Robinson, "Students Against Scanning," *Gotham Gazette*, May 25, 2006.

2. Barbara Cervone, *Taking Democracy in Hand: Youth Action for Educational Change in the San Francisco Bay Area* (Providence, RI: What Kids Can Do and the Forum for Youth Investment, 2002).

3. Excerpts from New York City Youth Organizing Institute 2006 participant speeches.

4. SCYEA Interview, February 26, 2005, Los Angeles.

5. Jennifer A. Fredericks, Phyllis C. Blumenfeld, and Alison H. Paris, "School Engagement: Potential of the Concept, State of the Evidence." *Review of Educational Research* 74, no. 1 (2004): 59–109; National Research Council, *Engaging Schools: Fostering High School Students' Motivations to Learn* (Washington DC: National Academies Press, 2004); Christina Norris, Jean Pignal, and Garth Lipps, "Measuring School Engagement," *Education Quarterly Review* 9, no. 2 (2003): 25–34.

6. High School Survey of Student Engagement, *What We Can Learn from High School Students* (Bloomington, IN: Center for Evaluation and Education Policy, 2005).

7. Karen J. Pittman and Michele Cahill, *Pushing the Boundaries of Education: The Implications of a Youth Development Approach to Education Policies, Structures, and Collaborations* (New York: Academy for Educational Development, Center for Youth Development and Policy Research, 1992).

8. "Youth Engagement and Voice: A Definition" (accessed January 23, 2007, at YouthEngagementandVoice.org/about.cfm).

9. Gail Robinson, "Students Against Scanning."

10. Joseph Kahne, Meredith I. Honig, and Milbrey W. McLaughlin, "The Civic Components of Community Youth Development." *New Designs for Youth Development* 14, no. 3 (1998): 8–12.

11. Susan Seigel and Virginia Rockwood, "Democratic Education, Student Empowerment and Community Service: Theory And Practice," *Equity and Excellence in Education* 26, no. 2 (1993): 65–70.

12. Kavitha Mediratta and Norm Fruchter, *From Governance to Accountability: Building Relationships that Make Schools Work* (New York: Drum Major Institute for Public Policy, 2003).

13. Michelle Lamont and Annette Lareau, "Cultural Capital: Allusions, Gaps and Glissandos in Recent Theoretical Developments," *Sociological Theory* 6, no. 2 (1988): 153–168; Pierre Bourdieu, *Outline to a Theory of Practice* (London: Cambridge University Press, 1977);

Pierre Bourdieu and Jean Claude Passeron, *Reproduction in Education, Society and Culture* (Thousand Oaks, CA: Sage, 1977).

14. SCYEA Interview, February 26, 2005, Los Angeles.

15. Seema Shah and Nina Johnson (untitled manuscript, New York, Institute for Education and Social Policy, 2006).

16. Linda Camino and Shepherd Zeldin, "From Periphery to Center: Pathways for Youth Civic Engagement in the Day-to-Day Life of Communities," *Applied Developmental Science* 6, no. 4 (2000): 213–220.

17. Daniel Hosang, "Youth and Community Organizing Today" (occasional paper no. 2; New York: Funders' Collaborative on Youth Organizing, 2003).

18. Kevitha Mediratta, "A Rising Movement," *National Civic Review* 95, no. 1 (Spring 2006): 15–22.

19. Advancement Project, *Education on Lockdown: The Schoolhouse to Jailhouse Track* (Washington, DC: Advancement Project, 2005); Hosang, "Youth and Community Organizing Today."

20. Jeremy Lahoud, *Suspended Education* (Chicago: Southwest Organizing Collaborative, 2000).

21. Mamie Chow, Carol Dowell, and Laurie Olsen, *Organizing for School Improvement in Los Angeles and the Bay Area* (New York: Institute for Education and Social Policy, 2001); Nsombi Lambright, *Community Organizing for School Reform in the Mississippi Delta* (New York: Institute for Education and Social Policy, 2001); Kevitha Mediratta and Norm Fruchter, *Mapping the Field of Organizing for School Improvement* (New York: Institute for Education and Social Policy, 2001).

22. Mediratta, "A Rising Movement."

23. District interview, March 1, 2006, Philadelphia.

24. Shawn Ginwright and Taj James, "From Assets to Agents of Change: Social Justice, Organizing, and Youth Development," in *Youth Participation: Improving Institutions and Communities*, ed. Benjamin Kirshner, Jennifer L. O'Donoghue, and Milbrey W. McLaughlin, New Directions for Youth Leadership, no. 96 (San Francisco: Jossey-Bass, 2003); Roderick J. Watts, Nat Chioke Williams, and Robert J. Jagers, "Sociopolitical Development," *American Journal of Community Psychology* 31, no. 1/2 (March 2003): 185–194.

8. Civic Capacity and Education Reform

Jeffrey R. Henig and Clarence N. Stone

1. Donald McAdams, *Fighting to Save Our Urban Schools . . . and Winning!* (New York: Teachers College Press, 2000).

2. Anthony S. Bryk, Penny Sebring, David Kerbow, Sharon Rollow, and John Q. Easton, *Charting Urban School Reform* (Boulder, CO: Westview Press, 1998).

3. We use the term "social class" to refer to standing in the system of social stratification. It therefore commingles matters of race with economic position. Each is important, but the two factors are intertwined in ways that have a special impact on educational opportunity. Both contribute to marginality and negative stereotyping, and in combination they pose a formidable barrier to quality education.

4. See Edmund W. Gordon, Beatrice Bridglall, and Aundra Meroe, eds., *Supplementary Education: The Hidden Curriculum of High Academic Achievement* (Lanham, MD: Rowman and Littlefield, 2005).

5. Colbert I. King, "A Tour the Mayor Should Make," *Washington Post*, July 28, 2001.

6. Meredith I. Honig, ed., *New Directions in Education Policy Implementation* (Albany: State University of New York Press, 2006).

7. Dan Goldhaber, Kacey Guin, Jeffrey R. Henig, Frederick M. Hess, and Janet A. Weiss, "How School Choice Affects Students and Families Who Do Not Choose," in *Getting Choice Right*, ed. Julian R. Butts and Tom Loveless (Washington, DC: Brookings Institution Press, 2005).

8. Archon Fung, *Empowered Participation: Reinventing Urban Democracy* (Princeton, NJ: Princeton University Press, 2004).

9. Martie Theleen Lubetkin, "How Teamwork Transformed a Neighborhood," *Educational Leadership* 53, no. 7 (April 1996): 10–12.

10. Lisbeth B. Schorr, *Common Purpose: Strengthening Families and Neighborhoods to Rebuild America* (New York: Doubleday, 1997).

11. Eva Gold, Amy Rhodes, Shirley Brown, Susan Lytle, and Diane Waff, *Clients, Consumers, or Collaborators? Parents and Their Roles in School Reform During Children Achieving, 1995–2000* (Philadelphia: University of Pennsylvania, Consortium for Policy Research in Education, 2001).

12. Gold et al., *Clients, Consumers, or Collaborators?*, p. 30.

13. Gold et al., *Clients, Consumers, or Collaborators?*, p. 30.

14. Howell S. Baum, *Community Action for School Reform* (Albany: State University of New York Press, 2003).

15. Clarence N. Stone, "Civic Capacity: What, Why, and from Whence," in *The Public Schools*, ed. Susan Fuhrman and Marvin Lazerson (New York: Oxford University Press, 2005), p. 230.

16. Joel F. Handler, *Down from Bureaucracy* (Princeton, NJ: Princeton University Press, 1996).

17. See, for example, Jean Anyon, *Ghetto Schooling: A Political Economy of Urban Educational Reform* (New York: Teachers College Press, 1997).

18. Larry Cuban and Michael Usdan, eds., *Powerful Reforms with Shallow Roots* (New York: Teachers College Press, 2003), p. 160.

19. Daphna Bassock and Margaret E. Raymond, "Performance Trends and the Blueprint for Student Success," in *Urban School Reform: Lessons from San Diego*, ed. Frederick M. Hess (Cambridge, MA: Harvard Education Press, 2005); Jane Hannaway and Maggie Stanislawski, "Flip-Flops in School Reform: An Evolutionary Theory of Decentralization," in Hess, *Urban School Reform*. Also see chapter 6 of this volume for examples of community engagement that supported reforms.

20. Albert O. Hirschman, *Exit, Voice, and Loyalty* (Cambridge, MA: Harvard University Press, 1970).

21. Robert Halpern, *Rebuilding the Inner City* (New York: Columbia University Press, 1995).

22. Sidney Verba, Kay L. Schlozman, and Henry E. Brady, *Voice and Equality: Civic Voluntarism in American Politics* (Cambridge, MA: Harvard University Press, 1995).

23. See, for example, Ron Suskind, *A Hope in the Unseen* (New York: Broadway Books, 1998), p. 7.

24. McAdams, *Fighting to Save Our Urban Schools*, p. 61.

25. Robert D. Putnam, *Bowling Alone: The Collapse and Revival of American Community* (New York: Simon & Schuster, 2000).

26. Quoted in Kristina Smock, *Democracy in Action: Community Organizing and Urban Change* (New York: Columbia University Press, 2003), p. 71.

27. Quoted in Smock, *Democracy in Action*, pp. 79–80.

28. Quoted in Smock, *Democracy in Action*, p. 81.

29. Frank F. Furstenberg Jr., Thomas D. Cook, Jacquelynne Eccles, Glen H. Elder Jr., and Arnold Sameroff, *Managing to Make It* (Chicago: University of Chicago Press, 1999); Adrie Kusserow, *American Individualisms: Child Rearing and Social Class in Three Neighborhoods* (New York: PalgraveMacmillan, 2004).

30. See Annette Lareau, *Home Advantage* (Lanham, MD: Rowman and Littlefield Publishers, 2000); Annette Lareau, *Unequal Childhoods* (Berkeley: University of California Press, 2003).

31. Mark R. Warren, "Communities and Schools: A New View of Urban Education Reform" *Harvard Educational Review* 75, no. 2 (Summer 2005): 133–165.

32. One of the complications is that lower SES groups do not have the luxury of a two-way struggle with education professionals. The professionals themselves may feel pressure from upper SES groups to abide by "meritocratic" standards rather than pursue social-equity goals. See Jeannie Oakes and John Rogers, *Learning Power: Organizing for Education and Justice* (New York: Teachers College Press, 2006).

33. See chapter 6 of Jeffrey R. Henig, Richard C. Hula, Marion Orr, and Desiree S. Pedescleaux, *The Color of School Reform* (Princeton, NJ: Princeton University Press, 1999).

9. What Mayors Can Do

Michael K. Grady and Audrey Hutchinson

1. Francis X. Shen, *Political Incentives and Mayoral Takeover of Urban School Districts*, paper presented at the annual meeting of the American Educational Research Association, Chicago, April 2003; Paul T. Hill, Christine Campbell, and James Harvey, *It Takes a City: Getting Serious about Urban School Reform* (Washington, DC: Brooking Institution Press, 2000); Michael W. Kirst, *Mayoral Influence, New Regimes and Public School Governance* (Philadelphia: Consortium for Policy Research in Education, 2002); National League of Cities, *Improving Public Schools: Action Kit for Municipal Leaders* (Washington, DC: National League of Cities).

2. Michael W. Kirst and Katrina Bulkley, "Mayoral Takeover: The Different Directions Taken in Different Cities," in *A Race Against Time: The Crisis in Urban Schooling*, ed. James Cibulka and William Boyd (Westport, CT: Praeger, 2003).

3. David Tyack, *The One Best System: A History of American Urban Education* (Cambridge, MA: Harvard University Press. 1974); Michael Usdan, "The Surprise Architects of an Intrusive Federal Role," *School Administrator* 62, no. 9 (October 2005): 49–50.

4. Larry Cuban and Michael Usdan, *Powerful Reforms with Shallow Roots* (New York: Teachers College Press. 2003); Kenneth K. Wong and Francis X. Shen, "Big City Mayors and School Governance Reform: The Case of School District Takeover," *Peabody Journal of Education* 78, no. 1 (2003): 5–32; Jeffrey Henig and Wilbur C. Rich, eds., *Mayors in the Middle: Politics, Race, and Mayoral Control of Urban Schools* (Princeton, NJ: Princeton University Press,

2004); Paul T. Hill and Mary Beth Celio, *Fixing Urban Schools* (Washington, DC: Brookings Institution Press, 1998).

5. Kenneth K. Wong and Francis X. Shen, "When Mayors Lead Urban Schools: Assessing the Effects of Mayoral Takeover," in *Besieged: School Boards and the Future of Education Politics,* ed. William G. Howell (Washington, DC: Georgetown University Press, 2004); Fritz Edelstein, *Mayoral Leadership and Involvement in Education: An Action Guide for Success* (Washington, DC: U.S. Conference of Mayors, 2006); Shen, *Political Incentives and Mayoral Takeover;* Hill et al., *It Takes a City.*

6. Michael W. Kirst and Fritz Edelstein, "The Maturing Mayoral Role in Education," *Harvard Educational Review* 76, no. 2 (2006): 152–163; Kenneth K. Wong, "The Political Dynamics of Mayoral Engagement in Public Education," *Harvard Educational Review* 76, no. 2 (2006): 164–177.

7. Wong, "Political Dynamics of Mayoral Engagement"; Michael D. Usdan, "Mayors and Public Education: The Case For Greater Involvement," *Harvard Educational Review* 76, no. 2 (2006): 147–151; Kirst and Edelstein, "The Maturing Mayoral Role."

8. Warren Simmons, Ellen Foley, and Marla Ucelli, "Using Mayoral Involvement in District Reform to Support Instructional Change," *Harvard Educational Review* 76, no. 2 (2006): 189–200.

9. The following case studies are taken from Michael K. Grady, Robert Rothman, and Hal Smith, *Engaging Cities: How Municipal Leaders Can Mobilize Communities to Improve Public Schools* (Providence, RI: Annenberg Institute for School Reform, 2006); this publication was produced in partnership with the National League of Cities. The publication also includes a case study of New York City.

11. "We Are Each Other's Business"

Dennie Palmer Wolf and Jennifer Bransom

1. Don Adams and Arlene Goldbard, *Creative Community: The Fine Art of Cultural Development* (New York: Rockefeller Foundation, 2001).

2. Mark Stern, *Is All the World Philadelphia? A Multi-City Study of Arts and Cultural Organizations, Diversity, and Urban Revitalization* (working paper no. 9, Philadelphia: University of Pennsylvania, 1999).

3. Dennis Palmer Wolf, "Arts Education as a Setting for Equitable Opportunity and Outcomes. A Report to the Ford Foundation" (grant no. 1020-1592), 2005.

4. Donna Bearden, *Final Report: ArtsPartners Program 2000–01* (Dallas: Dallas Independent School District, Division of Evaluation and Research, 2001).

5. David M. Fetterman and Abraham Wandersman, *Empowerment Evaluation Principles in Practice* (New York: Guilford, 2005).

6. Anthony S. Bryk and Barbara Schneider, *Trust in Schools: A Core Resource for Improvement* (New York: Russell Sage Foundation, 2002).

7. Dennie Palmer Wolf, Jennifer Bransom, and Katy Denson, *More Than Measuring: Program Evaluation as an Opportunity to Build the Capacity of Communities* (Dallas: Big Thought, 2007).

8. David K. Cohen and Deborah Loewenberg Ball, *Instruction, Capacity, and Improvement,* CPRE Research Report Series RR-43 (Philadelphia: University of Pennsylvania, Consortium for Policy Research in Education, 1999).

9. Shirley Brice Heath, "Three's Not a Crowd: Plans, Roles, and Focus in the Arts," *Educational Researcher* 30, no. 7 (2001): 10–17; Reed Larson, "From 'I' to 'We': The Development of the Capacity for Teamwork in Youth Programs," in *Approaches to Positive Youth Development,* ed. Richard M. Lerner and Rainer K. Silbereisen (Thousand Oaks, CA: Sage, in press).

10. This framework is based on the dimensions of "scale" described in Cynthia Coburn, "Rethinking Scale: Moving Beyond Numbers to Deep and Lasting Change," *Educational Researcher* 32, no. 6 (August/September 2003): 3–12.

11. Martha Nussbaum and Amartya Sen, eds., *The Quality of Life.* (Oxford: Oxford University Press, 1993).

12. From Smart Districts to Smart Education Systems

Warren Simmons

1. For Boston, see Aspen Institute and Annenberg Institute for School Reform, *Strong Foundation, Evolving Challenges* (Providence RI: Annenberg Institute for School Reform, March 2006); for Charlotte and Houston, see Jason Snipes, Fred Doolittle, and Corinne Herlihy, *Foundations for Success: Case Studies of How Urban School Systems Improve Student Achievement* (Washington, DC: Manpower Demonstration Research Corporation and Council of the Great City Schools, 2002); for San Diego, see Jennifer O'Day, "Standards-Based Reform and Low-Performing Schools: A Case of Reciprocal Accountability," in *Urban School Reform: Lessons from San Diego,* ed. Frederick M. Hess (Cambridge, MA: Harvard Education Press, 2005); for Christina, see Community Training and Assistance Center, New Directions in Christina: Accomplishments for Children, Challenges Ahead (Boston: Community Training and Assistance Center, June 2006); for Philadelphia, see Jolley Bruce Christman, Eva Gold, and Benjamin Herold, *Privatization "Philly Style": What Can Be Learned from Philadelphia's Diverse Provider Model of School Management?* (Philadelphia: Research for Action, June 2006).

2. National Assessment of Educational Progress, *2005 Trial Urban District Results*, available online at http://nces.ed.gov/nationsreportcard/nrc/tuda_reading_mathematics_2005/t0002.asp?printver = (accessed October 12, 2006).

3. Education Trust, *Yes We Can: Telling Truths and Dispelling Myths about Race and Education in America* (Washington, DC: Education Trust, September 2006).

4. Richard Elmore and Deanna Burney, *Investing in Teacher Learning: Staff Development and Instructional Improvement in Community School District #2, New York City* (New York: National Commission on Teaching and America's Future and Consortium for Policy Research in Education, 1997).

5. Milbrey W. McLaughlin and Joan Talbert, *Reforming Districts: How Districts Support School Reform.* (Seattle: University of Washington, Center for the Study of Teaching and Policy, September 2003).

6. Aspen Institute and Annenberg Institute, *Strong Foundation, Evolving Challenges.*

7. Center for Research on the Context of Teaching, *Bay Area School Reform Collaborative Phase One Evaluation* (Palo Alto, CA: Stanford University, Center for Research on the Context of Teaching, August 2002).

8. Christman et al., *Privatization "Philly Style,"* p. 15.

9. Council of the Great City Schools, "Urban School Superintendents: Characteristics, Tenure, and Salary," *Urban Indicator* 7, no. 1 (October 2003): 1–8.

10. Lea Hubbard, Mary Kay Stein, and Hugh Mehan, *Reform as Learning: When School Reform Collides with School Culture and Community Politics* (New York: Routledge, 2006).

11. Warren Simmons, "The Fading Promise of Standards-Based Reform," in *Shaping the Future of American Youth: Youth Policy in the 21st Century*, ed. Anne Lewis (Washington, DC: American Youth Policy Forum, 2003); Thomas Sobol, "Beyond No Child Left Behind," *Education Week*, September 20, 2006, pp. 38, 44.

12. See, for example, Education Trust, *Gaining Traction, Gaining Ground: How Some High Schools Accelerate Learning for Struggling Students* (Washington, DC: Education Trust, November 2005).

13. Gloria Ladson-Billings, "Now They're Wet: Hurricane Katrina as Metaphor for Social and Educational Neglect," *Voices in Urban Education* 10 (Winter 2006): 5–10; Jonathan Kozol, "Segregation and Its Calamitous Effects: America's 'Apartheid' Schools," *Voices in Urban Education* 10 (Winter 2006): 20–28.

14. Edmund W. Gordon and Beatrice Bridglall, "The Challenge, Context, and Preconditions of Academic Development at High Levels," in *Supplementary Education: The Hidden Curriculum of High Academic Achievement*, ed. Edmund W. Gordon, Beatrice Bridglall, and Aundra S. Meroe (Lanham, MD: Rowman and Littlefield, 2005).

15. Gordon and Bridglall, "The Challenge, Context, and Preconditions," p. 19.

16. Richard Rothstein, *Class and Schools* (Washington, DC: Economic Policy Institute, 2004).

17. Lisa Delpit, "Educators as 'Seed' People: Growing a New Future," *Educational Researcher* 7, no. 32 (2003): 14–21; James A. Banks, *Teaching Strategies for Ethnic Studies* (Boston: Allyn and Bacon, 1991); Shirl E. Gilbert and Geneva Gay, "Improving the Success in School of Poor Black Children," in *Culture, Style, and the Educative Process*, ed. Barbara J. Robinson Shade (Springfield, IL: Thomas, 1989); Theresa Perry, "Up from the Parched Earth: Toward a Theory of African-American Achievement," in *Young, Gifted, and Black: Promoting High Achievement Among African-America Students*, ed. Theresa Perry, Claude Steele, and Asa Hilliard (Boston: Beacon Press, 2003).

18. Patricia A. Wasley, Robert L. Hampel, and Richard W. Clark, *Kids and School Reform* (San Francisco: Jossey-Bass, 1997).

19. Gordon and Bridglall, "The Challenge, Context, and Preconditions," p. 27.

21. Valerie E. Lee and David T. Burkam, *Inequality at the Starting Gate: Social Background Differences in Achievement as Children Begin School* (Washington, DC: Economic Policy Institute, 2002); Forum for Youth Investment, *After School for All? Exploring Access and Equity in After-School Programs*. Out-of-School Time Policy Commentary #4 (Washington, DC: Forum for Youth Investment and Impact Strategies, 2003; accessed October 12, 2006, from http://www.forumfyi.org/Files/ostpc4.pdf).

22. Susanne James-Burdumy, Mark Dynarski, Mary Moore, John Deke, Wendy Mansfield, Carol Pistorino, and Elizabeth Warner, *When Schools Stay Open Late: The National Evaluation of the 21st Century Community Learning Centers Program, Final Report* (Washington, DC: U.S. Department of Education, Institute of Education Sciences, April 2005).

23. Constancia Warren, Michelle Feist, and Nancy Neverez, *A Place to Grow: Evaluation of the New York City Beacons, Summary Report* (New York: Academy for Educational Development, 2002); Elizabeth Reisner, Christina Russell, Megan Welsh, Jennifer Birmingham, and Richard White, *Supporting Quality and Scale in After-School Services to Urban Youth: Eval-*

uation of Program Implementation and Student Engagement in the TASC After School Program's Third Year, Report to the After-School Corporation (Washington, DC: Policy Studies Associates, March 2002).

24. Thomas J. Kane, "The Impact of After-School Programs: Interpreting the Results of Four Recent Evaluations" (working paper, William T. Grant Foundation. January 16, 2004).

25. See, for example, Jonathan Kozol, *The Shame of the Nation* (New York: Crown Publishers, 2005).

26. Mark Warren, "Communities and Schools: A New View of Urban Education Reform," *Harvard Educational Review* 75, no. 2 (Summer 2005): 133–165.

27. Luis C. Moll and Norma Gonzalez, "Engaging Life: A Funds-of-Knowledge Approach to Multicultural Education," in *Handbook of Research on Multicultural Education, 2nd Edition,* ed. James A. Banks and Cherry A. McGee Banks (San Francisco: Jossey-Bass, 2003).

28. Center for the Study of Social Policy, *Building New Futures for At-Risk Youth: Findings from a Five-Year Multi-Site Evaluation* (Washington, DC: Center for the Study of Social Policy, 1995).

29. Douglas W. Nelson, "Foreword," in *The Path of Most Resistance: Reflections on Lessons Learned from New Futures* (Baltimore: Annie E. Casey Foundation, 1995), p. 1.

29. Warren Simmons, Ellen Foley, and Marla Ucelli, "Using Mayoral Involvement in District Reform to Support Instructional Change," *Harvard Educational Review* 76, no. 2 (2006): 189–200; Michael W. Kirst and Fritz Edelstein, "The Maturing Mayoral Role in Education," *Harvard Educational Review* 76, no. 2 (2006): 152–163.

30. Carolyn Akers, "Developing a Civic Infrastructure," *Voices in Urban Education* 9 (Fall 2005): 14–21.

31. McLaughlin and Talbert, *Reforming Districts*; Thomas J. Sergiovanni, *Leadership for the Schoolhouse* (San Francisco: Jossey-Bass, 1996).

32. Jody Kretzman and John McKnight, *Building Communities from the Inside Out: A Path to Finding and Mobilizing the Community's Assets* (Evanston, IL: Northwestern University, Institute for Policy Research, 1993).

32. Robert Kronley and Claire Handley, *Reforming Relationships: School Districts, External Organizations, and Systemic Change* (Providence, RI: Annenberg Institute for School Reform, April 2003).

34. Casey Foundation, *The Path of Most Resistance.*

35. Annenberg Institute for School Reform, *Reasons for Hope, Voices for Change* (Providence, RI: Annenberg Institute for School Reform, 1998); Public Education Network and *Education Week, Accountability for All: What Voters Want from Education Candidates* (Washington, DC: Public Education Network, 2002).

ABOUT THE AUTHORS

Jennifer Bransom directs the program accountability department of Big Thought, an arts learning organization. She is the coauthor of "360 Degrees of Literacy: A Look at a Community Partnership in Dallas" (2005). She has also coauthored an online "Arts Toolkit" for the U.S. Department of Education. Bransom codirected a longitudinal study that assessed how teaching and learning changes when arts and cultural programming is integrated into mandated curriculum. Most recently, she collaborated with a team of national consultants and researchers to conduct policy leader interviews and a citywide census of art learning opportunities in Dallas. Bransom has a bachelor's degree in English, with a minor in art, from Southwestern University.

Deanna Burney is an educational researcher and consultant who has combined classroom and administrative experience with scholarly study. For many years Burney was a teacher, counselor, and principal in the School District of Philadelphia. She also served as assistant superintendent for curriculum and instruction in the Camden, New Jersey, school district. As a researcher, Burney has worked on the High-Performance Learning Communities study, which focused on Community School District #2 in New York City and on which she has published numerous papers in collaboration with Richard Elmore. Burney has also worked as a senior researcher at the Consortium for Policy Research in Education at the University of Pennsylvania.

Amy Cohen is a collaborative coordinator at the Annenberg Institute for School Reform's Community Involvement Program, where she coordinates the Urban Youth Collaborative, a coalition of youth organizations aimed at influencing high school reform in New York City. She works with youths to create meaningful, youth-led change in their schools and throughout the school system. Cohen previously taught high school social studies in the Bronx and in Jackson, Mississippi. She has also worked as a community organizer for the grassroots community organization ACORN in several cities on the west and east coasts. This work included a variety of education campaigns that focused on community participation in school policy, administration, and development. She holds a bachelor's degree in history from Oberlin College and a master's of education degree from Fordham University.

Ellen Foley is a principal associate at the Annenberg Institute for School Reform, where she serves as research manager for the Institute's work in district redesign. She was previously a research specialist at the Consortium for Policy Research in Education, where she worked on the evaluation of Children Achieving, Philadelphia's districtwide education reform effort. Her primary research interest is urban education reform, with a focus on the connection between academic, social, and health supports for students and the central office's role in leading reform efforts. She cochairs the American Educational Research Association's Special Interest Group on Districts in Research and Reform. Foley holds a bachelor's in political science from Boston College and a master's in education and a doctorate in education policy from the University of Pennsylvania.

Michael K. Grady is the deputy director of the Annenberg Institute for School Reform. He also serves as principal investigator of a major collaboration between the Institute and the National League of Cities that works with mayors, municipal leaders, and their education policy advisers on strategies to increase the public's awareness, participation, and stake in local school-improvement initiatives in the context of No Child Left Behind. Grady previously was a senior research associate at the Annie E. Casey Foundation, where he managed the research and evaluation portfolio. He also has conducted research on the Comer School Development Program, educational equity initiatives, and school-based management at the district level. He holds master's and doctorate degrees from the Harvard Graduate School of Education.

Richard Gray has been a coleader of the Community Involvement Program at the Annenberg Institute for School Reform since 1998. His work includes giving presentations, facilitating strategic plans, and conducting site visits in support of community school reform groups in Boston, Baltimore, Detroit, and Kansas City. He has been involved with New York University's Institute for Education and Social Policy from its inception in 1995 and was a visiting fellow with the Citizens Planning and Housing Association in Baltimore in 1997. Gray holds a bachelor's degree from Brown University and a J.D. from Boalt Hall School of Law. He has published extensively on education reform, including *The Good Common School: Making the Vision Work for All Children.*

Heather A. Harding is a principal associate in Opportunity and Accountability at the Annenberg Institute for School Reform. Her work focuses on developing culturally relevant tools in the Institute's teaching and learning review process and on supporting the Institute's equity focus in other Opportunity and Accountability initiatives. Harding previously taught in the Harvard Graduate School of Education's Teacher Education Program and at Lesley University in the Out of School Time Master's Program. Harding began her education career as a secondary teacher in rural North Carolina and has served in numerous roles in school reform organizations.

She earned her master's and doctoral degrees in education from the Harvard Graduate School of Education, and attended the Medill School of Journalism at Northwestern University.

Jeffrey R. Henig is a professor of political science and education at Teachers College, and a professor of political science at Columbia University. He was previously a professor at George Washington University, where he also served as director of the Center for Washington Area Studies. His research has focused most recently on the politics of school choice, charter schools, and coalition-building for urban school reform. His numerous published works include the coauthored *Building Civic Capacity: The Politics of Reforming Urban Schools* (2001), named the best book written on urban politics in 2001 by the Urban Politics Section of the American Political Science Association. He earned his bachelor's degree at Cornell University and his doctorate at Northwestern University.

Audrey Hutchinson is the program director of education and afterschool initiatives at the Institute for Youth, Education, and Families of the National League of Cities. She directs three major initiatives that assist mayors and city council members who are interested in improving the quality of K–12 education in urban school districts. For more than twenty years, her work has focused on K–12 and higher education, federal and local governments, and the nonprofit sectors. Hutchinson previously held several senior positions under the Clinton administration, working on key initiatives such as school-to-work transition, higher education, and international education. She also has held several positions at the City University of New York and was a special assistant and policy analyst for the president of the New York City Council. Hutchinson holds two master's degrees from Columbia University, in social work and public health.

Kenneth Klau managed curriculum development for an organization providing comprehensive education reform services to public schools. His research interest is the relationship between policy, practice, and research. He has also taught at the secondary school level. Klau completed a master's degree in education and policy from the Harvard Graduate School of Education in 2006.

Lamson Lam is currently a research assistant at the Community Involvement Program at the Annenberg Institute for School Reform, where his work focuses on community engagement and youth organizing. He is also an adjunct professor at Mercy College and recently completed his fourth year as a teaching fellow at the Teachers Network Leadership Institute. His article "Test Success, Family Style" appeared in *Educational Leadership* (2004). Lam received his bachelor's degree from the University of California at San Diego and his master's from the Steinhardt School of Education at New York University, where he is currently enrolled in the doctoral program in educational leadership.

Kavitha Mediratta is a principal associate at the Annenberg Institute for School Reform's Community Involvement Program (CIP), which she initiated in 1995. She was instrumental in developing CIP's strategy of building community-driven education policy reform coalitions. In New York City she facilitated citywide coalitions that have shaped the city's school policy, and she spent a year in India documenting the work of grassroots organizing groups and exchanging information on strategies. Mediratta previously served as a Warren Weaver Fellow at the Rockefeller Foundation and has taught elementary and middle school science in southern India and in the United States. She holds a bachelor's degree from Amherst College and a master's of education from Teachers College.

Jacob Mishook is a research analyst in district redesign at the Annenberg Institute for School Reform. Mishook's work includes research, analysis, and report writing in the areas of district redesign, effective central office practices, and data-informed decisionmaking. Previously, he worked as an educational researcher in the Center for Technology in Learning at SRI International. His interests include school reform, assessment, and arts education. His doctoral dissertation examined the impact of high-stakes testing on arts education at both arts-focused and non–arts-focused elementary schools. He holds a bachelor's degree with honors in education from Stanford University and a doctorate from Pennsylvania State University.

Jesse B. Register is the Annenberg senior advisor for district leadership at the Annenberg Institute for School Reform. From 1997 through 2006, he was superintendent of the combined city/county district of Chattanooga/Hamilton County, Tennessee, where he led a successful merger of the two districts, restructured nine low-performing schools, and launched a major redesign of all the district's high schools. Before coming to Hamilton County, Register was superintendent of two different districts in North Carolina. He has also worked as an English teacher, principal, and district administrator. He earned a bachelor's degree and a master's of education from the University of North Carolina at Charlotte. He also holds an Advanced School Administrator's Certificate from the University of North Carolina at Chapel Hill and a doctorate from Duke University.

Robert Rothman is a principal associate at the Annenberg Institute for School Reform. He is responsible for writing Institute publications and editing the Institute's quarterly journal, *Voices in Urban Education*, a "roundtable-in-print" designed to air diverse viewpoints and share new knowledge on vital issues in urban education. He has written for numerous education publications and organizations and was previously a reporter and editor for *Education Week*. He was also a senior project associate for Achieve, a study director for the National Research Council, and the director of special projects for the National Center on Education and the Economy. He is the author of *Measuring Up: Standards, Assessment and School Reform* (1995), and numerous book chapters and articles on testing and education reform. Rothman holds a bachelor's from Yale University.

Seema Shah is a research associate and study director for the Community Involvement Program at the Annenberg Institute for School Reform, where she codirects a national study on community organizing and school reform. Over the years, Shah has worked extensively with public schools and nonprofit organizations as an evaluator and researcher. Before joining the Institute, Shah completed a postdoctoral fellowship in mental health policy at the Consultation Center, Yale University School of Medicine. She earned a bachelor's from Duke University and a doctorate from DePaul University, where her dissertation research focused on the acculturation experiences of immigrant and refugee youth.

Warren Simmons is executive director of the Annenberg Institute for School Reform. He was previously executive director of the Philadelphia Education Fund. Over his twenty-five-year career in education, Simmons has worked on urban education issues from several vantage points: as a grant-maker at the National Institute of Education and the Annie E. Casey Foundation; as director of equity initiatives for the New Standards Project; and as special assistant to the superintendent of schools in Prince George's County, Maryland, where he designed and implemented reforms that improved the achievement of disadvantaged students. He serves on the boards of several education organizations, including the Public Education Network, the National Center on Education and the Economy, and the Rhode Island Children's Crusade. He received a bachelor's degree from Macalester College and a doctorate from Cornell University.

Clarence N. Stone is a research professor of political science and public policy at George Washington University. His teaching interests center on urban politics and comparative local politics, and his research interests include the theory and practice of local democracy, urban education, and the local agenda-setting process. His most recent book, the coauthored *Building Civic Capacity: The Politics of Reforming Urban Schools,* won the 2001 award for best book on urban politics from the Urban Politics Section of the American Political Science Association. Stone's other books include *Changing Urban Education* (1998), *Regime Politics* (1989), and *Economic Growth and Neighborhood Discontent* (1976). Stone is also Professor Emeritus at the University of Maryland. He received a bachelor's degree from the University of South Carolina and a doctorate from Duke University.

Marla Ucelli is director of district redesign for the Annenberg Institute for School Reform. In that capacity, she responds to district requests to build their capacity in key areas. She previously directed School Communities that Work: A National Task Force on the Future of Urban Districts, which produced resources to help school districts make the transition to becoming a "smart district." Before joining the Institute, she was associate director in the Equal Opportunity Division at the Rockefeller Foundation and special assistant for education to the governor of New Jersey. She frequently speaks and writes on issues related to urban district redesign, philanthropy in education, and urban community colleges. Ucelli holds a bachelor's degree from New York University and a master's degree from Rutgers.

David Wishnick is a senior at Brown University, where he is concentrating in urban studies. While at Brown, he has pursued independent research on urban school systems.

Dennie Palmer Wolf is director of Opportunity and Accountability at the Annenberg Institute for School Reform, where she heads a team that examines excellence and equity issues related to opportunity to learn and outcomes for students in K–12 urban systems. She previously taught at the Harvard Graduate School of Education and was codirector of the Harvard Institute for School Leadership. Her professional areas of interest include standards, assessment, and school reform, and cultural policy for youth. She has served three terms as a member of the National Assessment Governing Board. Wolf is the recipient of numerous awards and grants and has published extensively in the field of education. She received a master's degree and a doctorate from the Harvard Graduate School of Education.

Kenneth K. Wong is the Walter and Leonore Annenberg Professor in Education Policy at Brown University. He is also a professor of education, political science, and public policy, director of Brown's Urban Education Policy Program, and director of the National Research Center on School Choice, Competition, and Student Achievement. Before coming to Brown, Wong was a professor in the Department of Leadership and Organizations at Peabody College, Vanderbilt University, associate director of the Peabody Center for Education Policy, and a professor in the Department of Political Science at Vanderbilt. He was previously an associate professor in the department of education at the University of Chicago. Wong is the author and editor of numerous books and articles on education and public policy, including the coauthored *Money, Politics, and Law* (2004) and *Successful Schools and Education Accountability* (forthcoming).

INDEX